OXFORD STUDIES IN LANGUAGE CONTACT

Series Editors: Suzanne Romaine, Merton College, Oxford, and Peter Mühlhäusler, Linacre College, Oxford

Dynamics of a Contact Continuum

OXFORD STUDIES IN LANGUAGE CONTACT

Most of the world's speech communities are multilingual, and contact between languages is thus an important force in the everyday lives of most people. Studies of language contact should therefore form an integral part of work in theoretical, social, and historical linguistics. As yet, however, there are insufficient studies to permit typological generalization.

Oxford Studies in Language Contact will fill this gap by making available a collection of research monographs which present case studies of language contact around the world. The series addresses language contact and its consequences in a broad interdisciplinary context which includes not only linguistics but also social, historical, cultural, and psychological perspectives. It will not only provide an indispensable source of data for the serious researcher, but will also contribute significantly to theoretical development in the field.

Dynamics of a Contact Continuum

Singaporean English

HO MIAN-LIAN
and
JOHN T. PLATT

CLARENDON PRESS · OXFORD
1993

Oxford University Press, Walton Street, Oxford OX2 6DP

Oxford New York Toronto
Delhi Bombay Calcutta Madras Karachi
Kuala Lumpur Singapore Hong Kong Tokyo
Nairobi Dar es Salaam Cape Town
Melbourne Auckland Madrid

and associated companies in
Berlin Ibadan

Oxford is a trade mark of Oxford University Press

Published in the United States
by Oxford University Press Inc., New York

British Library Cataloguing in Publication Data
Data available

Library of Congress Cataloging in Publication Data
Ho, Mian Lian.
Dynamics of a contact continuum: Singaporean English/Ho Mian-
Lian and John T. Platt.
(Oxford studies in language contact)
Includes index.
1. English language—Social aspects—Singapore. 2. Languages in
contact—Singapore. I. Platt, John Talbot. II. Title.
III. Series.
PE3502.S5H6   1993   427'.95957—dc20   92–19609
ISBN 0–19–824828–8

Typeset by Best-set Typesetter Ltd., Hong Kong

Printed in Great Britain
on acid-free paper by
Bookcraft (Bath) Ltd., Midsomer Norton, Avon

Acknowledgements

Various people have contributed to the research and preparation of this book. Their assistance is gratefully acknowledged.

Sincere appreciation is extended to the many informants who gave so much of their time for the interviews and recordings. Without their co-operation and interest in this study, the collection of such a vast corpus of data would not have been possible. In particular, special thanks must go to the informants with English-medium primary education, who, despite their feelings of inadequacy, valiantly kept the conversation going without lapsing into Chinese.

Thanks are also due to the following: Mr and Mrs J. Richardson and Mr H. S. Seah for their advice on computer software; Dr J. Hu and Mr H. Y. Guo, who pointed out various differences between Standard Mandarin and Singapore Mandarin; the staff of the Main Library, Monash University, as well as the staff of the RELC Library of the SEAMEO Regional Language Centre, Singapore.

H. M.-L.

Contents

Contents

List of Figures

List of Tables

Abbreviations, Symbols, and Explanatory Notes

1 Abbreviations and symbols

1.1 Abbreviations used in the classification of past forms of verbs

Phonetic types

(a) VC verbs—verbs whose stems undergo a vowel change (and in some cases other changes as well) in order to form the past form e.g. *fall-fell, eat-ate, go-went.*

(b) Id verbs—verbs whose stems end in an alveolar stop and require the allomorph /ɪd/ for their past form e.g. *wanted, started, treated.*

(c) Vd verbs—verbs which in their past tense form end in a *vowel + d*, e.g. *followed, paid, carried.* Included in this category are verbs like *have* and *make* because their past tense ends in a *vowel + d.*

(d) CC verbs—verbs whose past form ends in a consonant cluster e.g. *picked, robbed, punched.*

Semantic types

(e) NP verbs—non-punctual verbs

(f) P verbs—punctual verbs

(g) S verbs—stative verbs

1.2 Other abbreviations

Adj	adjective
Adj^c	adjective and passive environments have been combined
Aux	auxiliary (verb)
BA	bǎ ('disposal' form)
BEI	bèi (passive marker)
BEV	Black English Vernacular
CHP	Conversational Historical Present
Cl	clause
CL	classifier
CRS	currently relevant state (*le*)
D	demonstrative
DUR	durative aspect (*-zhe, zài*)

EP	emphatic particle
ESM	English in Singapore and Malaysia
GC	Guyanese Creole
GEN	genitive (*-de*)
HCE	Hawaiian Creole English
I	first person singular pronoun
LDOCE	*Longman Dictionary of Contemporary English* (1978)
Loc	locative
Loc^c	locative and temporal environments have been combined
M	marker
Nom	nominal
NOM	nominalizer (*de*)
NP	noun phrase
ORD	ordinalizer (*di-*)
P	particle
Pass	passive
PFV	perfective aspect (*-le*)
PFV/CRS	perfective aspect/currently relevant state (*LE*)
PL	plural (*-men*)
Pn	pronouns other than *I*, *he*, *she*, and *it*.
QP	question particle
REL	relativizer
SBrE	Standard British English
SgE	Singaporean English
T, A, O, S, P	These refer to the educational attainment of the informants: tertiary (T), A level (A), O level (O), secondary one to three levels (S) (also referred to as sec. 1–3), and primary level (P). For convenience, informants with different levels of education will be referred to simply as the 5 educational groups e.g. 'at the tertiary level', etc. refers to informants with tertiary level education
V-ing	Verb + ing
WH	WH and similar elements such as *that*, *who*, *which*, etc.
3sg	third person singular pronoun

1.3 Common abbreviations and acronymns used in Singapore

AEB	Adult Education Board
BEST	Basic Education for Skills Training
HDB	Housing and Development Board
MAS	Malaysian Airlines System
MGS	Methodist Girls' School
MO	Medical Officer
NTUC	National Trades Union Congress

PSA   Port of Singapore Authority
URA   Urban Redevelopment Authority
VITB   Vocational and Industrial Training Board
* Utterances which are unacceptable to native speakers.

2 Explanatory notes

2.1 Texts

Each utterance from an informant is coded as follows: the first letter stands for the educational attainment of the informant. The first number refers to the informant number, the second to the page number of Ho's transcription. I and J stand for interviewer and interviewee respectively. Appendix A gives further details of the informants.

2.2 Explanation of transcriptions

Explanation of transcriptions includes a gloss, translation, and some context where appropriate.

2.3 Notations

Mandarin: the pinyin romanized system is used for all Mandarin examples. Hokkien: all examples from Bodman (1955) remain as they are in their original notations. Ho's Hokkien examples are based in general on the romanized system used by Chiang (n.d.).

1

The Development of an Indigenized English in a Multilingual Setting

1.1 English-medium and non-English-medium English

Singaporean English is a particularly interesting indigenized, or nativized, speech variety because it is so widely used and fills so many functions. Unlike some indigenized varieties of English, which function among only a very restricted subset of the population and perform only a small range of functions, Singaporean English performs a complete range of functions, at least for some of its speakers. By *Singaporean English*, we mean English as used by Singaporeans. Unfortunately, the term *Singapore English* is sometimes used in a somewhat pejorative manner to suggest a 'substandard' variety of English, especially the type of local English spoken by those with lower standards of education. It therefore seems appropriate to refer to Singaporean English in the same way that other varieties are referred to as American English, Australian English, etc.

Singaporean English is also interesting because it is a continuum similar in many respects to what has been described of other continua such as in Jamaica (DeCamp 1971) and Guyana (Bickerton 1975). The more basilectal subvarieties share many of the features of a creole, e.g. serial verb structures, variable marking of past tense, variable occurrence of articles and replacement of the articles by other items, variable occurrence of *be* as copula or auxiliary. However, Singaporean English cannot be considered as a post-creole continuum as it did not develop from a pidgin to a creole with later or contemporaneous modification through education in the medium of the superstrate language. Rather, it developed from the beginning through the medium of education, the English-medium education.

The term 'creoloid' was used by Platt (1975, 1978), who defined a creoloid as follows:

A speech variety which has developed through the educational system such that a non-native or introduced prestige speech variety is taught to speakers of another speech variety (or other speech varieties) in a situation where the introduced variety comes to be used in everyday situations, to be acquired by some children before they commence school and to become virtual 'native' speech variety for some or all speakers. (Platt 1978:55)

'Educational system' in the Singapore context refers, of course, to English-medium education. Those who have gone through a Chinese, Malay, or

Tamil stream of education generally lack the fluency in English of the English-medium educated. Heaton (1979) comments on the spoken English of the Chinese-stream teachers who had to go for further training at the then Teachers' Training College in order to teach various academic subjects in English:

These Chinese-medium teachers had previously completed their teacher-training course in Chinese at the Teachers' Training College and had all attained at least a minimum level of proficiency in English, though few could speak English with any degree of fluency and even fewer used English in their daily lives. (Heaton 1979:57)

The following is another observation on the difference between the speech of those with an English-medium education and those with other than an English-medium background:

It appears that the first major distinction can be drawn between the English of those who have been educated in schools where English is the medium of instruction, and the English of those educated in schools where the medium of instruction is Mandarin, Tamil, or Malay, who have studied English as a second or third language. The latter can be further broken down according to the linguistic background of the speaker. These are the vertical cuts. (Ramish 1969:312)

This is captured in Fig. 1.1.

In summary, the English spoken by those from the Chinese, Malay, and Tamil streams is more a learner's language, which is often hesitant and phonologically more deviant from the Standard British norm than that spoken by those who have received an English-medium education. It is with the English spoken by the latter group that we are concerned in the following chapters and it is this which we shall refer to as Singaporean English (SgE).

1.2 The Singaporean English speech continuum

As in all speech communities, the type of language used by the speakers varies according to education, socio-economic class, and type of employment. Like the post-creole continua in Guyana, Hawaii, or Jamaica, the SgE continuum has a range of lects ranging from the acrolect through the mesolects to the basilect. The acrolect is spoken (and written), at least in formal situations, by those who have received a high level of education and who hold high-status positions. Those who speak a basilect will be Singaporeans with minimal education working in an environment where less English is used. A representation of the present SgE continuum is given in Fig. 1.2. Besides excluding the speech of speakers from the Tamil-, Malay-, and Chinese-stream schools, it also excludes the pidgin English spoken by an older generation, e.g. cooks and waiters working in places such as the Singapore Cricket Club, most of whom had previously worked on board ships. They have had no formal education and theirs is a simplified English acquired for communication with

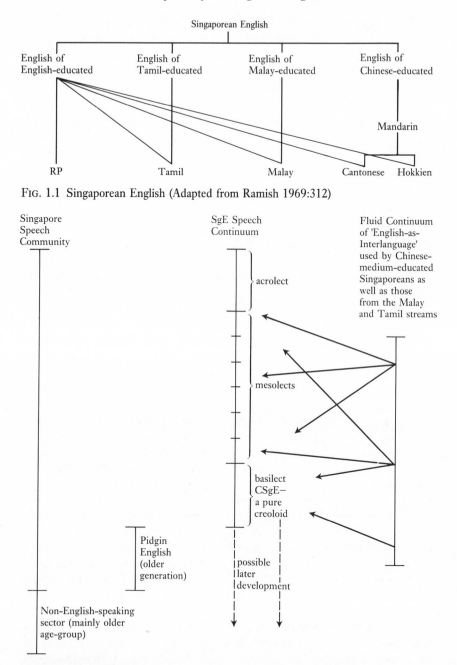

FIG. 1.1 Singaporean English (Adapted from Ramish 1969:312)

FIG. 1.2 The Singapore speech community and the SgE speech continuum. (Adapted from Platt 1978:57)

the British in the pre-independence period. Their numbers are, of course, diminishing and as English is now the major language of communication, the SgE speech continuum will expand and there will be a full SgE range.

Eventually the fluid continuum of 'English-as-interlanguage' used by those educated in the Chinese, Malay, and Tamil medium will also disappear. Previously, such speakers were hesitant about using English. However, with the increasing importance of English, they have made a conscious effort to use it. They will eventually acquire fluency in Singaporean English with constant exposure to it in the domains of friendship and employment. Interviews with informants from the Chinese-stream schools who have English-medium-educated spouses show that they have developed greater facility compared with their counterparts who have little exposure to SgE. Interviews with Chinese-medium informants with only primary education show that these informants have a desire to improve their English. Many of them are attending Basic Education for Skills Training (BEST) classes where English is one of the subjects taught, and many have expressed a desire to gain at least some oral competence in English because it is the major working language in Singapore. With the increase in English-medium-educated speakers over the past years who prefer to use SgE rather than the local languages in most domains, it is inevitable that Singaporeans who have had a non-English-stream education will soon gain at least some competence in SgE and be absorbed into the SgE continuum.

1.3 The subvarieties of Singaporean English

What is most interesting about the subvarieties of SgE is that not only do they indicate socio-economic class but they are also used for stylistic variation. Unlike a speech variety such as British, American, or Australian English, which has a 'fully developed stylistic range within each sociolectal range' (Platt, Weber, and Ho 1983*a*:16), a developing speech variety like SgE uses the range of lects on the continuum for stylistic variation. Therefore, an acrolectal speaker who may use a very formal type of English at a meeting or forum can drop very comfortably into the basilect when speaking to a tamby (messenger boy) or the car-park attendant. This is rather different from what happens in a 'native' variety of English. As indicated in Fig. 1.3, an acrolectal speaker of a 'native' variety such as British English can use a very colloquial style to a bartender but this style will still be within his or her sociolectal range. This can occur without a drop down the sociolectal scale although there are, of course, some speakers who can do this. It should also be mentioned that when Singaporeans with a command of higher lects drop down the scale in informal communication with their peers they do not

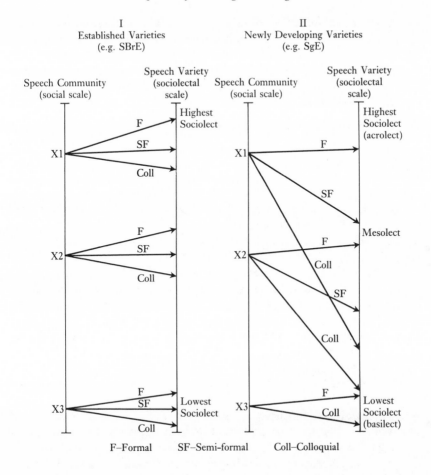

FIG. 1.3 Stylistic and social variation in established and newly developing varieties. (Adapted from Platt and Weber 1980:112)

necessarily drop to a basilectal subvariety. Furthermore, they may well use lexical items and expressions which would not be used by those with lower levels of formal education. Similar movement along the lectal scale is mentioned in connection with post-creole situations, e.g. Bickerton (1975), Minderhout (1977).

In the interviews, which were carried out by Ho, many of the speakers used a semi-formal style at the beginning but a more colloquial style as the interview progressed. On the whole, they felt relaxed speaking to a fellow Singaporean who, throughout the interview, used a speech style which was typically Singaporean.

1.4 The development of Singaporean English via English-medium education

The development of SgE via English-medium education is summarized in Fig. 1.4. The factors in this development include the types of teachers, learners themselves, language developmental processes, and the SgE speech community.

1.5 Types of teachers

A strong influence on SgE has been the type of teachers who were recruited in the early colonial era. At first, most of the teachers were from England and, to some extent, Scotland and Wales. There were also many from various Catholic orders in Ireland who came to staff the Catholic schools in Singapore, such as the Convent of the Holy Infant Jesus and St Joseph's Institution. Several possible Irish influences have been noted such as the pronunciation of the letter 'h' as 'haitch' by some ex-students of these schools and the use of the progressive aspect with stative verbs (cf. Bliss 1984). However, as this is also a well-known feature of Indian English, the influence of the English of Indian teachers is also likely. Another possible factor is, of course, overgeneralization.

With the expansion of English-medium education, many teachers were recruited from Ceylon (now Sri Lanka) and India, which were under British rule much earlier than Singapore. Since then, Indians have always been well represented in the teaching profession. Ramish, stressing the importance of the Indian languages on SgE, comments: 'Their importance derives from the fact that most teachers of English in primary and secondary schools have been English educated Tamils or Malayalees' (Ramish 1969:1). It would not be wrong to surmise that they have contributed in some way to the distinctive stress and intonation patterns of SgE, which has often been described as having a staccato rhythm (cf. Ho 1989*a*). This could also be attributed to influence from Chinese. However, it is noticeable that the SgE rhythm and stress patterns are very different from those of Hong Kong English, despite the fact that Hong Kong, like Singapore, has a predominantly Chinese population.

There appears to be Indian influence on SgE syntax as well. Syntactically, SgE and Indian English exhibit certain similarities. For example, the auxiliary *would* is often used instead of *will* in both varieties as it is felt to be a more polite form:

I hope you would expedite matters. (SgE—our example)
I hope that the Vice-Chancellor would investigate this matter.
(Indian English—Trudgill and Hannah 1982:108)

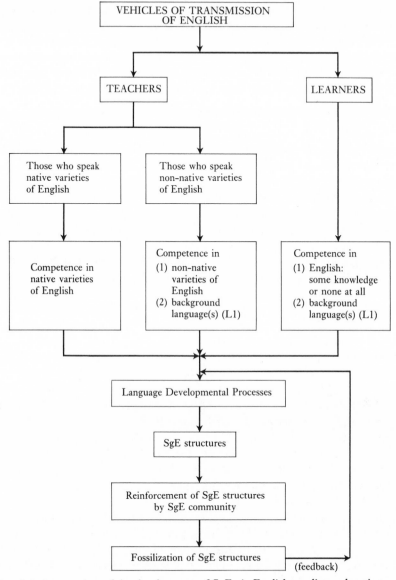

FIG. 1.4 An overview of the development of SgE via English-medium education

As Singapore was part of the British colony of the Straits Settlements, an idealized SBrE has been the norm for teaching purposes since the earliest days of English-medium education. However, a more formal variety of SgE is used by local teachers in the classroom. Phonetically, the local variety is very different from the British norm, while syntactically and lexically there are varying degrees of deviation from the norm. For discussions, a less formal style is used. The degree of informality also depends on the type of lesson; for example, in laboratory lessons and physical training lessons a more informal style is used. No doubt, once outside the classroom, exchanges between teachers and pupils will often be in more racy, colloquial SgE.

1.6 Learners and the transference of features from the substrate languages

One of the characteristics of SgE is that it shows the transference of features from the various speech varieties spoken by the different ethnic groups. The population of Singapore comprises 76.9% Chinese, 14.6% Malays, 6.4% Indians and other groups (Khoo 1980). However, as will be shown later, the dominant substratum influence on Singaporean English syntax as spoken by those with lower levels of education, and by others in informal situations, is Chinese. This is also true of semantics, such as the semantics of verbs of movement and, to a great extent, phonology. The use of Chinese-derived discourse particles is also a noticeable feature of the less formal subvarieties (Platt and Ho 1982, 1989; Richards and Tay 1977;. Smith 1985).

The influence of the Indian languages on SgE has already been discussed in Section 1.5. It should be pointed out that Tamil lexical items are not a feature of Singaporean English, except in reference to religious festivals such as *Deepavali* or food, e.g. *Murtabak*, a Muslim Indian speciality, and in any case such words are not a part of everyday speech.

As far as Malay is concerned, the influence is indirect. Earlier on when English-medium schools were established, few Malays except for the sons of royalty and the aristocracy attended them. It was mainly the Indians and Chinese who sent their children to these schools, often at great financial sacrifice. They could see that such an education could lead to employment in government departments and in the British-owned banks and trading companies. However, the indirect influence of Malay via Bazaar Malay and Baba Malay is noticeable, and it is from these two speech varieties that Malay lexical items such as *hantam* (beat), *bodoh* (stupid), and *makan* (food) came into colloquial Singaporean English. Bazaar Malay is a pidginized form of Malay and has many features transferred from Chinese. It was used mainly for inter-ethnic communication before the widespread use of SgE (cf. Platt and Weber 1980). Baba Malay has 'a more clearly defined linguistic system' and is recognized 'by certain syntactic characteristics peculiar to it and by its sizeable lexicon of Chinese loan-words' (Lim 1981:17). It was used mainly for intra-group communication but is disappearing under the influence of English-medium education in Singapore and of Bahasa Malaysia-medium education in Malaysia. As Baba Malay has had considerable influence on SgE, some details about its origins are warranted.

Prior to the large-scale immigration of Chinese from South China to the

Malay Peninsula in the nineteenth century, there were already Chinese traders who had settled in several parts of the region, the first settlement being in Malacca (cf. Lim 1981:8). A pidginized form of Malay was used for inter-ethnic communication and when the Chinese settlers married local Malay women, Baba Malay, a hybrid of Malay and Hokkien, developed as the native language of the descendants of these inter-ethnic marriages. The Babas had a high regard for English-medium education and preferred to send their children to English-medium schools, recognizing the financial benefits and upward social mobility that came via such an education. Many of them, like Song, who published *One Hundred Years' History of the Chinese in Singapore* (1923), used the English language with great dexterity. The Straits Chinese British Association comprised an élite group of successful, enterprising English-educated professionals and 'the kind of example they embodied extended the prestige of the English language throughout the community' (de Souza 1977:21).

Naturally, the English as spoken by the Babas and their native language, Baba Malay, would have had a very important influence on SgE. In the following chapters, mention is made of the influence of Baba Malay on SgE structures wherever relevant. For the present, it will be sufficient to give some examples of this influence. One is to be seen in the use of *one* in the more basilectal and colloquial subvarieties of SgE. This particle is realized as *punya* in Baba Malay, *de* in Mandarin, *kè* in Cantonese, and *ê* in Hokkien. What is interesting is that this particle is absent in Hong Kong English (Budge, personal communication) as well as Taiwan English (Chen, personal communication). Both varieties are influenced by Chinese, Cantonese in the first variety and Taiwanese (which is a variety of Hokkien) as well as Mandarin in the latter variety. One can surmise that in the case of SgE, the syntax of Baba Malay has had a strong influence. Furthermore, unlike Hong Kong and Taiwan English, SgE is an indigenized variety. A few examples of the influence of Baba Malay, which in turn is influenced by Hokkien syntax, on SgE are given below. It is noticeable that these structures are quite different from those of Malay.

1. *One* in SgE can be used as a relative marker (REL) showing the influence from Baba Malay and Hokkien:

Basilectal SgE: pray one t(h)ing
                  REL
Baba Malay: Sembayang punya barang
                Pray   REL thing
Hokkien: Pai sîn ê   mì-khīa^n
                Pray god REL thing
Malay: Barang-barang sembahyang
                Thing (plural) pray
                'The things that are used for praying'

In Malay the postmodifying clause *sembahyang* occurs after the noun *barang-barang*. Note also that the reduplication of the noun *barang* is absent in Baba Malay. This is an influence from Hokkien, which does not mark nouns for plural. The modifying clause in both Hokkien and Baba Malay as well as in SgE occurs before the noun.

2. *One* is also used for emphasis in sentence final position, which again is an influence from Baba Malay and Hokkien:

Basilectal SgE
A: You sit car come here ah? (ah = yes/no QP)
   'Did you come here by car?'
B: No lah! I walk come here *one*.
   'No, I *walked* here.'
   (*lah* is an emphatic particle. *One* emphasises the information *walked*,
   whereas in SBrE stress is used instead: I *walked* here.)

Hokkien
A: lí   chē chhia lâi   chit-tau ah?
   you sit car   come here   QP
   'Did you come here by car?'
B: bo la, góa kîaⁿ lō   lâi   chit-tau ê
   no EPI   walk road come here   EP
   'No, I walked here.'

Baba Malay
A: Lu datang sini dengan kereta kah?
   you come here with   car   QP
   'Did you come here by car?'
B: Bukan, goa jalan sini punya
   no,   I   walk here EP
   'No, I walked here.'

Malay
A: Awak datang ke sini dengan kereta kah?
   you   come to here with   car   QP
   'Did you come here by car?'
B: Tidak, saya berjalan (kaki) ke sini
   no,   I   walk   (foot) to here
   'No, I walked here.'

Note that the particle *punya* is absent in the Malay version.

1.7 Language developmental processes

The English of a Singaporean learner shows transference of features not only from L1 but also from L2. Language learning strategies such as simplification, hypercorrection, analogies, and blends will be discussed, where relevant, with regard to the acquisition of the variable under study.

1.8 The Singaporean English speech community

With the expansion of English-medium education after the Second World War, the number of SgE speakers has increased over the years. Many school-children would have picked up SgE from their elder siblings even before starting school. As discussed earlier, their English shows many features trans-ferred from their respective background languages. Such SgE structures have then been reinforced through constant use in the playground and in the friendship domain, causing fossilization of certain expressions and con-structions and leading to further innovative use of language (cf. feedback in Fig. 1.4).

Overall, SgE is increasingly used for inter- and intra-ethnic communication as well as in various other domains such as in transactions, in employment, and in the media. Certainly, the switch to a national stream of education (English is now the main medium of instruction) ensures the vitality of a SgE speech community and the growth in the number of native speakers of SgE. There is evidence that stylistic ranges are developing and this process will obviously continue.

2

Research on Singaporean English

2.1 Early research

Although it is difficult to be precise about exactly when research on SgE commenced, the first book on the subject was published in 1974: Tongue, *The English of Singapore and Malaysia*. The work, which is 'designed for the general reader and not for the specialist' (p. v), includes a wide range of features typical of the local variety of English. However, it is unfortunate that one of the chapters is entitled 'Some Frequent Sub-Standard Forms' which he claims (p. lll) are 'found, generally speaking, in the language of the less well-educated members of society but adopted by educated people when communicating with the latter and sometimes among themselves for humorous effect'. Actually, many of these forms occur in the speech of the highly (English-medium) educated in informal situations, e.g. the use of discourse particles, especially la(h) and a(h), and some of them even in quite formal situations, e.g. omission of *be* as copula or auxiliary, variation in the use of prepositions. There is no suggestion in Tongue's book that SgE is in any sense a continuum and that there is system in the occurrence or non-occurrence of certain features. Despite these reservations, however, Tongue deserves credit as a pioneer and the book is a valuable source of examples. Furthermore, Tongue makes some interesting comments on the development of this localized variety and on the legitimacy of such varieties.

An argument of relevance to any research on non-native varieties of English is that since 'ESM [the English of Singapore and Malaysia] is closely related to British English, it seems most sensible to use the latter as the point of reference' and he adds: 'It is the deviations in grammar and usage from standard British usage taken together which distinguish the ESM variety' (p. 7).

2.2 The need for quantitative research

In recent years, a number of writers on nativized varieties of English have argued strongly against the legitimacy of any comparison between such varieties and a prescriptive native speaker standard. This argument can be understood, as any comparison could be taken to imply the inferiority of the nativized variety. However, apologists for the 'no comparison' type of description never explain how quantitative research can be undertaken. Works such as Labov (1969) on *be* occurrence in Black English Vernacular are based on comparison with a standard and it is difficult to see how any quantitative research on morpho-syntactic variation can be undertaken without reference to some norm. Our own quantitative research naturally implies comparison with a norm, namely Standard English. However vague the concept of 'Standard English' may be, it would be generally agreed that features of Standard English would include the following:

1. the marking of nouns for plural (except in irregular cases such as *deer*, *sheep*);
2. the occurrence of forms of *be* in various structures, e.g. between the subject and adjective or predicate nominal;
3. the marking of verbs for past tense when reference is made to a past state or event (except when the present perfect is appropriate).

It is with variation as compared with these norms that we are concerned in the following chapters.

2.3 The expansion of research

The first publications based on a quantitative analysis of linguistic variables in spoken SgE were by Platt (1977*a*, *b*). The former work compared a number of variables—definite and indefinite article occurrence and noun plural, past tense, and third person singular present tense marking—and demonstrated a considerable amount of systematicity. The latter discussed past tense marking of various verb types and demonstrated an implicational relationship among them. As could be expected, the lowest degree of marking in the spoken form was for the 'C + d/t' verbs such as *work*. This is because in all the substratum languages there are no words ending in a consonant cluster. However, under 'Problems for Further Research' mention was made (1977*b*:80) of 'the variation in past tense marking of stative as opposed to non-stative verbs'. As will be seen in Chapter 7, this is a very important factor.

In Platt (1979) it was demonstrated that there are implicational relationships in *be* occurrence according to four following environments: Adjective (Adj), Predicate Nominal (Nom), Verb+ing (V-ing), and Locative (Loc), with the implicational relationship in that order. This ordering was based on the recorded speech of 59 Singaporeans, 41 of whom were English-medium educated. However, for these 41 the overall occurrence of *be* before a predicate nominal was slightly higher than before V-ing. Later research by Ho (1986) on 100 ethnically Chinese, English-medium-educated Singaporeans has indicated that overall occurrence of *be* before V-ing is very similar to its occurrence in the pre-adjective environment. Some of the results of the earlier investigations were published in Platt and Weber (1980).

Newbrook (1987) is a collection of papers based on research by Newbrook and students at the National University of Singapore on aspects of the syntax of educated SgE. Most of the research is based on written English and there are also reports of attitude tests. It provides interesting information on local norms and usage.

Foley (1988) is a collection of articles on various features of SgE. One of the articles (Bradshaw and Hew) contains results of quantitative analysis of a number of morpho-syntactic variables in spoken SgE. It compares the speech of one woman when speaking to adults and to her 1-year-old child. Her education level is GCE O level (four years of secondary education). For speech to adults the highest occurrence of *be* is pre-Loc, but there is only one token of this. For three other environments the highest score is for Pre-Adj (90.9%), followed by Aux (= pre-V-ing), followed by pre-NP (noun and embedded clauses). As will be seen in Chapter 6, occurrence of *be* before a clause is considerably higher than before a predicate nominal. Bradshaw and Hew's ordering is at variance with Platt (1979) and with Ho (1986) but, of course, it is based on the speech of only one person and a total of only 27 occurrences out of a possible 31.

For past tense, the speaker marks the verb 12 times out of a possible 15, i.e. 80%. This is slightly less than the percentage for the 10 speakers with higher than GCE O level investigated by Platt (1977b) but considerably higher than the overall percentage for the 20 GCE O level speakers investigated by Ho (1986). However, the purpose of Bradshaw and Hew's investigation was to compare talk to adults with talk to children and as only one speaker is involved, no meaningful comparison can be made.

Foley (1988) provides a useful 'Bibliography of English in Singapore/ Malaysia'. Many of the works referred to are unfortunately not widely available, being theses and academic exercises or local publications. However, Gupta (1986) 'A Standard for Singapore English?', Richards (1982a, b) on rhetorical and communicative styles, and Tay (1982) 'The Phonology of Educated Singapore English', are more accessible.

Unfortunately, Foley's bibliography includes a considerable number of publications which seem to have little or no relationship to English in Singapore or Malaysia, such as 'Salient Segmental Features in the Mandarin Spoken in Singapore', 'A Fifth Tone in the Mandarin Spoken in Singapore', or 'Handbook of Malay Colloquial as Spoken in Singapore: Being a Series of Introductory Lessons for Domestic and Business Purposes'. The claim on the back cover that the volume contains 'the largest bibliography so far published on Singapore English with over 700 titles listed' is no doubt true as far as size is concerned, but as quite a number of the references deal only with Malaysia and a considerable number of the others do not deal with Singaporean English, the number seems somewhat inflated.

SgE is unique among non-native varieties both in the degree to which it is used as a spoken as well as a written/printed medium and in the extent to which it is used in informal situations among the population. It is therefore particularly worthy of research, not only for practical purposes such as the preparation of materials for the teaching of 'standard' English but also for the insights to be gained concerning the processes of language indigenization, the influence of substrate languages, learning strategies and possible universals on language acquisition, and the interrelationship between semantic factors and morpho-syntax. It can be expected that the pace of research will increase.

In Platt and Ho (1988) and Ho (1989*b*, 1990), we gave some indication of the relationship between certain semantic factors and the marking of past tense, and in Platt (1989) the contributions of substratum influences, creativity, and universals to the nature of indigenized varieties of English are considered. In Chapter 4, below, we discuss some factors involved in the degree of noun plural marking, in Chapter 6 we discuss the systematic nature of *be* occurrence in SgE, in Chapter 7 we consider factors contributing to or inhibiting past tense marking, and in Chapters 9 and 10 we consider the influence of Chinese semantics on verb usage, considering in particular verbs of movement and verb repetition.

There are some academics in Singapore who feel that research should concentrate on the speech and writing of the more educated members of society. However, we agree with Ritchie (1986:27) that 'basilectal SE shows considerable promise . . . as a locus for the study of second-language acquisition and use'. In fact, it seems to us that there is a need to investigate the whole range of SgE in order to understand the degree to which various factors operate in the English of those with different levels of English-medium education.

3

Substratum or Universals?

3.1 Bickerton's 'bioprogram' hypothesis

Bickerton's 'bioprogram' hypothesis (Bickerton 1981) was greeted with a good deal of adverse criticism, e.g. Aitchison (1983), Holm (1982), Le Page (1983). Much of the 'Open Peer Commentary' following Bickerton (1984*a*) is also highly critical, e.g. Seuren (1984:208): 'Bickerton's argument for "biological determination of linguistic properties" (Section 4.0) suffers from factual incorrectness as well as tendentious and often fanciful analyses.'

Certainly, some of Bickerton's claims may be, or have been, proven incorrect and even if they are correct they may be difficult to substantiate. However, one interesting claim in Bickerton (1981) seemed worth pursuing empirically and quantitatively. This is the claim (p. 165) regarding past tense marking of verbs in two decreolizing situations, Guyana and Hawaii, that 'what was being marked in both sets of data was not really pastness but rather punctuality' and that the distinction between punctual and non-punctual affected the degree of past tense marking.

It is necessary here to quote Bickerton at some length:

In creoles, past tense is not a category. But when creoles begin to decreolize, past-tense markers begin to be introduced, occurring sporadically just as they do in child acquisition.

At first, one might interpret such data just as similar child language data have been interpreted—the speakers have an established past category but do not always mark it. However, analyses of decreolization in both Guyana and Hawaii (Bickerton 1975: 142–61; 1977:36–51), with a data base of a thousand past-reference verbs in both cases, suggest quite a different picture.

On the assumption that speakers had a past category, one would have to conclude that decreolizing GC (Guyanese Creole) speakers randomly inserted past morphemes 27 percent of the time while decreolizing HCE (Hawaiian Creole English) speakers did so 30 percent of the time. However, when all past-reference verbs were divided into two categories—those that referred to SINGLE, PUNCTUAL EVENTS, and those that referred to iterative or habitual events—insertion rates were shown to vary widely between the two categories, as shown in Table 3.2 ... (Bickerton 1981:164)

The figures in Bickerton's Table 3.2 are presented in Table 3.1 below along with figures for Singaporean English. These are based on interviews with 100 English-medium-educated ethnically Chinese Singaporeans (Ho 1986). In the corpus there were 8,725 verbs which, prescriptively, should be marked for past tense. Clearly, the punctual–non-punctual distinction is

TABLE 3.1. *A comparison of Bickerton's figures for past tense marking in Guyanese Creole and Hawaiian Creole English with Singaporean English* (%)

	Punctual	Non-punctual
Guyanese Creole	38	12
Hawaiian Creole English	53	7
Singaporean English	56	23

Sources: Bickerton (1981) and Ho (1986).

highly relevant for Singaporean English and, as will be seen later, the difference in past tense marking between punctual and non-punctual is even more dramatic for those with lower levels of formal English-medium education.

Of course, Bickerton's earlier claims about the bioprogram are restricted to the genesis of creoles and even in a later work (1984a:173) he states of the Language Bioprogram Hypothesis (LBH) that it 'claims that the innovative aspects of creole grammar are inventions on the part of the first generation of children who have a pidgin as their linguistic input, rather than features transmitted from pre-existing languages'. However in Bickerton (1984b: 154 ff.) he raises the question of whether the bioprogram influences secondary acquisition and mentions (p. 156) that 'in their acquisition of English articles, native speakers of Spanish are influenced by the specific–nonspecific distinction, one of the linchpins of the bioprogram'. On the other hand, he mentions (p. 155) that 'native speakers of Hindi frequently make mistakes such as **I am liking it* or **He is wanting to see you* (Gordon Fairbanks, p.c. [personal communication]). Use of nonpunctuals with statives is a bioprogram as well as an English violation . . .' and he continues (p. 156) 'Thus in this case mother-tongue influence clearly overrides the bioprogram in nonprimary acquisition.'

He also refers to Huebner's (1982) description of the acquisition of the English definite article by a Hmong speaker and concludes (p. 157) that this study 'does strongly suggest that in nonprimary acquisition the promptings of the bioprogram are by no means extinguished but rather overlaid by subsequent learning'. It is certainly the case with Singaporeans that it is the speech of those with low levels of English-medium education which fits more closely to what Bickerton claims to be features of the bioprogram. As can be expected, those Singaporeans with high levels of English-medium education approximate much more closely to Standard English in matters such as past tense marking and the use of definite and indefinite articles, at least in more formal situations. In unmonitored speech there is greater deviation from prescriptive norms.

3.2 Chinese substratum features

However, some features of Singaporean English, especially of basilectal Singaporean English, show a marked resemblance to Chinese. Ritchie (1986), referring to Platt and Weber (1980) and Platt, Weber and Ho (1983a), suggests that basilectual Singaporean English is, in some respects, typologically closer to Chinese than to English and he considers three particular features (1–3 below). Further substratum features are given in 4–8.

1. Topic-comment structures, e.g.
   Is very interesting I find geography.

   (Platt and Weber 1980)

2. Zero pronouns, e.g.
   ___is just at the back of this Sago Lane.
   We don't have___.

   (Platt and Weber 1980)

3. No pleonastic subjects, e.g.
   In China where___got people go to English school?

   (Platt, Weber and Ho 1983*a*)

4. The use of discourse particles, e.g.
   A: That machine very hard to operate—so many buttons.
   B: Easy ma! Come I show you.

   (Platt, Weber and Ho 1984)

   The use of other Chinese particles is discussed and exemplified in Platt and Ho (1989).

5. Semantic changes, e.g.
   Come, I'll send you to the airport.
   (Meaning 'I'll give you a lift to the airport.')

   (Platt, Weber and Ho 1984)

6. Chinese-type serial verb construction, e.g.
   That book on the TV, take come here, can or not?
   (Father to son, both sitting on the sofa and the latter is sent to get a book.)

   (Platt, Weber and Ho 1984)

7. Chinese-type question tagging as exemplified in 6 and in:
   Our chicken also the same—all came from one chicken, right or not?

   (Platt, Weber and Ho 1983*a*)

8. Repetition for emphasis, e.g.
   I find find find don' have.
   (Meaning 'I've looked everywhere but haven't found it.')

   (Platt, Weber and Ho 1984)

In this last example, there is also Chinese influence in the use of *find* for 'look for'. Of course, topic-comment structures, serial verbs, and repetition are also common in many creoles and therefore Chinese influence cannot be proved.

However, one important difference between the typical creole speaker and the typical speaker of basilectal Singaporean English is that whereas the former is not typically bilingual in the creole and one or more of the substratum languages, the latter is and will, if ethnically Chinese, use a Chinese dialect and/or Baba Malay as well as English. In fact, he or she may speak and listen to a non-English language for the major part of everyday communication.

Other obvious Chinese substratum features of the more basilectal sub-varieties of Singaporean English will be mentioned and exemplified in later chapters. However, it will also be seen that by no means all the variation in Singaporean English can be explained by substratum influences.

4

Noun Plural Marking in Singaporean English

4.1 Noun plural marking in creoles and Chinese

It is a well-known feature of typical creoles that nouns are not marked for plural. It is only when there is influence from a superstrate language which does mark nouns for plural, whether through frequent contact with its speakers or through formal teaching of and through the medium of it, that noun plural marking appears. Of course, reference of a noun to more than one item of the referent *may* be indicated by a different demonstrative or by a quantifier, as in the Australian Cape York Creole, e.g.

Plenti dog i bin singaut.
Some dogs were barking.

(Crowley and Rigsby 1979:177)

Chinese, the main substratum language of Singaporean English and still the main first language of most, although by no means all, Singaporean Chinese, does not mark plural on the noun either. As with creoles, reference of the noun to more than one item of the referent may be indicated by a quantifier where appropriate but when it is clear from the context, from shared knowledge, or from general knowledge that several items are being referred to then a quantifier may not be required.

The first quantitative investigation of noun plural marking in Singaporean English (Platt 1977a) was actually a comparison of noun plural marking with four other variables: definite article occurrence, indefinite article occurrence, past tense marking, and third person singular present tense marking. It was also a comparison of these variables in the speech of 20 English-medium-educated speakers and 14 Chinese-medium-educated speakers. One interesting finding was that noun plural marking was always higher than third person singular present tense marking, except in the case of two of the Chinese-medium-educated speakers. In both cases the number of tokens of third person singular present tense was too low to be considered a reliable indicator (Table 4.1).

Interestingly, Wolfram (1969:143), reporting on variation in the speech of Detroit Negroes, states that 'the incidence of z plural absence is very low for all Negro social classes, even the working class'. Compared with third person singular z, z plural absence is lower for each of the four social classes, strikingly so in the upper and lower working-class groups.

TABLE 4.1. *Noun plural and third person singular marking of two Chinese-medium-educated speakers*

Speaker	Noun plural		3 sg	
	Marking rate	%	Marking rate	%
B2	16/24	66.7	2/2	100
B13	3/32	9.4	1/4	25

One reason for the higher degree of marking of noun plural as compared with third person singular present tense is that the former marks an obvious distinction. Bickerton (1981:149), referring to child language acquisition, mentions that 'the plural morpheme marks a single, straightforward distinction—one/more than one—and it does so bi-uniquely'. Third person singular, on the other hand, is the only marked form of the verb in the present tense (except in the case of *be*) and to the learner it must be confusing that whereas nouns are (except in irregular cases) marked with an affix to indicate plural, verbs are marked with the *same* affix forms when the subject of the verb is singular. In fact, marking of verbs when the subject is plural is fairly common in the speech of some second and foreign language speakers of English. The difference in degree of marking between noun plural and third person singular present tense is also confirmed by Ho (1981) for 15 ethnically Chinese Singaporeans in a pilot study for her research on noun plural marking. Furthermore, the overall scores for the 15 speakers were higher for noun plural marking for every one of 13 phonetic environments.

4.2 Phonological environments

However, although the rules of noun plural marking in English can be considered as making 'more sense' for the learner/acquirer than some other rules of English, there are clearly constraints on the degree to which nouns are marked for plural. One of these could be expected to be phonological environment. This was one of the independent variables in Ho's investigation (1981) of noun plural marking in the recorded speech of 50 English-medium-educated, ethnically Chinese Singaporeans, 10 in each of 5 educational levels:

Group I   tertiary graduates
Group II   A levels (6 years secondary education)
Group III   O levels (4 years secondary education)
Group IV   1–3 years of secondary education
Group V   primary school only.

Scores were calculated for three following environments and two preceding environments. The three following environments were:

1. when potential plural marker is followed by a pause;
2. when potential plural marker is followed by a vowel;
3. when potential plural marker is followed by a consonant.

Overall and for each of the five educational groups there was very little difference according to following environment and individual scores showed no consistent pattern.

Unlike in most 'native' varieties of English, there is very little liaison between words in Singaporean English. This explains why there is no systematic difference in noun plural marking according to following environment.

The two preceding environments investigated were Consonant and Vowel. Noun plural marking was higher following a vowel for 37 of the 50 speakers (74%): 9 of the 10 A level speakers and 7 of the 10 in each of the other groups.

4.3 Semantic-syntactic environments

What appears to have a greater influence than phonological environment on the degree of noun plural marking for individual speakers is the syntactic-semantic environment. In Ho's investigation, scores were calculated for eight preceding environments but we shall consider only three:

A   Zero Determiner, the environment preceding an indefinite plural count noun, e.g. 'We get customer(s) like that.'

D   + or − Count Noun Modifiers, e.g. *any, some, all, other, such, what, no, certain, more, most.* These may occur before count nouns as in *any books* or before non-count nouns as in *any money.*

F   + Count Noun Modifiers, e.g. numerals higher than one, *both, (a) few, several, many,* which occur only before count nouns.

Group scores for the three environments are given in Table 4.2.

Noun plural marking in environment F is higher than in environment A for 41 of the speakers (82%) and it is also higher in environment F than in environment D for 41 speakers (82%). It is higher in environment D than in environment A for only 26 speakers (52%).

In environment F, categorical noun plural marking occurs for eight of the tertiary level speakers, five of the A level speakers, and one of the O level speakers.

For environment D, categorical marking occurs for five of the tertiary level speakers, one of the A level speakers, and one of the secondary 1–3 level speakers.

For environment A there was no speaker with categorical marking of noun plural.

TABLE 4.2. *Noun plural marking for three syntactic-semantic environments for the five educational levels*

	A		D		F	
	Marking rate	%	Marking rate	%	Marking rate	%
Tertiary	296/335	88.4	151/162	93.2	150/153	98.0
A levels	350/411	85.2	142/159	89.3	204/215	94.9
O levels	283/383	73.9	105/175	60.0	187/219	85.4
Sec. 1–3	148/280	52.9	73/160	45.6	133/226	58.8
Primary	78/292	26.7	40/122	32.8	71/196	36.2
TOTAL	1155/1701	67.9	511/778	65.7	745/1009	73.9

Notes: A Zero Determiner;
D + or − Count Noun Modifiers;
F + Count Noun Modifiers.

What is the explanation for the different rates of noun plural marking? As Chinese does not mark plural by affixation no matter what the preceding syntactic-semantic environment it is obviously not a direct substratum influence. In Chinese it is often to be understood from context or from previously acquired knowledge that more than one item is referred to. For example, in the following, if it is known that the speaker is an avid reader who reads several books a day, then *shū* will be understood to refer to more than one book:

wǒ měi   tiān kàn   shū
I   every day read book
'I read books/a book every day.'

Therefore, when no particular numeral or a quantifier implying 'more than one' co-occurs with the noun it is understandable that, particularly at the lower end of the continuum, the marking of nouns for plural is lower. A very strong reason for the low degree of noun plural marking can be attributed to the fact that this is a non-specific environment. As mentioned in Platt, Weber, and Ho (1984:54), it seems that many indigenized varieties of English make a specific–non-specific rather than a definite–indefinite distinction. This, of course, is claimed by Bickerton (1981) to be a feature of typical creoles and of the 'bioprogram'.

However, where there is a quantifier which co-occurs *only* with count nouns there seems to be a considerable reinforcement of the English rule of marking the noun for plural. Scores at the lower end of the educational scale are still low—for one speaker only 2 nouns were marked out of a total of 16 tokens and for another none at all out of 48 tokens, but for those with four years of secondary education (O levels), the lowest score is 24 out of 34: 70.6%. It would seem that once a higher level of English-medium secondary education has been reached then the rule of noun plural marking in this environment has been fairly well internalized. It must be remembered too that some of the non-marking in spoken English is due to phonetic factors, particularly when the plural affix occurs after a consonant.

The determiners of environment D are, as mentioned before, those which may co-occur not only before a count noun referring to more than one item, in which case plural marking occurs in Standard English, but also before non-count nouns as in *more water, some rice*, and, in some cases, before a singular count noun as in *the other book, a certain person, no opportunity*. When nouns which should prescriptively be marked for plural were preceded by one of these determiners, marking for plural was quite high among the tertiary and A level speakers, the lowest degree of marking being 10 out of 14 (71.4%) for the tertiary-level speakers and 4 out of 6 (66.7%) for the A level speakers. However, below this level of education, the degree of marking is very variable, e.g. from 13.3% to 88.9% among the O level speakers, from 20% to 100% among the sec. 1–3 level speakers and from 0 to 82.4% among the primary-level speakers.

The effect of a preceding quantifier on noun plural marking is also in evidence in the speech of a group of adult Hong Kong Chinese. In an investigation based on recorded interviews with 80 speakers, Budge (1986) also found that nouns referring to more than one of the same item were more frequently marked for plural if preceded by a quantifier (category 2) than if not (category 1). Of the 80, 5 produced fewer than 5 tokens in category 2 but of the remaining 75, 61 (81.3%) had a higher rate of marking in category 2 than in category 1. Two subjects had the same scores for both categories, one of them having 100% in each category (26 tokens in category 1 and 10 tokens in category 2).

It seems that some speakers acquire the overall rule for noun plural marking quite early while others may find it difficult to internalize, even with a considerable amount of further training.

From a purely formal viewpoint, the rule of noun plural marking is not a particularly difficult one as, to quote Bickerton (1981:149) again, 'the plural morpheme makes a simple straightforward distinction—one/more than one—and it does so bi-uniquely, that is to say, in a one-morpheme one-meaning relationship: when the morpheme is present, one meaning is entailed; when it is absent, the other meaning is entailed.' However, with the D group of determiners, it is not a straightforward matter for the speaker of a Chinese dialect. After all, these are sometimes followed by nouns marked for plural and sometimes not. When co-occurring with count nouns, some of them are very much like quantifiers, e.g. *all, most, some* (unstressed) and in Standard English are followed by a noun marked for plural. Others such as *other, such, certain, more* are also quantifier-like in some environments, e.g. *other books*, but not when preceded by certain other determiners in the noun phrase, e.g. *one other book*, *my other brother*, while others again such as *any*, *some* (stressed), *what*, *no* may co-occur with singular or plural count nouns.

In reading school texts and in some cases reading English-language newspapers and magazines, someone of a Chinese dialect background will sometimes see *no*, *any*, *more*, etc. followed by a plural noun and sometimes by a singular noun. The rule for when to add a plural marker is certainly not a simple one and it is doubtful whether, in the teaching of English, particular attention can be given to the teaching and practice of noun plural marking in the more problematic environments—at least not at primary and lower secondary levels.

Of course, there are many other factors which may influence a person's speech, whether in a more permanent way or on a particular occasion. Among the more permanent sociological factors are type of occupation and type of interlocutor with whom the speaker frequently communicates.

For example, Speaker 4 in the tertiary level group, a civil engineer with an overall rate of noun plural marking of 73.1%, the lowest in the tertiary level group, used a great deal of Hokkien dialect in his work. On the other hand, Speaker 3, with an overall rate of 98.5%, had English-medium-educated parents and English was used in the family, friendship, media, and transactions domains, with only a little Cantonese and Bazaar Malay used where necessary at food stalls. At the other end of the educational scale, Speaker 44's rate of 75.4% may well be related to her employment as an amah (general domestic) at an X-ray clinic, where she would have picked up technical terms and heard a good deal of English spoken.

Among the more temporary sociological factors, those related to the particular occasion of the recorded interview, are attitudes to being interviewed, attitudes to the interviewer, and the environment in which the interview takes place. State of health, alertness, and tiredness are, of course, other factors. Speaker 16 in the A level group had an overall noun plural marking rate well below the 88.6% mean for this group—only 51.6%. He was interviewed just before his evening shift began. The atmosphere was very informal and he spoke very fast. There was also the more permanent factor of the home environment. He spoke Hokkien and Mandarin with his Chinese-medium-educated parents and siblings.

To summarize, it seems that the independent variables related to the degree of noun plural marking are:

1. educational level;
2. phonetic environment, particularly preceding phonetic environment;
3. semantic factors, in particular the occurrence of a preceding quantifier which, in Standard English, co-occurs only with a noun marked for plural;
4. 'permanent' sociological factors; and
5. temporary sociological factors.

It is, of course, impossible to quantify all of these variables, especially 4 and 5. Even in 1, there is a wide range within each educational level in terms of field of study, and in 2 there are differences in degree to which various preceding consonants may inhibit or facilitate the addition of the plural marker. In Ho's investigation it was found that plural marking was lower for stops, particularly after voiceless stops. This was particularly so for those with lower levels of education.

For the researcher undertaking a quantitative investigation there is always a problem concerning the degree of 'delicacy' (to use Halliday's term) to which data may be subjected. The finer the degree of delicacy, the fewer are the linguistic tokens in each 'cell'. The coarser the degree of delicacy, the more masking of possibly important differences there will be. The best the researcher can do is to opt for a middle course and analyse to the extent that the relationship between the various independent variables and the dependent variable being investigated becomes apparent.

5

Research on the Verb

5.1 The corpus

In the following chapters, variation in the verb in SgE, based on extensive, detailed research by Ho, is discussed. The one hundred subjects under study are all ethnically Chinese Singaporeans who have had English-medium education. A list of the informants and their particulars is found in Appendix A. Ho's investigation shows the extent to which SgE is influenced by the substrate language, Chinese, and in particular the Hokkien dialect,[1] as well as by other factors such as simplification and other learning strategies and universals of language acquisition, all of them factors which need to be taken into consideration when examining an interlanguage such as SgE, which is 'an ordered dynamic system' (Platt 1978:61) advancing towards a target norm. However, it must be stressed that SgE is not just a learner's language like the language of a learner of French in England. As the latter does not usually have a community of French-speaking English people with whom he or she can interact, it is less likely that the learner's French will be petrified at a level at which communication can adequately take place but which is far from native speaker competence. The situation is entirely different in Singapore. Learners of English are continually exposed to SgE. At the same time, they can practise using SgE with other speakers of SgE. This constant exposure to and use of SgE has led to a petrified system which is available for informal use.

In what follows, the systematicity of SgE is demonstrated and the degree to which certain variables occur at different levels of education and whether there is any implicationality are investigated. The variables under examination are *be*, past tense marking, non-standard use of verbs of movement, and repetition of verbs. It is also shown that the variable use of these linguistic features is socially diagnostic and, indeed, as Labov and other linguists have shown, there is a close correlation between these features and social class. Features found in the corpus are substantiated wherever possible by examples found in written English, such as newspapers and the written assignments of students.

[1] Although in the spoken form, the Chinese dialects (including Mandarin) are in general mutually unintelligible, Chao (1968:13) points out that 'in matters of grammar', one finds 'the greatest degree of uniformity'. In view of this and the paucity of published material on Hokkien, many examples cited in the book are in Mandarin. However, where there are distinct differences between Mandarin and Hokkien, exemplifications will be given in the latter dialect.

5.2 The data

Tape recordings of spontaneous speech of 150 ethnically Chinese English-medium-educated Singaporeans were made by the interviewer, Ho. These informants were mostly friends of the interviewer or had been recommended to the interviewer by friends. They were recorded at their places of work, at their homes, or at the home of the interviewer.

5.3 Selection of informants

1. There is strict control where educational qualifications are concerned. For example, an informant who has had two years of pre-university education, but has not passed the General Paper, is excluded from the sample. As we are looking at variation in English according to educational levels, it is essential that every informant should have a pass in English and be assigned a group according to educational qualifications. An informant who failed the General Paper cannot be put in the O level group as he or she has had an advantage of two additional years of education. However, it has been decided that with the group of informants with primary education, those with additional training at a vocational institute should be included. Likewise, secretaries with O level qualification and having an additional secretarial diploma are placed under the O level group.

2. All the informants are working or have worked before as it is felt that the working environment is one of the major factors affecting competence in English.

3. As far as possible, informants from different types of occupations have been chosen to see whether the type of occupation affects the features under study. It is felt that if all the informants are chosen from lower-status occupations it will give a rather distorted picture of the performance of the group. Thus, although many recordings of informants with O level education from less prestigious occupations were made, these have not been used. They are, however, used where relevant, to point out other features not extracted from the corpus of the hundred tape recordings chosen.

4. All the informants are ethnically Chinese, although they may belong to different dialect groups. It has been decided to keep a homogeneous group as it is felt that background languages have a very marked influence on SgE. As 76.9% of the population of Singapore is Chinese, it is felt that the type of features found in this dominant group will probably affect the English of the other ethnic groups.

5. All informants have received an English-medium education. As pointed out before, most of those who have been through a non-English medium education are not fluent speakers of SgE.

6. An attempt was made to have a balance of male and female informants. The present corpus comprises recordings of 51 females and 49 males.

5.4 Selection of recordings

A hundred tapes were selected based on the above criteria and the quality of the recording as described below.

1. There must be good rapport between the interviewer and the informant.

2. There must be a substantial amount of speech by the informant. At the basilectal end, many of the informants were not able to carry on a conversation at length. A tape is discarded if the pause button is used too frequently because speech is not forthcoming from the informant.

3. The tape recording must be clear to allow easy extraction of data.

5.5 Transcription

All tapes were transcribed by Ho in ordinary orthography. Phonetic transcription was used only where the pronunciation was markedly deviant from SBrE.

5.6. The questionnaire

A questionnaire was personally administered by Ho at the end of each interview to obtain information on the occupation and linguistic background of each informant.

6

To Be or Not to Be: Variation in *Be* Occurrence

6.1 Previous studies on *be*

One of the distinctive syntactic features of Black English Vernacular (BEV) is the variable use of *be*. Among the more detailed studies on variation in the copula in BEV are Labov (1969, 1972), Wolfram (1969, 1974), and Baugh (1980). Perhaps the best-known work in this area is Labov's (1969) 'Contraction, Deletion, and Inherent Variability of the English Copula'. In this article, Labov argues that the deletion of *be* is largely a result of phonological processes. After the present tense full forms of *be* in constructions such as *he is*, *they are* have been contracted, the remaining *'s* and *'re* are deleted. However, deletion does not apply to *'m* as 'there are phonological processes which operate upon final [z] and [r] in BEV, but not upon final [m]' (Labov 1969:721). He further states that 'wherever SE [standard English] can contract, NNE [non-standard Negro English] can delete *is* and *are*, and vice versa; wherever SE cannot contract, NNE cannot delete *is* and *are*, and vice versa' (Labov 1969:722). This analysis lends support to the hypothesis that BEV does not have creole origins, but is in fact a 'dialect' of English and has an underlying copula.

Various linguists however, e.g. Bickerton (1973*a*, 1975), Romaine (1979, 1988), Baugh (1980), Alleyne (1980), and Holm (1975, 1984, 1988), are critical of Labov's approach. In fact Baugh's (1980) detailed and insightful analysis of Labov's data provides compelling evidence of the creole ancestry of BEV. As Labov had originally combined the predicate adjective and locative environments, the effects of the former environment had not been apparent. When the two environments had been separated by Baugh, it was found that the predicate adjective environment strongly favoured the deletion of *be* but had minimal effect on contraction (deletion = 1.00; contraction = 0.116). The locative environment, on the other hand, did not favour deletion. This suggests that deletion must have pre-dated the emergence of contracted forms for the predicate adjective environment and that a zero copula did exist in protoforms (Baugh 1980:100). Besides commenting on structural similarities, Baugh also points out similar constraints on the adjective and locative environments when comparing his data to those found in Holm's (1975) investigation of the copula in Jamaican Creole English and Gullah, as well as in Bailey's (1966) study of Jamaican Creole. He then concludes decisively that the creole ancestry of contempory BEV is established beyond any doubt (Baugh 1980:103).

This conclusion is also supported later by Labov, who acknowledges that 'It [BEV] shows evidence of derivation from an earlier Creole that was closer to the present-day Creoles of the Caribbean' (Labov 1982:192). Fasold, however, feels that 'Labov's analysis might be the outcome of very late stages of decreolization' and maintains that 'contraction-deletion is part of modern VBE [BEV]' (Fasold 1990:212, 222).

Apart from research on the BEV copula, other interesting works on *be* include Day's (1972) investigation of the Hawaiian post-creole continuum and Bickerton's research on Guyanese Creole (Bickerton 1973*a*, 1973*b*, 1975). Bickerton states that the copulative post-creole continuum is not 'an area of random variation' but one which shows 'a series of developmental stages ordered in accordance with basic principles of linguistic change' (Bickerton 1973*b*:640).

Platt's (1976, 1979) investigation of the copula in SgE shows a similar systematicity. The occurrence of *be* was examined in four syntactic environments: pre-adjective, pre-nominal, pre-V-ing, and pre-locative. His findings show that there is a high degree of implicationality between the four environments and that *be* is acquired in the following order:

1. Invariant non-realization in all 4 environments.
2. Variable realization in all 4 environments.
3. Invariant realization pre-Locative; variable elsewhere.
4. Invariant realization pre-Locative, pre-Nominal; variable elsewhere.
5. Invariant realization pre-Locative, pre-Nominal, pre-V-ing; variable pre-Adjective.
6. Invariant realization in all 4 environments.

(Platt 1976: 55–6)

6.2 The present study

The corpus comprises 10,311 instances of potential *be* tokens, of which 8,896 (or 86.3%) are observed occurrences. All potential occurrences were classified according to 5 educational levels as well as 7 environments following *be* and 7 environments preceding *be*. The 5 educational levels are: tertiary level, A level, O level, secondary 1–3 (henceforth sec. 1–3) level, and primary level. The 7 environments following *be* are:

1. Before adjectives or adjectival groups: __Adj, e.g.
   P10.3. I damn naughty.
2. In passives: __Pass, e.g.
   S12.13. She punished.
3. Before -ing forms of the verb: __V-ing, e.g.
   S6.30. I still finding.

4. Before nominal groups: __Nom, e.g.
   S10.15. De one de wife lah.
      'That lady is his wife.'
5. Before locatives: __Loc, e.g.
   T13.2. Another (brother) in de NS (National Service).
6. Before temporals: __Temp, e.g.
   P12.13. Breaktime in de morning.
7. Before clauses: __Cl, e.g.
   T2.15. Dat is what dey are trying to do.

The 7 preceding environments are:

1. After the pronoun *I*: I__ .
2. After third person singular pronouns *he, she*: 3sg__. (The environment It__ has been excluded because of a phonetic problem. This is discussed under Section 6.4 'The contracted form of *it is* in SgE'.)
3. After all pronouns other than those in (2), *you, they, we, one, some, all*, etc.: Pn__.
4. After nominals and nominal groups, e.g. *my friends, some of them*, etc.: Nom__.
5. After WH and similar elements, such as *that, who, which*, etc.: WH__.
6. After clauses: Cl__, e.g.
   What I hate is . . . (or in basilectal SgE: I hate most is . . .)
7. After demonstratives *this/that, these/those*: D__.

6.3 Environments that have been excluded

The following environments have been excluded:

1. Environments with invariant *be* constructions, e.g.

   P10.8. So I *be* ba(ck) again (in Singapore) so I pay me I fly to Bangkok again.
   P20.11. I was the only one to be scolded and my brother and sisters never *be* scolded so that I always objected.

While it is possible that *be* in P10.8 occurs after a deleted *would*, the second token resembles the use of 'distributive *be*' in BEV, e.g.

Well, see, I *don't be* with them all the time so I can't pick out one specific leader.

(Fasold 1972:154)

It is beyond the scope of this book to examine such tokens. However, it should prove an interesting area for further research. Note that the second type of *be* is used mainly by basilectal informants. The first type is used even by acrolectal speakers, e.g.

T1.14. (Once the stock market turns bullish) property (prices) will follow behind, because people *be* getting a lot of money.

2. Environments where *be* occurs in question tags, e.g.
He doesn't drink any more, *is* it?

3. Environments where *be* is in final position, e.g.
Yes, he is.
Interestingly, the categorical use of *be* in this environment is also found in BEV.

4. Environments where the subject, such as *it*, other pronouns, or NPs are omitted, e.g.

P1.27. He tot (he) was as(ked) to proceed.

P14.11. Mostly (it) is fix(ed) price.

P2.14. Not that (it) is a must.

This is another example of the categorical use of *be* which is also found in BEV.

5. Environments where the subject follows *be*:

P3.19. Here is our working place.

6. Environments where the contracted form of *be* is used with demonstratives and the WH elements e.g. *that's* [dæs], *what's* [wʌs], where prescriptively *be* ought not to be used:

S12.5. I feel boring—I want to see wha(t)'s de society is—is like—to meet the people you see.

S15.23. (talking about safety boots) So dat da(t)'s boot is a preven(t)—er preven(t) also—our foot from hurting.

It is found that the phrase *that's why* [dæswaɪ] occurs very frequently as a filler. Such tokens are not tabulated.

7. Environments where WH occurs after *be*, e.g.

Go and see, hiding behind the car there is who.

It is found that basilectal informants and some O level informants tend to move WH elements to the end of an utterance, e.g.

S18.5. She teach us—about t(h)ree subje(ct)s lah, English, literature, and another one is what ah?

6.4 The contracted form of *it is* in SgE

The almost categorical realization of the contracted form of *it is* as [ɪs] is one of the distinctive features of SgE. *Is* is also found in written SgE, such as in students' written assignments, e.g. *Is very fun*. In Ho's corpus [ɪs] is used by informants with primary-level up to tertiary-level education, although informants with higher levels of education sometimes use [ɪts]. Another variant used is [ɪz]. Sometimes both the alveolar stop and fricative are deleted leaving [i:], e.g.

O14.10. Previously [i:] (it was) just a shop house.

At the lower end of the continuum there is clearly little or no distinction between the voiceless alveolar stop and voiceless alveolar fricative in final position in monosyllabic words, as shown in the following examples:

S5.22. I take dis type of bus ah. *Is* cost you sixty cen(ts).
S15.20. Oh ah, *is* normally happen.
O7.7. Dat's what *it* call X Committee.
O16.17. My mother *as* present is not working.

The use of *is* in initial position has sometimes been attributed to influence from Chinese where it is frequent to omit the subject, which is understood in context.

6.5 The *be* + *stem/past* environment in SgE

Before working out implicational scales, Ho excluded two environments following *be*. They are *be* + *stem* and *be* + *past*. It is interesting to note that *be* realization in these environments occurs only in the speech of the primary, sec. 1–3, and O level interviewees. A total of 92 tokens was found. They did not occur in the speech of the A level and tertiary level interviewees. There were only 2 tokens of *be* + *past*. Both were used by O level informants.

Interestingly, these examples bear a close resemblance to those given by Andersen (1979) quoted by Schumann (1979:59). These exemplifications show how adult second-language learners 'create a non-native form-meaning relationship under conditions of restricted access to the TL [target language] norm' (p. 16). The following are his examples of *is* and *are* used as preverbal markers of tense:

> That room *is belong* to Christine, too. (That room *belongs*...)
> That part on top *is go* down. (That part on top *goes* down.)
> The house *was belong* to his son. (The house *belonged*...)
> I *was live* in New York about 6 years ago. (I *lived*...)
> I *was be* a student all my life. (I have been...)

The examples from Ho's corpus show that the present and past forms of *be* are also used as preverbal markers. When the past is referred to, the past forms of *be* are used, e.g.

P1.5. I *was improve* my English.
　'I improved my English.'

S3.8. My mother *was sold* away it (piano).
'My mother sold my piano.'
O16.12. I *was study* in primary school.
'I studied in a primary school.'

The following examples refer to events in the present:

P4.26. My father *is stay* here what.
'My father lives here.'
P13.25. Dey *are put* on new clothes.
'They (the children) put on new clothes (during the Lunar New Year).'

There are, however, instances of deviation from the norm, where the present form of the pre-verbal marker *be* is used for past events. In such cases it was found that these events were almost always habitual or iterative or else that the main verb used was a stative verb e.g.

P10.4. I's *bring* the tings with me. (Informant is referring to his frequent trips to Indonesia in the past.)
P10.4. Whilst dis *is look* like Eurasian.
'He looked like a Eurasian.'
P12.3. We *are feel* so shy. (Informant is referring to her schooldays in a mixed school.)

It is noticed that the structure *non-past be + stem/past* occurs with very high frequency when adverbial adjuncts such as *just* and *already* are used, e.g.

S15.2. De gues(t) *is check* out already.
P15.17. She *is resign* already.
O15.12. My youngest one (brother) *is* just *left* his Sec. (Secondary) Four.

What is interesting is that such structures indicate a 'change of state'. The influence of Chinese is seen in the use of *already*, a literal translation of the Chinese particle *le* (Mandarin) or *liáu* (Hokkien), which in final position can convey the meaning of a change of state. Prescriptively, in SBrE the present perfect aspect would have been used.

The *be + stem/past* structure can also express duration; for example inform-ant S7 wavered between the use of the *be + V-ing* form and the *be + stem* form:

S7.13. Dey *are* now *practising* the coupon system also y'know (referring to Housing and Development Board car parks) Like ours ah ('ours' refers to URA car parks). Yah, dey *are practise* now.

It can also be used to express emphasis. *Be* in the *be + stem* structure is an emphatic marker, showing the informant trying to make a point that it is quite easy to tell apart the type of cutlery each airline has:

S16.17.... you must know all that—by the look y'know—dis *is belong* to MAS, *belongs* to aah QANTAS, or *belongs* to BOAC.

Schumann (1974:148) explains the use of *be + stem* and *0 + V-ing* in a learner's interlanguage as 'a rejection of redundancy' which 'leads to a pidgin-like simplification in morphology'. He quotes H. V. George (1972):

> The difficulty of teachers of English to Asian children is that many of the children accept the features of English which seem to them to be nonredundant, and with these features make a *language of communication* which is more efficient than the standard English which they, the teachers, are attempting to teach. In other words, what for the teacher is 'wrong' is for the learner psychologically correct. (p. 14; emphasis Schumann's)

Lastly, it must not be forgotten that Chinese, a predominantly topic and comment language, probably exerts considerable influence on the *be + stem* structures used by the informants.

6.6 Two linguistic tools: implicational scaling and Varbrul analysis

6.6.1 *Implicational scaling*

Implicational scaling, developed by Guttman (1944), is a particularly useful technique for analysing variation in language. DeCamp (1971:355), for example, applied implicational scaling to his data on Jamaican English. The six linguistic features selected 'are among the many which define the continuum of Jamaican English'. These features are given below:

+A child	−A pikni
+B eat	−B nyam
+C /θ~t/	−C /t/
+D /ð~d/	−D /d/
+E granny	−E nana
+F didn't	−F no ben

The acrolectal form of each linguistic feature is represented by a plus sign and its basilectal variant by a minus sign. Thus [+A] indicates the habitual use of *child* while [−A] shows the use of *pikni* or *pikini* in equivalent contexts. [+B] indicates the habitual use of *eat* instead of *nyam*, which is represented by [−B]. [+C] indicates a phonological contrast in pairs such as *thing/ting* while [−C] shows its absence. Again, while [+D] indicates another phonological contrast in pairs such as *den/then*, [−D] shows its absence. [+E] shows the habitual use of *granny* instead of *nana*, [−E]. [+F] indicates the use of *didn't* in negative past tense constructions, while [−F] shows the use of other alternatives like *no ben, no did*. The combination of these features in the speech of the seven informants from DeCamp's survey of 142 Jamaican communities is as follows:

Speakers   Features
1.   +A +B +C +D +E +F
2.   −A +B −C −D +E +F
3.   −A +B −C −D −E −F
4.   −A −B −C −D −E −F
5.   +A +B +C +D +E +F
6.   +A +B −C −D +E +F
7.   −A +B −C −D +E −F

The construction of an implicational scale of the seven speakers arranged according to the use of the six linguistic features placed in the order D, C, A, F, E, B enables one to see immediately a clear and definite pattern in the co-occurrence of these features for each idiolect (cf. Table 6.1). As DeCamp (1971:357) has commented: 'If all the *n* varieties of a speech community are thus arranged in an ordered series such that the difference between any variety and its neighbours is minimal, the result is a significant spectrum.'

As shown in Table 6.1 there is a great deal of systematicity in the use of the linguistic features, which are now ordered implicationally. Speaker 6, who uses the acrolectal form 'child' [+A], also uses all the acrolectal forms of features to the right of A: 'didn't' [+F], 'Granny' [+E], and 'eat' [+B]. Likewise speaker 7, who uses the basilectal form 'no ben' [−F], also uses all the basilectal forms to the left of F: 'pikni' [−A], /t/ [−C] and /d/ [−D].

We have just seen how implicational scaling has been used effectively to order linguistic features as well as isolects of speakers, ranging from the most basilectal to the most acrolectal. What is most interesting is that the position of the speakers on the continuum also corresponds with their respective socio-economic backgrounds. Thus the most acrolectal speaker, informant 5, who uses all the acrolectal forms of the features, is a young and well-educated proprietor of a successful radio and appliance shop. Speaker 4, who uses all

TABLE 6.1. *Implicational scale for six linguistic features of Jamaican Creole*

Speaker	Linguistic feature					
	D	C	A	F	E	B
5	+	+	+	+	+	+
1	−	+	+	+	+	+
6	−	−	+	+	+	+
2	−	−	−	+	+	+
7	−	−	−	−	+	+
3	−	−	−	−	−	+
4	−	−	−	−	−	−

the basilectal forms, is an illiterate peasant in an isolated mountain village. Similarly, for the rest of the informants, it is found that their backgrounds roughly match their different positions on the continuum (DeCamp 1971:358).

Various other works which show the use of implicational scaling analysis in the study of linguistic data include, among others, Stolz and Bills (1968), Elliot, Legum, and Thompson (1969), Bailey (1973), Fasold (1970, 1973, 1975), Ross (1973), Bickerton (1971a, 1973a, 1973b, 1975), Platt (1976, 1977b), Andersen (1978), and Romaine (1980, 1982).

There are, however, problems arising from the use of this linguistic tool. Romaine (1982:177–82, 1988:186–7) discusses a number of these problems concerning deviant cells and indices of scalability. She points out that 'if empty cells do not count as deviations (and in Bickerton's 1975 data for Guyanese creole, they very often do not), and full freedom is given to manipulate rows and columns, then virtually any set of data is scalable to an acceptable level, possibly as high as 90 percent' (Romaine 1982:177). She also mentions the problem of 'where to draw' the line (both figuratively and literally) between cells defining the variables. Overall, she feels that there should be some constraints on the ordering of rows and columns in implicational scaling (otherwise the device is far too powerful), more consistency from scale to scale should be observed, and there should be an agreement on the threshold of significance for whatever index of scalability one adopts (Romaine 1982:181).

Nevertheless, despite these problems, implicational scaling is a valuable tool. It unravels and displays the underlying systematicity of variable linguistic data and enables one to examine individual as well as group performance. It is also useful for pedagogic purposes; for example, Platt's investigation of *be* realisation in Singaporean English shows how the results of scaling may be of value in the structuring of language-teaching courses (Platt 1976:48).

6.6.2 *Varbrul analysis*

Varbrul analysis is another tool used for analysing variable linguistic data. This technique employs a variable rule program developed by Henrietta Cedergren and David Sankoff. The program calculates the probabilistic aspects of a rule on the basis of frequency data. The use of maximum likelihood estimation finds those values of the coefficients which maximize the probability that the observed data would be produced by a given variable rule model (Cedergren and Sankoff 1974:343).

Both techniques, implicational scaling and Varbrul 2 (the third of the five versions of the Varbrul program) were used to analyse the Singaporean data on *be*. As will be seen in the following sections, each technique gives various illuminating linguistic insights.

6.7 Data used in Varbrul analysis and implicational scaling

The following environments have been excluded in the data used for the Varbrul program because of colinearity and knock-out factors:

preceding environments: WH__, Cl__, D__
following environments: __Cl

Although there are knock-out factors under the Temp environment, the latter has not been excluded. Rather, data under the Temp environment have been combined with the Loc environment. There are many common features under these two environments in terms of similar forms. For example, one can say *at 6 o'clock* and *at that place*. Data under the Adj and Pass environments have also been combined as there is sometimes very little distinction between a passive and an adjective. Granger (1983) describes some adjectives as pseudopassives, e.g.

/194/ We *were engaged* at the time. (p. 134)

She further mentions that the 'statal category' (p. 152), of which sentences 296 and 290 are examples, 'does not only display a relationship with the passive (and consequently with the active), but that it also partakes of the adjectival and verbal pseudopassives' (p. 155). However, she continues: 'It would be hard to prove that the V-ed form in /296/ ... is an adjectival form, since none of the criteria for adjectives applies' (p. 155).

/296/ At the beginning of this chapter fifteen from which my text *is taken* ...
(p. 154)
/290/ 'Earlier' *is misspelt* towards the bottom of this page of the proof.
(p. 154)

Another reason for combining the Temp and Loc environments is that there are fewer tokens in the Temp environment compared to the other environments:

Adj	4,137	tokens
Pass	560	tokens
V-ing	1,561	tokens
Nom	2,305	tokens
Loc	859	tokens
Temp	96	tokens
Cl	793	tokens

In the implicational tables, the preceding environments WH, Cl, and D and the following environment Cl have not been excluded as was done for the Varbrul input. Thus data under environment Adj include all environments with an Adj following a potential *be* irrespective of whether the preceding environment is I, 3sg, Pn, Nom, WH, Cl, or D. It is felt that this would clearly reflect to what extent Adj as a following environment is related to the omission of *be*. Similarly, when I is considered as a preceding environment, all Is irrespective of the following environment have been included.

6.8 Implicational scaling, group averages, and the proportion of speakers with categorical and non-categorical realization of *be*

6.8.1 Environments following be

Table 6.2 gives the percentage-group scores of *be* according to following environments.

Generally, the overall scores for *be* realization increase from the primary to the tertiary level. In the __Pass and __Loc environments the A level scores are slightly higher than the Temp level scores. The preceding environment Pn brings the scores of the tertiary informants down (cf. discussion in Section 6.8.2). The scores for Pn *be* Pass (88.4%) and Pn *be* Loc (85.4%) are much lower than those for the A level for Pn *be* Pass (96.2%) and Pn *be* Loc (100%). In the __Cl environment the score for the tertiary informants is lower than that of the A, O, and S informants. This is due mainly to the lower score of 93.1% (67/72) of the tertiary informants in the D *be* Cl environment (cf. discussion in Section 6.8.2). There is categorical realization of *be* before Cl in all the other preceding environments in the tertiary group.

Two implicational tables—Tables 6.3 and 6.4—have been constructed. The scalability for Table 6.3 is 89.1%, the calculation of which is based on the formula:

$$\frac{\text{number of filled cells} - \text{number of deviations}}{\text{number of filled cells}} \times 100$$

i.e. $\dfrac{634 - 69}{634} \times 100 = 89.1\%$

This is an acceptable degree of scalability, as in general, 85% perfect scales or better are considered efficient approximations to perfect scales (Guttman

TABLE 6.2. Be *realization according to educational levels and seven syntactic environments following* be (%)

	__Adj	__Pass	__V-ing	__Nom	__Loc	__Temp	__Cl
Tertiary	94.2	94.1	91.9	97.1	95.3	100.0	97.4
A level	91.6	94.9	91.9	96.4	96.0	100.0	98.8
O level	85.1	87.4	87.8	92.9	92.2	96.6	98.1
Sec. 1–3	68.9	82.8	65.9	89.1	80.0	88.2	97.7
Primary	59.4	65.7	58.5	79.5	61.6	93.8	95.4
Overall	81.8	87.3	81.7	91.9	88.6	95.8	97.9

TABLE 6.3. *Implicational scaling of speakers in regard to* be *realization in seven following syntactic environments* (scalability = 89.1%)

Informant	_Adj	_V-ing	_Nom	_Loc	_Pass	_Cl	_Temp
A3	+	+	⊗	+	+	+	+
T7	+	+	+	⊗	⊙	+	+
O4	+	+	+	⊗	+	+	—
T1	+	⊗	+	+	⊗	+	—
T12	+	⊗	+	+	+	⊗	+
A20	x	+	+	+	+	+	+
A6	x	+	+	+	+	+	—
T11	x	+	+	+	⊗	+	—
A11	x	+	⊗	+	+	+	—
O11	x	+	+	⊗	+	+	—
T19	x	+	+	⊗	+	+	+
A12	x	+	+	+	⊗	+	+
A19	x	+	+	+	⊗	+	—
T6	x	+	⊗	+	+	⊗	—
A14	x	+	⊗	+	+	⊗	+
O17	x	+	+	⊗	⊗	+	+
T15	x	+	+	⊗	⊗	+	—
T18	x	x	+	+	+	+	+
A10	x	x	+	+	+	+	+
O5	x	x	+	+	+	+	+
T14	x	x	+	+	+	+	—
T16	x	x	+	+	+	+	—
A13	x	x	+	+	+	+	—
A18	x	x	+	+	+	+	—
A9	x	x	+	+	+	+	—
T9	x	x	+	+	+	⊗	—
O16	x	x	+	+	—	+	+
O3	x	x	+	+	⊗	+	+
A1	x	x	+	⊗	+	—	—
S3	x	x	+	+	—	⊗	—
S2	x	x	+	+	⊗	+	+
S18	x	x	+	⊗	+	+	+
O14	x	x	+	⊗	+	⊗	+
P1	x	x	+	⊗	+	+	+
P7	x	x	+	⊙	—	—	—
T20	x	x	x	+	+	+	+
A5	x	x	x	+	+	+	+
O18	x	x	x	+	+	+	+
O12	x	x	x	+	+	+	+
T10	⊕	x	x	+	+	+	+
T5	x	x	x	+	+	+	—
S19	x	x	x	+	+	+	+
S4	x	x	x	+	+	+	—

TABLE 6.3. *Continued*

Informant	_Adj	_V-ing	_Nom	_Loc	_Pass	_Cl	_Temp
A15	x	x	x	+	⊗	+	+
A8	x	x	x	+	+	⊗	−
T4	x	x	x	+	⊗	+	−
S15	x	x	x	+	+	⊗	+
S5	x	x	x	+	−	+	+
P5	x	x	x	+	⊗	+	+
O19	x	x	x	+	⊗	+	+
O2	x	x	x	+	⊗	+	−
O10	x	x	x	+	⊗	+	−
P12	x	x	x	+	+	+	⊗
P17	x	x	x	+	−	−	−
P18	x	⊙	x	+	−	+	+
P4	x	x	x	+	⊙	⊙	+
T2	x	x	x	x	+	+	+
T13	x	x	x	x	+	+	+
A2	x	x	x	x	+	+	+
A7	x	x	x	x	+	+	−
A17	x	x	x	x	+	+	−
T17	x	⊕	x	x	+	+	−
S13	x	x	x	x	+	+	−
S14	x	x	x	x	+	+	−
P20	x	x	x	x	+	+	−
T8	x	x	x	x	+	⊗	+
S8	x	⊕	x	x	+	+	−
P2	x	−	x	⊙	+	⊗	+
O6	x	⊕	x	x	+	+	⊙
P13	x	x	x	x	+	⊗	−
T3	x	x	⊕	x	x	+	+
A16	x	x	x	x	x	+	+
A4	x	x	x	x	x	+	+
O9	x	x	x	x	x	+	−
O7	x	x	x	x	x	+	+
O1	x	x	x	x	x	+	+
O15	x	⊕	x	x	x	+	+
S17	x	x	x	x	x	+	+
S1	x	⊕	x	x	x	+	+
S11	x	x	⊕	x	x	+	+
P10	x	x	x	x	−	+	+
S6	x	x	x	x	x	+	−
P3	x	x	x	x	x	+	−
P15	x	x	x	x	x	+	−
P19	x	x	x	x	x	+	−
P8	x	x	x	x	x	+	−
S12	x	x	⊕	x	x	+	−

TABLE 6.3. *Continued*

Informant	__Adj	__V-ing	__Nom	__Loc	__Pass	__Cl	__Temp
S7	x	x	x	x	x	+	⊗
S9	x	x	x	x	x	+	—
P11	x	x	x	x	◎	+	—
S20	x	x	x	x	◎	+	—
S10	x	x	x	x	◎	+	—
P9	x	x	x	x	◎	+	—
O8	x	x	x	⊕	x	x	+
O20	x	x	x	x	x	x	+
S16	x	x	x	⊕	x	x	—
O13	x	x	x	x	x	x	—
P6	o	o	x	—	x	—	—
P16	⊗	o	⊕	x	—	—	—
P14	⊗	o	⊗	o	o	—	—

Key: +   categorical occurrence of *be*.
    x   variable occurrence of *be*.
    o   categorical non-occurrence of *be*.
    —   empty cell.

Note: Deviations are ringed.

1944:140). Table 6.3 has been constructed with __Adj and __Temp as separate environments as it is felt that this table will give some insight into the order of acquisition of *be* in these environments as well as in the environments __Pass and __Loc. In general, Table 6.3 shows that *be* is acquired in following environments __Loc and __Pass before the __Nom environment. However, Table 6.5, which shows the proportion of speakers with categorical realization and categorical non-realization of *be*, provides fresh insights into the acquisition process.

Table 6.3 shows that in the acquisition of *be*, the environment __Temp is much easier than __Loc. A comparison of the __Pass and __Adj environments shows that the former environment is easier compared to the latter environment. Table 6.5 provides additional information on *be* realization in these environments. An examination of the number of speakers with lower education who have categorical non-realization of *be* shows that for some informants, the rule for *be* insertion has not been acquired at all; but with higher levels of education the rule is acquired very swiftly and fully as shown by the larger number of speakers with categorical realization of *be*. The lower number of speakers with categorical realization of *be* in the __Adj environment as compared to the __Pass environment indicates that even with tertiary education, the rule is not fully grasped by most informants. A similar situation to the __Pass environment is applicable to the __Loc environment, where the rule is not fully grasped by informants with lower levels of education. As will

TABLE 6.4. *Implicational scaling of speakers in regard to* be *realization in five following syntactic environments* (scalability = 91.7%)

Informant	__Adj	__V-ing	__Nom	__Loc^c	__Cl
O4	+	+	+	⊗	+
A3	+	+	⊗	+	+
T12	+	⊗	+	+	⊗
T11	x	+	+	+	+
A6	x	+	+	+	+
A12	x	+	+	+	+
A19	x	+	+	+	+
A20	x	+	+	+	+
A11	x	+	⊗	+	+
T7	x	+	+	⊗	+
T19	x	+	+	⊗	+
T15	x	+	+	⊗	+
O11	x	+	+	⊗	+
O17	x	+	+	⊗	+
T6	x	+	⊗	+	⊗
T18	x	x	+	+	+
A9	x	x	+	+	+
A10	x	x	+	+	+
T14	x	x	+	+	+
T1	x	x	+	+	+
T16	x	x	+	+	+
A13	x	x	+	+	+
A18	x	x	+	+	+
O3	x	x	+	+	+
O5	x	x	+	+	+
O16	x	x	+	+	+
S2	x	x	+	+	+
T9	x	x	+	+	⊗
T3	x	x	+	⊗	+
S3	x	x	+	+	⊗
S11	x	x	+	⊗	+
S12	x	x	+	⊗	+
S8	x	x	+	⊗	+
P1	x	x	+	⊗	+
P7	x	x	+	⊙	—
T20	x	x	x	+	+
T10	⊕	x	x	+	+
T4	x	x	x	+	+
T8	x	x	x	+	+
A5	x	x	x	+	+
A15	x	x	x	+	+
O2	x	x	x	+	+
O10	x	x	x	+	+

Table 6.4. *Continued*

Informant	__Adj	__V-ing	__Nom	__Loc[c]	__Cl
O12	x	x	x	+	+
O18	x	x	x	+	+
O19	x	x	x	+	+
S4	x	x	x	+	+
S5	x	x	x	+	+
S19	x	x	x	+	+
P5	x	x	x	+	+
P18	x	◎	x	+	+
P17	x	x	x	+	—
S15	x	x	x	+	⊗
S16	x	x	x	+	⊗
O8	x	x	x	+	⊗
A8	x	x	x	+	⊗
A14	x	⊕	x	+	⊗
P4	x	x	x	+	◎
T17	x	⊕	x	x	+
O6	x	⊕	x	x	+
O5	x	⊕	x	x	+
S1	x	⊕	x	x	+
S8	x	⊕	x	x	+
T2	x	x	x	x	+
T13	x	x	x	x	+
A2	x	x	x	x	+
A4	x	x	x	x	+
A7	x	x	x	x	+
A16	x	x	x	x	+
A17	x	x	x	x	+
O1	x	x	x	x	+
O7	x	x	x	x	+
O9	x	x	x	x	+
S6	x	x	x	x	+
S7	x	x	x	x	+
S9	x	x	x	x	+
S10	x	x	x	—	+
S13	x	x	x	x	+
S14	x	x	x	x	+
S17	x	x	x	x	+
S20	x	x	x	x	+
P3	x	x	x	x	+
P8	x	x	x	x	+
P9	x	x	x	x	+
P10	x	x	x	x	+
P11	x	x	x	x	+
P12	x	x	x	x	+

TABLE 6.4. *Continued*

Informant	__Adj	__V-ing	__Nom	__Loc^c	__Cl
P15	x	x	x	x	+
P19	x	x	x	x	+
P20	x	x	x	x	+
O14	x	x	⊕	x	x
A1	x	x	⊕	x	—
T8	x	x	x	x	x
O13	x	x	x	x	x
O20	x	x	x	x	x
P2	x	—	x	x	x
P13	x	x	x	x	x
P6	⊗	o	x	—	—
P14	⊗	o	x	◎	—
P16	⊗	o	⊕	x	—

Key: +   categorical occurrence of *be*.
     x   variable occurrence of *be*.
     o   categorical non-occurrence of *be*.
     —   empty cell.
Note: Deviations are ringed.

be discussed later, the rule application for *be* in the __Loc and __Pass environments follows Chinese rather than English syntax.

In Table 6.4 the environments __Adj and __Pass as well as __Loc and __Temp have been combined (now called Adj^c and Loc^c respectively). The reasons for combining the data have been mentioned in Section 6.7. This gives an improved scalability of 91.7%, calculated as follows:

$$\frac{\text{number of filled cells} - \text{number of deviations}}{\text{number of filled cells}} \times 100$$

i.e. $\dfrac{491 - 41}{491} \times 100 = 91.7\%$

Table 6.6 shows a great deal of implicationality between the environments. The least implicationality is found in the __V-ing and __Adj^c environments, where the proportion of speakers with scores in the __V-ing equal to or greater than in the __Adj^c environment is only 48.5%. In general, the overall scores for the two environments are about the same: 82.4% for __Adj^c and 81.7% for __V-ing. Table 6.7 gives a breakdown of the percentage-group scores.

In the sec. 1–3 and primary levels, the scores for __V-ing are lower than for __Adj^c. In the primary group (see Table 6.8) there were even four speakers with categorical non-realization of __V-ing. However, the picture changes in the A and O level groups, with 60% of the speakers in the A level

TABLE 6.5. *The proportion of speakers with categorical realization and categorical non-realization of* be *in the environments* __Loc, __Temp, __Pass, *and* __Adj

		__Loc	__Temp	__Pass	__Adj
Tertiary	R[a]	12/20	10/10	14/20	3/20
	N[b]	—	—	—	—
A level	R	14/20	10/10	15/20	1/20
	N	—	—	—	—
O level	R	9/20	13/14	7/19	1/20
	N	—	1/14	—	—
Sec. 1–3	R	7/19	7/8	7/18	—
	N	—	—	2/18	—
Primary	R	5/19	6/7	5/15	—
	N	3/19	—	4/15	1/20

[a] Categorical realization of *be*.
[b] Categorical non-realization of *be*.

TABLE 6.6. *The proportion of speakers with scores in a particular environment equal to or greater than in another environment*

	(Cl ≥ Loc[c])	(Loc[c] ≥ N)	(Nom ≥ V-ing)	(V-ing ≥ Adj[c])
Tertiary	17/20 (85.0)	15/20 (75.0)	16/20 (80.0)	8/20 (40.0)
A level	17/19 (89.5)	15/20 (75.0)	15/20 (75.0)	12/20 (60.0)
O level	19/20 (95.0)	11/20 (55.0)	15/20 (75.0)	14/20 (70.0)
Sec. 1–3	16/19 (84.2)	9/19 (47.4)	16/20 (80.0)	7/20 (35.0)
Primary	14/15 (93.3)	5/19 (26.3)	17/19 (89.5)	7/19 (36.8)
Overall	83/93 (89.3)	55/98 (56.1)	79/99 (79.8)	48/99 (48.5)

Notes: Loc[c] = combined data for environments __Loc and __Temp.
Adj[c] = combined data for environments __Adj and __Pass.
Relative frequencies are in parentheses.

group and 70% in the O level group having scores where __V-ing is equal to or higher than __Adj[c] (see Table 6.6). In the T group the overall score for Adj[c] is again slightly higher than __V-ing (see Table 6.7). This is because the informants in the tertiary-level group did not monitor their speech closely, and scores where a potential *be* is preceded by Nom or Pn are low.

An examination of the number of speakers with categorical non-realization and categorical realization of *be* in the __V-ing environment (see Table 6.8) shows that for those in the primary-level group, the *be* insertion rule in this environment is a difficult one, but it is more frequently fully acquired at the higher levels.

TABLE 6.7. Be *realization: percentage group scores in the environments* __V-ing *and* __Adj^c

	__V-ing	__Adj^c
Tertiary	91.9	94.2
A level	91.9	92.0
O level	87.8	85.5
Sec. 1–3	65.9	69.1
Primary	58.8	59.7
Overall	81.7	82.4

TABLE 6.8. *Proportion of speakers with categorical realization and categorical non-realization of* be *in the environments* __Cl, __Loc^c, __Nom, __V-ing, *and* __Adj^c

		__Cl	__Loc^c	__Nom	__V-ing	__Adj^c
Tertiary	R[a]	16/20 (80)	14/20 (70)	11/20 (55)	6/20 (30)	2/20 (10)
	N[b]	—	—	—	—	—
A level	R	17/19 (89.5)	14/20 (70)	9/20 (45)	7/20 (35)	1/20 (5)
	N	—	—	—	—	—
O level	R	16/20 (80)	9/20 (45)	7/20 (35)	5/20 (25)	1/20 (5)
	N	—	—	—	—	—
Sec. 1–3	R	17/20 (85)	7/19 (36.8)	5/20 (25)	2/20 (10)	0/20 (0)
	N	—	—	—	—	—
Primary	R	12/15 (80)	4/19 (21.1)	3/20 (15)	0/19 (0)	0/20 (0)
	N	1/15 (6.7)	2/19 (10.5)	—	4/19 (21.1)	—

[a] Categorical realization of *be*.
[b] Categorical non-realization of *be*.

Notes: Loc^c = combined data for environments __Loc and __Temp.
       Adj^c = combined data for environments __Adj and __Pass.
       Relative frequencies are in parentheses.

The proportion of speakers with scores where __Loc^c ⩾ __Nom is 47.4% for the sec. 1–3 level informants and 26.3% for the primary-level informants (see Table 6.6). If we compare group scores (see Table 6.9), the __Loc^c scores are always lower or equal (in the case of A level informants) to the __Nom scores.

However, when we compare the number of speakers with categorical realization and non-realization of *be* (see Table 6.8), there are more speakers with categorical realization of *be* in the __Loc^c environment than in the __Nom environment. This shows that the *be* insertion rule in the __Loc^c environment is difficult to acquire for some but once mastered it is fully acquired, unlike the __Nom environment, where the scores are consistently high for all informants but *be* is not as frequently fully acquired.

TABLE 6.9. Be *realization: percentage group scores in the environments* __Nom *and* __Loc^c

	__Nom	__Loc^c
Tertiary	97.1	95.6
A level	96.4	96.4
O level	93.0	92.4
Sec. 1–3	89.1	80.8
Primary	79.5	66.7
Overall	91.9	89.3

6.8.2 *Environments preceding* be

It is found that the order of overall percentages of *be* realization according to preceding environments is the same as the order in Table 6.11, which has a scalability of 88.3%, derived as follows:

$$\frac{\text{number of filled cells} - \text{number of deviations}}{\text{number of filled cells}} \times 100$$

i.e. $\dfrac{642 - 75}{642} \times 100 = 88.3\%$

The average percentages of *be* occurrences according to preceding environments, arranged in ascending order, are given below:

Pn__	80.3%
Nom__	83.3%
I__	88.1%
3sg__	90.4%
WH__	90.7%
D__	95.3%
Cl__	96.1%

Table 6.10 gives the percentage group scores of *be* in seven preceding environments. In general, the scores increase from the primary to the tertiary level in preceding environments except in the Pn__ environment, where the A level has a higher score (91.7%) than the T level (89.5%), and in the D environment, where the A, O, and S level scores are higher than those for the tertiary level. This is because the tertiary informants spoke more informally. They monitored themselves less. In SBrE *they're* is pronounced as [ðeə], *you're* as [jɔ:] or [jʊə], and *we're* as [wɪə].

As the reduced spoken forms are seldom or never taught in school, most informants either use the full forms or pronounce the contractions as shown in the list following Table 6.10.

TABLE 6.10. Be *realization according to educational levels and seven syntactic environments preceding* be (%)

	Pn__	Nom__	I__	3sg__	WH__	D__	Cl__
Tertiary	89.5	95.1	98.7	97.5	97.1	94.9	100.0
A level	91.7	91.1	96.1	97.4	88.6	97.4	100.0
O level	83.7	88.3	93.1	90.4	88.1	95.3	95.3
Sec. 1–3	65.9	72.7	76.0	80.1	84.8	95.6	93.5
Primary	54.0	66.9	64.4	79.8	78.6	90.5	85.7
Overall	80.3	83.3	88.1	90.4	90.7	95.3	96.1

they're [deɪə]
      [deɪ:]
      [deɪr]
you're [ju:]
      [jʊr]
we're [wi:ə]
      [wi:]
      [wɪr]

The pronunciation with [r] is probably influenced by the spelling or written forms and also by American pronunciation frequently heard on TV. The forms *they're, you're*, and *we're* are often realized as [deɪ:], [ju:], and [wi:] by tertiary level informants.

In the D__ environment, the percentage score for the T informants is lower than those in the A, O, and sec. 1–3 levels. *This* is often realized as [dɪs] or [dɪz]. A number of informants had problems pronouncing *this is* [ðɪsɪz] in fast speech. In the other three levels, *this* and *be* are often realized as separate morphemes. At the tertiary level, the two morphemes are collapsed into one and realized as [di:s] or [di:z].

Both implicational scaling (see Table 6.11 where a scalability of 88.3% is obtained) and the data in Table 6.12, showing the proportion of speakers with scores of a particular environment equal to or greater than another environment, indicate very strongly that there is a great deal of implicationality between the different environments preceding *be*. In Table 6.12, we find that the overall scores for all the environments are above 60%. If we compare group scores we find that they are all above 55% except for the A level group, where Pn__ has a higher score than that of Nom__. There are several reasons for this. Non-insertion of *be* is high in environments where words ending in sibilants precede the potential copula, e.g.

A2.7. My work place at Hong Kong Shanghai Bank.
A5.12. New things coming up.
A19.14. So points already given.

TABLE 6.11. *Implicational scaling of speakers in regard to* be *realization in seven preceding syntactic environments* (scalability = 88.3%)

Informant	Pn__	Nom__	I__	3sg__	WH__	D__	Cl__
A2	+	⊗	+	+	+	+	+
O6	+	⊗	+	+	+	+	—
A13	+	+	⊗	+	⊗	+	—
O4	+	⊗	+	+	+	+	+
T18	x	+	+	+	+	+	+
A6	x	+	+	+	+	+	+
O19	x	+	+	+	+	+	+
T6	x	+	+	+	+	⊗	+
T19	x	+	+	+	⊗	+	+
T9	x	+	+	+	+	⊗	—
T10	x	+	+	—	+	⊗	+
T11	x	+	+	⊗	+	+	+
T12	x	+	+	⊗	+	⊗	+
T16	x	+	⊗	+	+	+	+
A10	x	+	+	+	◎	+	—
A12	x	+	⊗	+	⊗	+	+
T1	x	x	+	+	+	+	+
T15	x	x	+	+	+	+	+
T17	x	x	+	+	+	+	+
A18	x	x	+	+	+	+	+
A19	x	x	+	+	+	+	+
O3	x	x	+	+	+	+	+
O5	x	x	+	+	+	+	+
S2	x	x	+	+	+	+	+
A16	x	x	+	+	—	+	+
T2	x	x	+	+	+	⊗	—
T4	x	x	+	+	+	⊗	+
T14	x	x	+	+	⊗	+	+
T5	x	x	+	⊗	+	+	+
T8	x	x	+	+	+	⊗	—
A9	x	x	+	⊗	+	+	+
A14	x	x	+	+	+	⊗	+
A8	x	x	+	+	⊗	⊗	+
T20	x	x	+	⊗	+	⊗	+
O12	x	x	+	⊗	+	⊗	+
O11	x	x	+	⊗	+	+	—
O13	x	x	+	⊗	+	+	⊗
S17	x	x	+	+	◎	+	—
S8	x	x	+	+	⊗	⊗	+
S1	x	x	+	⊗	+	⊗	+
S16	x	x	+	⊗	+	+	—
P13	x	x	+	⊗	—	+	+
A5	⊕	x	x	+	+	+	+

TABLE 6.11. *Continued*

Informant	Pn__	Nom__	I__	3sg__	WH__	D__	Cl__
T7	⊕	x	x	+	+	+	+
A1	x	x	x	+	+	+	−
O18	x	x	x	+	+	+	+
S18	x	x	x	+	+	+	+
P12	x	x	x	+	+	+	+
P1	x	x	x	+	−	+	−
P5	x	x	x	+	−	+	+
A15	x	x	x	+	+	−	+
O8	x	x	x	+	+	+	⊗
A7	x	x	x	+	⊗	+	−
A3	⊕	x	x	+	+	+	+
P17	x	x	x	+	+	−	−
P16	⊕	x	x	+	−	−	−
P7	x	x	x	+	−	−	−
S4	x	x	x	+	⊗	+	+
S5	x	x	x	+	⊗	+	+
A17	x	x	x	+	+	⊗	−
S19	x	x	x	+	−	⊗	+
O7	x	x	x	+	−	⊗	−
P15	x	x	x	+	⊙	⊗	+
A4	x	x	x	x	+	+	+
O3	x	x	x	x	+	+	+
S12	x	x	x	x	+	+	+
O14	x	x	x	x	+	⊗	+
O2	x	x	x	−	+	⊗	+
T3	x	x	x	x	+	⊗	+
S10	x	x	⊙	x	+	+	+
S7	x	x	x	x	+	⊗	+
S11	x	x	x	x	+	⊗	+
P8	x	x	x	x	+	⊗	+
T13	x	x	x	x	x	+	+
P10	x	x	x	x	x	+	+
P18	x	x	x	−	x	+	+
O16	x	x	x	x	−	+	+
P9	x	x	x	x	−	+	+
S2	x	x	x	x	−	+	+
P11	x	x	x	−	−	+	+
O17	x	x	x	x	x	+	+
P3	x	x	x	x	−	+	−
O20	x	x	⊕	x	x	+	+
S14	x	x	⊙	x	−	+	⊗
S13	x	x	x	−	⊙	+	−
P19	x	x	x	x		+	−
S9	x	x	⊕	x	x	+	−

TABLE 6.11. *Continued*

Informant	Pn__	Nom__	I__	3sg__	WH__	D__	Cl__
A11	⊕	x	⊕	x	x	x	+
A2	x	x	x	x	x	x	+
O9	x	x	x	x	x	x	+
O10	x	x	⊕	x	x	x	+
O15	x	x	⊕	x	x	x	+
S6	x	x	x	x	—	—	+
P4	x	x	x	◎	—	—	+
P20	x	x	x	x	—	x	—
S15	x	x	x	x	⊕	x	x
O1	x	x	x	◎	x	x	—
P2	x	x	x	—	⊕	x	◎
P14	x	x	◎	x	—	—	x
P6	o	x	x	◎	—	—	—

Key: + categorical occurrence of *be*.
    x variable occurrence of *be*.
    o categorical non-occurrence of *be*.
    — empty cell.

Note: Deviations are ringed.

A20.13. All the crime rates so high.

A20.9. But in the States yes—cosmetics very very cheap.

When the head noun is far away from the verb, *be* often tends to be omitted, e.g.

A2.20. Other subjects, I would say, just above average.

Be is also frequently omitted in *found that* clauses:

A9.14. I found dat de company a little slow in dis kind of approaches.

This is possibly due to the influence of a fairly similar structure in English: *I found the company a little slow.*

6.9 Varbrul analysis of *be*

The Varbrul 2 program was used for the data on *be* as presented in Table 6.13, to calculate the effect of each factor on the insertion of *be*. Table 6.14 displays the relative effects of the various factors.

Two preceding environments, I__ and 3sg__, and two following environments, __Nom and __Loc, exert considerable influence on the insertion of *be*. In contrast, the other preceding environments (Pn__ and Nom__) and following environments (__Adj and __V-ing) have an opposite effect. Such effects

TABLE 6.12. *The proportion of speakers with scores of a particular preceding environment equal to or greater than in another preceding environment* (%)

	Cl ≥ D	D ≥ WH	WH ≥ 3sg	3sg ≥ I	I ≥ Nom	Nom ≥ Pn
Tertiary	100.0	55.0	84.2	68.4	95.0	80.0
A level	100.0	83.3	66.7	80.0	75.0	45.0
O level	87.5	66.7	76.5	52.6	80.0	75.0
Sec. 1–3	93.3	75.0	66.7	84.2	55.0	55.0
Primary	90.0	66.7	60.0	55.6	60.0	65.0
Overall	94.5	69.2	73.0	68.4	73.0	64.0

TABLE 6.13. *Frequency of occurrences of* be *over total number of tokens of* be *according to four preceding and four following environments and educational levels of informants*

	—Adj	—V-ing	—Nom	—Loc
Tertiary				
I—	160/164 (97.4)	88/88 (100.0)	43/44 (97.7)	90/90 (100.0)
3—	123/126 (97.6)	43/47 (91.5)	66/66 (100.0)	41/41 (100.0)
Pn—	225/251 (89.6)	98/116 (85.5)	85/88 (96.6)	42/49 (85.7)
N—	316/342 (92.4)	45/49 (91.8)	169/170 (99.4)	59/62 (95.2)
A level				
I—	170/182 (93.4)	125/127 (98.4)	41/42 (97.6)	79/81 (97.5)
3—	97/101 (96.0)	50/51 (98.0)	54/54 (100.0)	25/26 (96.2)
Pn—	240/259 (92.7)	90/106 (84.9)	57/60 (95.0)	25/25 (100.0)
N—	323/367 (88.0)	49/54 (90.7)	139/145 (95.9)	37/41 (90.2)
O level				
I—	127/145 (87.6)	87/90 (96.7)	48/51 (94.1)	68/68 (100.0)
3—	101/119 (84.9)	45/47 (95.7)	58/59 (98.3)	21/24 (87.5)
Pn—	247/298 (82.9)	107/137 (78.1)	82/88 (93.2)	42/49 (85.7)
N—	334/392 (85.2)	72/82 (87.8)	157/171 (91.8)	47/52 (90.4)
Sec. 1–3				
I—	81/125 (64.8)	62/78 (79.5)	46/50 (92.0)	33/39 (84.6)
3—	77/110 (70.0)	34/47 (72.3)	63/65 (96.9)	18/18 (100.0)
Pn—	141/217 (65.0)	52/92 (56.5)	45/55 (81.8)	20/28 (71.4)
N—	307/449 (68.4)	41/73 (56.2)	145/169 (85.8)	50/66 (75.8)
Primary				
I—	59/105 (56.2)	44/68 (64.7)	36/47 (76.6)	19/26 (73.1)
3—	31/45 (68.9)	17/24 (70.8)	33/34 (97.1)	6/6 (100.0)
Pn—	62/112 (55.4)	35/67 (52.2)	23/40 (57.5)	7/17 (41.2)
N—	153/257 (59.5)	18/35 (51.4)	140/173 (80.9)	25/41 (60.9)

Note: Relative frequencies are in parentheses. 3 = 3sg, N = Nom.

TABLE 6.14. *Contribution of each factor influencing the occurrences of* be *according to Varbrul* (input = 1.00)

Effect of

Educational level		Preceding environment		Following environment	
T	0.79	I—	0.63	—Adj	0.50
A	0.77	3sg—	0.68	—V-ing	0.49
O	0.65	Pn—	0.48	—Nom	0.74
S	0.40	Nom—	0.54	—Loc	0.62
P	0.30				

are reflected in the scores for *be* realization according to preceding and following environments (cf. Table 6.13).

Naturally, the educational attainment of the informants is important too. This is reflected in the influence different educational attainment exerts on *be* occurrence. For instance, the effect computed by Varbrul 2 for tertiary-level informants is 0.79. In contrast, the effect of a primary-level education is 0.30. It can, therefore, be seen that the mastery of the rule for *be* insertion increases with higher levels of education.

Table 6.15 shows a very good match between the frequencies predicted by Varbrul 2 and the observed frequencies. The statistic values resulting from the chi-squared test are highly insignificant.

6.10 The influence of Chinese and/or the target language on *be* occurrences in preceding and following environments

6.10.1 Be + Adjective

The following are some characteristic features found in the *be* + *Adj* environment in SgE. Where applicable, the Chinese influence is shown.

1. As observed in the data, the highest number of non-occurrences of *be* is before predicate adjectives. The influence from Chinese is obvious. In Chinese all words equivalent to adjectives in English are stative verbs. *Shì* (often referred to as the copula in Chinese) is usually absent in adjectival predicates, except when used for emphasis, contrast, or contradiction.

2. Omission of *be* is particularly high if the adjectival predicate contains an intensifier or an additive adjunct:

P14.13. Our father *also* sick.
P18.5. I *very* scared.
P5.9. De teacher *so* fierce.

TABLE 6.15. *Frequency of occurrences of be predicted by Varbrul, compared with observed frequencies (cf. totals in Table 6.13)*

	__Adj		__V-ing		__Nom		__Loc	
	Predicted	Observed	Predicted	Observed	Predicted	Observed	Predicted	Observed
Tertiary								
I__	160.4	160	83.0	88	43.1	43	86.9	90
3sg__	120.2	123	44.8	43	64.9	66	39.8	41
Pn__	226.2	225	104.4	98	84.7	85	45.9	42
Nom__	314.8	316	45.1	45	165.0	169	58.9	59
$\chi^2 = 1.4385$	$\chi^2_{15,0.05} = 25.00$							
A level								
I__	170.4	170	118.8	125	41.0	41	77.8	79
3sg__	95.7	97	48.3	50	53.0	54	25.2	25
Pn__	229.9	240	93.9	90	57.4	57	23.2	25
Nom__	333.8	323	49.1	49	140.1	139	38.7	37
$\chi^2 = 1.6221$	$\chi^2_{15,0.05} = 25.00$							

O level

I—	129.2	127	80.1	87	48.9	48	63.3	68
3sg—	108.2	101	42.7	45	57.0	58	22.6	21
Pn—	242.7	247	111.3	107	81.4	82	43.1	42
Nom—	332.5	334	69.4	72	160.8	157	46.9	47

$\chi^2 = 2.2002$ $\chi^2_{15,0.05} = 25.00$

Sec. 1–3

I—	93.1	81	57.9	62	44.6	46	32.3	33
3sg—	85.9	77	36.6	34	59.1	63	15.4	18
Pn—	132.5	141	55.9	52	44.9	45	20.2	20
Nom—	299.1	307	48.4	41	143.6	145	50.6	50

$\chi^2 = 5.9056$ $\chi^2_{15,0.05} = 25.00$

Primary

I—	68.9	59	44.4	44	39.7	44	19.7	19
3sg—	31.5	31	16.7	17	29.5	33	4.8	6
Pn—	56.8	62	33.7	35	29.8	23	10.7	7
Nom—	145.6	153	19.7	18	136.2	140	28.0	25

$\chi^2 = 6.8320$ $\chi^2_{15,0.05} = 25.00$

Omission of *be* is almost categorical in environments containing several adverbials, e.g.

P5.28. Dat place *very* nice *also*.
P13.13. De first one *not quite so* daring.

All the above utterances are simple declarative sentences. In Chinese such structures co-occur with modifiers such as *hěn* (very), *dōu* (also), *tài* (too, so), etc. The absence of such modifiers implies that a contrast is intended, e.g.

nà-liang chē dà, zhè-liang chē xiǎo
that-CL car big this-CL car small
'That car is big, this one is small.'

Likewise, in basilectal SgE *be* is sometimes omitted in such contrastive environments, e.g.

P14.17. Like we talk Mandarin ah, talk easy. To write lah, write . . .

Where no contrast is intended, a particle is obligatory in declarative sentences in colloquial and basilectal SgE to convey emphasis:

P16.23. I: Were you sad when told the news?
    J: I sad lah.
P8.16. We busy at dis time lah.

It is interesting to note that while *hěn* (very) in Chinese is unstressed, in SgE *very* is often stressed for emphasis:

P14.5. Dis one *very* hard lah.
P10.10. One of de old man *very* sick.

Basilectal informants often use *damn* in place of *very*:

P10.3. I damn naughty.
P6.22. De road damn wide.

It appears that with emphasis shifted to the modifier and/or particle, *be* is more likely to be omitted in basilectal SgE. Chao (1968:693) mentions the use of *shì* when there is 'assertive stress', i.e. for emphasis, and 'when there is a contrast before two adjectives', e.g.

tā shì bèn, bú shi huài
3sg be stupid, not be bad
'S/He is stupid, not bad.'

In the corpus, it is only acrolectal speakers who insert *be* for emphasis in predicate adjectival environments.

6.10.2 Be *in Passives*

6.10.2.1 Environments where the omission of be *in passive constructions is high*
Be omission is high in the following environments:

1. In the presence of intensifiers and adverbial adjuncts such as *always*, *all*, *also*, etc.:

S9.1. De purse all taken away.
P3.23. Dey (the children) always confine at my in-law house.

2. In the presence of the adverbial *already* which often represents a translation of the Chinese particle *LE* which can indicate perfective aspect or change of state, depending on the context, e.g.

P14.19. His house pull down already.

3. In WH sentences:

A12.7. Thes (those) forms that submitted in.
O20.4. Some cases dat we do *who* sent by police.
S17.24. Dat's *what* connected.

Note that at the primary level no *be* tokens with WH are used.

4. In passive structures in the presence of stative verbs, particularly with the verb *call*:

S7.24. Dey all *call* 'aqua' or what.

5. In environments where words preceding the potential *be* end in a sibilant:

A19.14. So points already given.
O20.6. Priorities given to English.

6. In subordinate clauses, particularly conditional ones:

P9.10. (If) you injured . . .
P9.20. If de ang pow ah, put very high . . . ('Ang pow' in Hokkien means a gift of money in a red envelope.)

7. In the presence of verbs such as *born* where the verbs used in an active sentence and a passive sentence are different in English, e.g.

A4.6. Both of dem born in Singapore.
S16.1. He born . . .
P11.2. I born in . . .

6.10.2.2 *A discussion of the passive in Chinese and its influence on SgE*

In Mandarin, the passive is constructed by the use of the coverb *bèi*, meaning 'to cause to suffer', as shown in Li and Thompson (1981:492–3, /1/ to /5/). For example:

/1/ NP$_1$ *bèi* NP$_2$ verb
/2/ tā   bèi jiějie   mà   LE
    3sg   BEI elder:sister scold PFV/CRS
    S/He was scolded by (his/her) older sister.

Ta (S/He) is the patient. *Jiějie* (elder sister) is the agent. We may have a variant of /1/ without NP$_2$:

/3/ NP$_1$ bèi verb

For example:

/4/ tā   bèi mà   LE

3sg BEI scold PFV/CRS
S/He was scolded.
/5/ wǒ bèi qiǎng LE
    I   BEI rob   PFV/CRS
    I was robbed.

According to Li and Thompson (1981:493) *bèi* 'is used essentially to express an adverse situation', e.g.

/7/ qiáo   bèi (dà-shuǐ) chōng-zǒu LE
    bridge BEI (big-water) wash-away PFV/CRS
    'The bridge got washed away (by the flood).

Perhaps one of the most important things to note is that

the English passive often does not correspond to the *bèi* construction in Mandarin. In other words, what is normally best translated into an English passive sentence is often not a *bèi* sentence in Mandarin, and, conversely, an English passive sentence often does not translate into a *bèi* sentence in Mandarin. (Li and Thompson 1981:498)

An example of a Chinese non-passive sentence is given below:

/26/a nèi-běn shū yǐjīng   chūbǎn le
      that-CL book already publish CRS

The equivalent English passive sentence is:

That book has already been published.

If one were to translate /26/a using a Chinese structure employing *bèi* the sentence would be considered unacceptable:

/26/b *nèi-běn shū yǐjǐng   bèi chūbǎn le
       that-CL book already BEI publish CRS

The reason why /26/b is unacceptable is that there is nothing adverse or pejorative about the sentence. It can be construed as a topic and comment structure. The influence of Chinese on SgE is clearly shown by the fact that /26/b can be directly translated into SgE:

Dat book already publish already.

Other exemplifications in SgE which highlight the topic include:

A16.4. De standard raised very high.
O8.2. I sen(t) to dis places.
P14.19. His house pull down already

Notice that no agent is mentioned as it is not the main focus.

6.10.2.3 The use of 0 + born *in SgE*
In SBrE the expression *to give birth* is used in the active voice. However *be + born* is used with passives, e.g.

She gave birth to a son in Malacca. (Active)
Her son was born in Malacca. (Passive)

In SgE one finds that 'give birth' and 'born' can be used interchangeably in both active and passive voice structures:

P18.18. Aah I *gif birth* in—my mother *gif birth* me in Singapore.

The first part of the utterance is non-standard in that *I* is the patient. The informant then rephrases her sentence, putting *my mother* as the subject of *give birth* which is in the active voice.

In the interlanguage of Singaporean basilectal speakers 'born' and 'give birth' are still not stabilized and there is no distinction between the two. Informant S7, for example, first uses *born* in the active voice, switches to *give birth* still used in the active voice, and then uses *born* in the passive:

S7.3. I: How old are they? (her children)
　　　J: One in nineteen ... I *born* one—the first child is nineteen seventy-fi(ve). She's aroun(d) fi(ve) years plus ah, going to be six years ah ... den de other is abou(t)—dis aah—National Eve (eve of Singapore's National Day)—I gi(ve) bir(th) eigh(t) of Augus(t).

When she talks about her husband, the passive *born* is used:

S7.22. Because *he's born* like dat, his paren(t) ah, always never make coffee, never make breakfast for dem. ('born like that' is a typical Singaporean structure meaning 'this is one of his characteristics'. She meant that during her husband's childhood days his parents never gave him any breakfast.)

Since informant S7 is a Baba her speech must have been influenced by Baba Malay which, as mentioned in Chapter 1, displays many characteristic features from Chinese. In Baba Malay, the same verb appears in the active voice and in the passive:

Dia beranak anak betina di Melaka
she born   child female at Malacca
'She gave birth to a daughter in Malacca.'

Dia punya anak betina beranak di Melaka
she GEN child female born   at Malacca
'Her daughter was born in Malacca.'

Note that *jantan* in Malay is used for the male of animals. The terms *betina* (female) and *jantan* (male) are used in Bazaar and Baba Malay.

The above sentences are clearly different from those used in standard Malay, where a different prefix is used for the verb *lahir*.

Dia melahirkan anak perempuan di Melaka
she gave birth child female   at Malacca
'She gave birth to a daughter in Malacca.'

Anak perempuan nya   dilahirkan di Melaka
child female   GEN born   at Malacca
'Her daughter was born in Malacca.'

In colloquial spoken Malay *diberanakkan* may be used, especially in the kampongs (*kampung* in standard Malay orthography). However, the verb *beranak* is usually reserved for animals. In Chinese, the verb remains unchanged and unaffected, irrespective of whether the subject is the agent or the patient. For example the same verb *shēng* is used for 'to give birth' and 'to be born'.

> tā shēng-le yí-ge nǚ háizi
> 3sg born-PFV one-CL female child
> 'She gave birth to a baby girl.'

> háizi yǐjīng shēng-le
> child already born CRS
> 'The child has already been born.'

6.10.2.4 *The verb* call *in Chinese*

In Chinese, for certain stative verbs like *jiào* 'call' and *xìng* 'surname', the passive is never used. This is because *xìng* and *jiào* act in the same way as the copula *shì*, i.e. they serve as links in identifying the subject.

The following are illustrations from Chinese:

> wǒ xìng Hé
> I surname He
> 'I am surnamed He.'

or

> wǒ jiào Wáng Dà Míng
> I call Wang Da Ming
> 'I am called Wang Da Ming.'

The verb *call* may be used in an active sentence.

> tā men jiào wǒ Lǎo Wáng
> 3sg PL call I Old Wang
> 'They call me Old Wang.'

Like the above Chinese structures, the verb *call* in SgE seldom co-occurs with *be*, e.g. 'His name call Ah Beng' (He's called/His name is Ah Beng).

6.10.2.5 *WH in Chinese*

In Chinese relative clauses, 'the semantic properties of the head noun will determine the interpretation of the construction *relative clause + head noun*' (Li and Thompson 1981:581).

In the following sentence, the subject is missing:

/14/ jīntiān yíng de qián fù fáng-zū
   today win NOM money pay house-rent
   The money (we) won today goes to pay the rent.

The head noun *qián* or 'money'

cannot refer to the missing subject participant, 'the ones who won' since 'money' cannot do the winning; it can, however, refer to 'what was won'. The result is the meaning 'the money that (we) won today' for the relative-clause-plus-head-noun construction. (Li and Thompson 1981:581–2)

In SgE, when the relative clause is a lengthy one, the nominaliser *de* (realized as *one* in shorter relative clauses, such as *pray one thing*, 'things used for praying') is not used. *De* is then replaced by a relativizer such as *who* or *that*. The subject is not mentioned, *be* is not used, but the meaning is clear from the context:

A12.7. Thes (those) forms that submitted in . . .
O20.4. Some cases dat we do who send by police.
    'The cases that were brought to us by the police.'

These sentences are similar to the Chinese construction given in /14/ which rendered in Singaporean English, reads as follows:

    The money that won today goes to pay the rent.

In Chinese the direct object can also be missing in the relative clause:

/15/ jīntiān yíng de   rén   yùnqì hǎo
    today win NOM person luck   good
    The people who won today had good luck.

(Li and Thompson 1981:581)

From the context *rén* is normally interpreted as 'the ones who won'. However, *rén* could be ambiguous too, in that there would be another possible interpretation if the stakes at a gambling event were people. Then the sentence will read 'The people whom (we) won today had good luck'. Thus in SgE confusion can arise if the head word were [+animate], e.g. 'The dog that won was an Alsatian' can refer to the dog which won the prize or the dog which we won (more likely to be at a dog show than race).

    Another possible reason for the omission of *be* in the environment with a preceding WH and a following passive is that *be* is not salient in both native and Singaporean varieties of English. Hence a learner of English only hears WH and not *be*. The written work of Singaporean Chinese students also shows the omission of *be* in similar environments:

    Bottles with meat juice which ( ) prepared by Pasteur did not go bad.
    I'd like to introduce to you the 'Speak Mandarin Campaign' which ( ) held during October.
    She sold the goods which ( ) produced by prisoners.

6.10.3 Be + V-ing

6.10.3.1 Environments where be *is inserted*
As shown in the examples given below, *be* is frequently inserted to show emphasis in the environment __V-ing.

T4.9. She was always pestering.
A8.14. He himself is reading.
O8.15. I'm stopping at two!
   'I certainly do not wish to have more than two children!'
S12.7. I was really dying!

6.10.3.2 *Environments where* be *is frequently omitted*
The following are environments where the omission of *be* is found to be high.

   1. In structures where intensifiers and adverbial adjuncts such as *not, all, just, still, also*, etc. are used, e.g.

P17.24. My area—I *just* working aroun(d) my area only.
S6.13. So de kettle drop. De water *all* running out. So my leg all tight. (The informant was badly scalded on the legs.)
O7.1. I *still* working as a draughtsman.

   2. In subordinate clauses

S15.6. So if we living in de flat, we can mix a lot of frien(d)s.
P12.4. (If) you using the scope, you can see very big lah.

   3. In structures where the following types of verbs are used:

   (*a*) Verbs 'that denote postures or physical dispositions of an entity at a location' (Li and Thompson 1981:219) including those verbs that are relatively static, e.g.

   P19.3. We *waiting* for de flight to come in.
   O16.9. I still *sleeping.*

   (*b*) 'Activity verbs signalling states associated with their activity meanings' (Li and Thompson 1981:220), e.g.

   T3.12. Den he *carrying* an umbrella.
   S7.25. Some of dem *wearing* caps.

   (*c*) Verbs occurring frequently in the progressive form in colloquial SgE, e.g.

   P13.18. Like sometime dey *having* dinner.
   S18.18. Aroun(d) one hundred and ten (guests) *having* dinner.

   The use of the progressive aspect has also been extended to the stative verb *have*, where omission of *be* is high too.

   A18.5. You *having* excess (cash) in your box.

   (*d*) Verbs with the feature [+habitual] or [+iterative], e.g. *work, live, stay, speak*, etc.

   S14.7. Two eldes(t) brothers *working.*
   P5.1. I *living* here.

P20.37. Most of de time I *speaking* English down here. 'At work I speak to my colleagues in English.'

P10.4. I use(d) to go in and *flying* in and out.

6.10.3.3 The influence of the target language on the omission of be *in* be + V-ing *in SgE*

In SBrE there are many V-ing constructions where *be* is absent.

1. Participial phrases and gerunds, e.g.

   Climbing up the stairs, he slipped and fell.
   He works very hard, *starting* at 8 o'clock in the morning and *coming* home late in the evening.
   Beginning at page 1, we shall read until page 15.
   Going there by car will take 8 hours.

2. Elliptical constructions, e.g.

   Q: What are you doing in the garden?
   A: *Watering* the plants.

   Q: Where is Ali?
   A: *Having* a nap.

   Q: What did you see there?
   A: Oh! people *selling* all kinds of things.

Frequent exposure to such structures can lead to confusion, and learners of English often produce utterances like *he watering the plants.*

3. V-ing forms in *there is/are* constructions, and with verbs of perception, e.g.

   There's a patient *waiting* outside to see you.
   I heard her *shouting* for help.

These constructions are another source of confusion for EL2 learners.

6.10.3.4 The influence of Chinese on the use of the progressive aspect in SgE

In English, the progressive verbal form is used for continuing activities, e.g.

   The children are playing in the garden.
   I was writing letters the whole morning.

In Chinese, durative events are indicated by two aspect markers *zài* and *-zhe*. Li and Thompson (1981:217 ff.) illustrate the use of these aspect markers in the following semantic types of verbs: (A) activity verbs; (B) verbs of posture; and (C) activity verbs signalling states associated with their activity meanings.

A. Activity verbs

Most activity verbs take the durative marker *zài* meaning 'to be engaged in' indicating that an activity is still in progress, e.g.

Māma zài xǐ   yīfu
Mother DUR wash clothes
'Mother is washing clothes.'

Note that *be* is absent in Chinese. Likewise, in SgE, *be* is often omitted in verbal structures describing an activity in progress:

S20.14. Dey just beating each other y'know.

B. Verbs of posture
Verbs classified under this category include *zuò* 'sit', *zhàn* 'stand', *dūn* 'kneel', *xiē* 'rest', *guì* 'kneel', *tǎng* 'lie', *tíng* 'stop', and *shuì* 'sleep' (Li and Thompson 1981:219). The durative aspect marker *-zhe* is often used with such verbs, e.g.

/139/ Lǐsì zài kètīng-lǐ   shuì-zhe
      Lisi at living:room-in sleep-DUR
      Lisi is sleeping in the living room.
/141/ tā zài chuáng-shang tǎng-zhe
      3sg at bed-on   lie-DUR
      S/He is lying on the bed.

(Li and Thompson 1981:220)

Such verbs have the feature [+durative]. The omission of *be* is frequent with the progressive form of such verbs as well as other verbs which are inherently [+durative], e.g. *wait*. As shown in the above Chinese examples, the copula is absent and since *-zhe* is in the immediate environment following the verb in Chinese, this may have had an influence on the addition of *-ing* to the verb in SgE. For many basilectal speakers of SgE, *be* is redundant and it appears that the verbal *-ing* forms are treated as full finite verbs.

C. Activity verbs signalling states associated with their activity meaning
Illustrations from Li and Thompson (1981:220) include the use of the verb *ná* which can be used as an activity verb:

/142/ tā zài ná   bàozhǐ
      3sg DUR take newspaper
      S/He is $\begin{Bmatrix} \text{taking} \\ \text{picking up} \end{Bmatrix}$ newspapers.

or a verb denoting a state associated with *ná*, where the durative aspect marker used is *-zhe*:

/143/ tā ná-zhe   liǎng-běn shū
      3sg take-DUR two-CL   book
      S/He is holding two books.

Examples from SgE show a frequent omission of *be* with such durative verbs as *hold*, *wear*, *carry*, etc.

6.10.4 Be + Nominal

In Chinese 'equational verbs are verbs which connect or equate two nominal expressions on either side of the verb ... The verb *shì* (often pronounced *shi* with a neutral tone) is the most common equational verb' (DeFrancis 1976: 20), e.g.

> tā   shi Zhōngguo rén
> 3sg be China person
> 'S/He's a Chinese.'

The negative form of such substantive predicates is made by putting the negative adverb *bù* before *shì*, e.g.

> wǒ bú shi yīsheng
> I   not be doctor
> 'I'm not a doctor.'

However, if we examine colloquial or spoken Chinese, we find the frequent omission of *shì* 'in standard formulas giving place of origin, age, price etc.' (T'ung and Pollard 1982:24), as well as in response to informal questions. Thus *shì* is omitted in the following sentences:

> wǒ Xīnjiāpō   rén
> I   Singapore person
> 'I'm a Singaporean.'

> wǒ bāshísì   siù
> I   eighty-four age
> 'I'm eighty-four.'

> bā-zhī   bǐ sānkuài   qián
> eight-CL pen three dollar money
> 'Eight pens are three dollars.'

'In the corpus there is frequent omission of *be* in such environments:

P2.2. One 'wan tan mee' like dat ten dollars. 'One bowl of noodles is $10 (in Europe).'
P5.27. Your salary five or six hundred.
P18.18. I Singaporean.

It is noticed that although in Chinese, *be* is obligatory with the negative marker *bù*, it is not so in Singaporean English:

P2.1. Sim not Hailamese. 'Mr Sim is not a Hainanese.'
S1.4. We not shipbuilding yard. 'We are not a shipbuilding yard.'

One reason why *be* is omitted is that *bù* comes before *shì* in Chinese. Hence inserting *be* would mean reversing the word order for the informant, e.g.

> Sim *not is* Hainanese.

Another reason is that when *be* is used in SgE, some emphasis may be placed on it. However, when *not* is used, the emphasis is shifted to the adverbial modifier. In Chinese, stress can fall on the negator too, e.g.

  tā bú shi Rìbén rén
  3sg not be Japan person
  'S/He is not a Japanese.'

Omission of *be* is particularly high in the presence of other emphasizers and adverbial adjuncts such as *really, also, only, all, already,* all of which frequently receive stress in SgE:

S1.3. I apprentice *only.*
P8.16. His job *really* a driver.
O13.8. De rest *all* older teachers.

Emphasis may be conveyed through the use of a particle, e.g.

S10.15. De one de wife lah. 'That lady is his wife.'

Similarly in subordinate clauses, where emphasis falls near the pause, non-occurrence of *be* is frequent:

P4.3. If dey emergency *case* (loudness shows emphasis), you must pay lah. (If) you want to take taxi, you must pay lah.

6.10.5 Be + Locative/Temporal

6.10.5.1 Be + Locative
Chinese expresses location at a place as follows:

  N *zài* P
  'N is at P'

(DeFrancis 1976:83)

An example is given below:

  Mèimei   zài jiā
  Younger sister at home
  'Younger sister is at home.'

Zài '(be) at' can be used as a full verb as shown in the above example. The influence of *zài* may be a reason for the omission of *be* in locative environments in SgE:

S6.17. Once de person in jail, . . .
T8.1. Both of dem in school.
S11.17. We on land.

Naturally, it can be said that the preceding environment may also have influenced the omission of *be*, particularly when *be* is preceded by *you* and *we*, e.g.

T15.7. When you in MGS . . .
T19.2. We at Hyde Park.

Omission of *be* also occurs in environments where the locative expression does not have a preposition:

S13.10. Many people dere.
P2.2. All my friends overseas.

It is found that *be* omission is particularly high in the presence of various adverbial adjuncts such as *not, still, always, also, seldom*:

S13.28. I *seldom* at home.
S11.2. Some friends *still* dere.
O15.17. De customer *not* in.

At tertiary level, a possible reason for the non-insertion of *be* is the inadequate mastery of gapping in English, e.g.

T17.12. dey (my friends) went all over de place—some in US, some (in) Australia, some (in) New Zealand. (Her friends now live in the US, Australia, and New Zealand.)

A very noticeable feature of the locative phrase in SgE is the use of *dere, dat place, dat side*, following the locative phrase. This is deliberately used for emphasis. This feature is also found in Chinese. Examples in SgE include:

My house near the Changi airport *dat side*.
The hospital Toa Payoh *dere*.
That bank somewhere near Rochore Road, *dat area*.

6.10.5.2 Be + Temporal

In Chinese, temporal expressions may be preceded by *zài* and, as seen in locative expressions, *be* can be omitted in this environment too in SgE:

Dinner usually at 7 p.m. lah.

6.10.6 Clause + be *and* be + Clause *environments*

6.10.6.1 *Types of clauses preceding and following be in SgE*

The types of clauses preceding and following potential *be* used by informants with different levels of education are given below. The clause types are referred to in accordance with SBrE usage.

Tertiary level

Clauses used by informants with tertiary level education are generally similar to those used in SBrE. These include the following.

1. WH clauses:

   T5.10. What happen was I went . . .
   T20.8. What I wanted was . . .
   T2.15. Dat is what dey are trying to do.

2. Noun Phrase + *be* + Clause:

T7.6. The question is that ...
T18.3. The only encounter was ...

3. To-infinitive clauses:

T7.7. To go to work is a dislocation.
T10.11. Our objective is more to make ...

4. Gerunds:

T5.17. Having long lectures is nothing new.
Some non-standard usage includes:

T12.9. One of the tings I can learn is know more about X (a certain subject).

5. If clauses with *be* + to-infinitive:

T10.12. So even if I were to join de ...

A level
1. WH clauses. These structures are fairly stable and are similar to those used by tertiary level informants.
2. Noun Phrase + *be* + Clause. These are fairly stable too. Some non-standard usage includes:

A19.2. But my (i.e. mine) is that to make sure everyting is proper, ready for delivery.

3. To-infinitive clauses. Some non-standard usage includes:

A2.10. If the company were go into the red ...

4. Gerunds. These are not stable as yet and include usage such as:

A5.2. Give dem the basic foundation is important.

5. If clauses with *be* + to-infinitive. See 3 above for an example of non-standard usage.

O level
In all categories 1–5 there is standard usage. Only non-standard usage will be commented on.
1. WH clauses:

O12.19. Dey offer you is four plus.
    'What they offer you in salary ...'
O9.11. A person cook is always standardize(d).
    'What a person normally cooks is a standard meal.'

2. Noun Phrase + *be* + Clause:

O2.2. Dey employ most of them are Malaysians.
    'Most of the staff employed are Malaysians.'

O15.6. I like very much is de Domestic (Science) teacher. 'The teacher I liked best was the Domestic Science teacher.'

3. To-infinitive clauses:

   O10.5. Court her is quite difficult.
   'It is difficult to court her.'

4. Gerunds:

   O2.10. My work is make sure dat dey—you ask dem to do certain ting ah, dey do lah.
   'My job is making sure that . . .'

5. If clauses with *be* + to-infinitive. If-hypothetical clauses with *be* appear only at the O level.

   O4.3. If I were to talk to . . .

6. Topic-comment clauses:

   O5.11. Normally we bring out is when dey got regular buying all dis lah.
   'Normally we only take our regular clients out.'

Sec. 1–3 level

1. WH clauses:

   S7.24. She like the most is drawing.
   'What she likes most is drawing'.

2. Noun Phrase + *be* + Clause:

   S18.14. I went dere was a Saturday.
   'The day I went there . . .'

3. To-infinitive clauses:

   S16.13. (referring to business deals) The purpose is have connections.

4. Gerunds:

   S14.1. Work shift duty is very tired.
   'Working on the night shift is very tiring.'

5. If clauses with *be* + to-infinitive are absent.

6. Topic-comment clauses:

   S15.7. Shopping is: sometime I like to shop, sometime I don't like.
   'Talking about shopping, well, there are times I enjoy shopping and times when I don't.'

   S20.18. (Discussing her daughter's name. Hanyu pinyin notation is now used in all schools for the names of students.)
   Her name is: use Hanyu pinyin already.

Primary level

1. WH Clauses

   P14.22. We all talk in the house is Hokkien.
   'What we use at home is . . .'

2. Noun Phrase + *be* + Clause:

P10.17. The train arrive Jakarta is eight a.m.
'The time the train arrived . . .'

3. To-infinitive clauses:

P2.4. Earn dere easy, spend also de same.
'To earn a living there is easy, to spend all your money there is
just as easy.'

4. Gerunds:

P5.25. We work here is not bad lah.
'Working here isn't bad at all!'

5. If clauses with *be* + to-infinitive are absent.

6. Topic-comment clauses:

P11.2. Last time is: I'm not a Singaporean.
'I wasn't a Singaporean at that time.'

6.10.6.2 The influence of Chinese on the types of clauses used in SgE
In Chinese, a sentence may consist of two independent clauses. Li and
Thompson (1981:603–4) discuss structures where 'the first verb phrase/
clause can be the subject of the second verb' and cite the following examples:

/43/ xué Ménggǔ-huà   hěn bu róngyì.
study Mongolia-speech very not easy.
It is not easy to learn Mongolian.

or Learning Mongolian is not easy. (our gloss)

/44/ zài zhèli tíng chē   fàn-fǎ.
at here stop vehicle violate-law.
It is against the law to park here.

or Parking here is illegal. (our gloss)

/51/ tā kǎo   dì-yī   míng tài hǎo le
3sg take: exam ORD-one name too good CRS.
It's terrific that s/he got the top honor in the exam.'

or That/The fact that s/he topped the class is terrific. (our gloss)

or Her topping the class is terrific. (our gloss)

There is an obvious difference between clause patterns in English and
Chinese. In English, the clauses preceding *be* in the above sentences will have
to be clauses containing a gerund or a to-infinitive, or a *that clause* or one
containing an NP, e.g. *the fact* as in /51/. Finite clauses beginning with a verb
in its stem form or of the type *subject + verb* cannot be followed by *be*, e.g. *He
will resign is uncertain*. The influence of Chinese on the types of clauses used
in SgE is obvious. There is a close similarity between the Chinese structures
given above and those used by the basilectal informants (see 6.10.6.1).

The topic-comment clauses show the influence of Chinese structures,
where a 'loose relation' between subject and predicate is possible (Chao

1968:72). As shown in S7.13, meaning can only be inferred from the context:

S7.13 Housing Board is deir housing estate.

'The parking lots which belong to the HDB are those in the HDB housing estates. They do not belong to URA.'

In conclusion, the types of clauses used are a clear indicator of socio-educational class. For instance hypothetical structures with *if* and a copula are rarely used by basilectal informants. In most instances, *if* is omitted in hypothetical clauses. Certainly *if* + *NP* + *be* + *to-infinitive* clauses do not occur at all in the speech of informants with sec. 1–3 and primary level education. It is obvious that the use of *if* hypothetical structures is a diagnostic feature which reflects more acrolectal speech. On the other hand, the use of the 'loose' topic and comment type of clauses typifies the speech of the basilectal class.

7

The Acquisition of Past Tense

7.1 Problems in the acquisition of past tense

The acquisition of the tense-aspect system of a language by speakers of another language is often problematic, even if the languages are related. For example, English sentences with verbs in the simple past tense are often the appropriate translations of German sentences with a compound verb form which is structurally similar to the English present perfect, such as when an adverb of time occurs:

English: She *saw* him yesterday.
German: Sie *hat* ihn gestern *gesehen*
She has him yesterday seen.

With languages as far apart genetically and typologically as English and Chinese, the acquisition of the English tense-aspect system obviously presents considerable problems for the speaker of a Chinese-language background. It has been claimed, e.g. by Lyons (1977:687), that Chinese is among the languages which do not have tense but which grammaticalize aspectual distinctions. On the other hand, Comrie (1976:58) states that in Chinese (Mandarin) 'the verbal particle -*le* indicates perfective aspect and relative past time reference'. Later (p. 82) he explains that 'in many cases the use of -*le* is optional . . . but when it does occur -*le* indicates a past perfective situation'. In any case, Chinese is among those languages which do not mark tense or aspect on the verb itself by morphological means.

Of course, there are some Singaporean Chinese whose mother tongue is (Singaporean) English and there are many more who use English as much as or more than a variety of Chinese in everyday communication. None the less, the influence of various subvarieties of Chinese is pervasive and the colloquial subvarieties of SgE have many features which are clearly of Chinese origin.

However, the analysis of individual verbs by Ho demonstrates that very marked differences in the degree of past tense marking cannot always be explained by direct Chinese substratum influence.

7.2 The corpus and the categories

There are 8,725 verbs in the corpus which would prescriptively be marked for past tense. These verbs were classified under five educational levels, three semantic categories, and four phonetic types. The three semantic categories comprise verbs which are used in a punctual (P), non-punctual (NP), and stative (S) way. The four broad phonetic types are as follows.

1. VC verbs—verbs whose stems undergo a vowel change (and in some cases other changes as well) in order to form the past form, e.g. *fall–fell, eat–ate, go–went.*
2. Id verbs—verbs whose stems end in an alveolar stop and require the allomorph /ɪd/ for their past form, e.g. *wanted, started, treated.*
3. Vd verbs—verbs which in their past tense form end in a *vowel + d*, e.g. *followed, paid, carried.* Included in this category are verbs like *have* and *make* because their past tense ends in a *vowel + d.*
4. CC verbs—verbs whose past form ends in a consonant cluster, e.g. *picked, robbed, punched.*

7.3 Counting of verbs

7.3.1 Verbs that have been excluded

1. All verbs in the perfect aspect form are excluded e.g. if a present perfect were unmarked for past in a sentence such as

When I arrived, he has left.

This is because if we include all perfect aspect forms, we will actually be considering *have/has/had* as the finite part of the verb. This means that it could heavily increase the count of *have.*

2. Tokens of simple past occurring where the simple present or present perfect would have occurred in SBrE have been excluded, e.g.

S8.2. In the morning we came out also lah (describing a present habitual activity.)

O13.4. We can tell whether they (shoplifters) really *forgot* to pay or they have intention of taking. (Here the informant is talking about a present state of affairs—she is making a judgement about them.)

It is found that many informants (especially those at the upper end of the continuum) use the simple past with *already*:

I already *did* that.
I already *spoke* to him about the matter.

A plausible reason for such structures could be the influence of similar structures in SBrE. For instance, *already* can be used with past reference statives:

I already *knew* a great deal of maths when I started school.
I already *admired* his work before I met him.

Yet another reason for the use of the past form with *already* is that many of the English past forms, e.g. *told, bought, brought*, have similar past participle forms. Many SgE speakers could have heard *have/had* + *past participle* as just *0* + *past participle*:

We've already *told* them not to do it

could have been heard as:

We already *told* them not to do it.

This phenomenon has resulted in a stabilized *0* + *past participle* SgE structure:

S13.1. But we already *done* it y'see.

P9.29. One of the operator(s) seen (it) 'know.

Naturally, expressions such as *I seen him* also occur in non-standard speech of native varieties of English and such usage could have come through in films and television and have influenced SgE in general.

Those with higher levels of education also tend to use *just* with a past tense form verb, e.g.

I just *gave* a talk last Monday.

When *just* refers to *time* (i.e. 'not too long ago') then it should, prescriptively, co-occur with the perfect aspect. Again the target language may have an influence on the use of such structures because when *just* means *simply*, it can co-occur with the simple past:

He *just* (meaning 'simply') left the firm.

3. Structures with *ever/never* + *verb* are excluded if they are used in a non-standard way, e.g.

I ever/never go/went/gone dere.

In Standard English *ever* is used in only three environments:

(*a*) In question forms, e.g. 'Have you ever seen him?'

(*b*) In embedded questions, e.g. 'I asked her if she had ever seen him.'

(*c*) In embedded negatives, e.g. 'I don't think I've ever seen him.'

In SBrE *never* usually co-occurs with the perfect. However, in a narrative about the past, the past form can also be used:

After that terrible event he never spoke to her again.

In some native varieties of English there are non-standard structures such as:

I never *saw/seen* him (meaning I didn't see him).

As mentioned before, as with the adverb *just*, such usage could have influenced SgE in general through television and films.

4. Other auxiliary verbs that have been excluded include modals, such as *could* in *could sing* and *had to* in *I had to go*.

5. Because of the complex nature of *be* occurrence, it was decided to
exclude all forms of *be* from the investigation.

6. The past form of *get* is almost categorical in several environments in
SgE:

(a) *existential got*

Here *got* one stall selling very delicious noodles.

'There is a stall here selling very delicious noodles.'

(b) *emphatic got*

What for buy dis type of ting in Australia. Some more (i.e. in addition) so expensive. Singapore also *got* sell what (particle indicating
disapproval).

You shouldn't waste your money buying such things in Australia.
Moreover, they are so expensive. You certainly can get them in
Singapore!'

I also *got* go and learn

'I did go and learn.'

The above examples show the use of *got* as an emphatic marker in
basilectal SgE. This marker, strongly influenced by the Southern
Chinese dialects, rather than Mandarin, is replaced by *do/did* in the
speech of informants with higher levels of education, e.g.

I do/did learn.

Sometimes 'do/did + verb' are used even when no emphasis is
intended. This cannot be totally attributed to L1 influence because in
English *do* and *did* are often used to express emphasis.

(c) *passive got*

I *got* fired by the boss.

'My boss told me off.'

(d) *possessive got*

Everyting I *got* my own what (particle expressing disapproval and
disagreement about sharing cutlery with one's flatmates)—pots, pans,
spoon—what for share?—Wait (later on) get plenty problems only
(talking about the hassles of flatting).

'I've got everything of my own. I don't believe in sharing anything with
my flatmates. You never know what's in store for you—I can foresee
lots of problems ahead!'

Naturally, one cannot attribute the categorical use of *got* mainly to
background language influence. In L2 there is also the common use of
I've got in SBrE and in American English there is the strong influence
of *gotta* e.g. *I gotta tell X about . . .* as heard in American pop songs, TV
programmes, and films. Since the distinction between *I've got* and *I got*
is a very slight one in fast speech, the labio-dental fricative is almost

categorically deleted in the environments mentioned above. Such tokens have been excluded.

7. All verbs marked in a non-standard way are excluded, e.g.

S12.12. I *knowed* a girl.

However, verbs which are lexically non-standard are counted in the corpus, such as *friended* (instead of *befriended*, used by O16.22). Words like *dated* may have a semantic shift for the basilectal speaker. *To date* means to fix a date, e.g. for a fight. Such tokens are also counted.

8. Certain active transitive verbs in expressions such as *catch to X* are excluded. The structure *catch to* collapses two verbs into one, i.e. *to catch* and *to take to* X:

S9.1. Den de purse all taken away and den (the man) *caught* de girl *to* de penthouse.

9. The verb *say* has not been considered as the final consonant of its past form *said* is often realized as an unreleased stop in SgE. At times, the glottal stop [ʔ] is used in final position. In fast speech where there are expressions such as *said that*, the initial consonant [ð] in *that* is often realized as [d]. It is therefore very difficult to tell if *say* has been marked for past in such environments. Yet another reason for excluding *say* is that in SgE there are expressions such as *write/tell/ask me say/said*. One cannot consider such expressions as structures with a missing *and* because *a verb of communication plus say* is a single semantic unit in the more basilectal sub-varieties of SgE. The use of such structures is influenced by Chinese.

10. *Use to* is excluded from the count because of the difficulty of deciding whether *use* is marked for past or not. Moreover, *use to* is commonly used as a present habitual marker in SgE, e.g.

I *use to* speak English with my brothers and sisters at home (meaning she still does).

Sometimes the expression *would use to* marks the habitual in the past.

7.3.2 Verbs that have been included

In the following types of narratives, many of the verbs used are in the present tense. This may be related to an informant's belief that certain persons, places, and situations are still the same. In SBrE, if one has visited a place very recently and has reason to believe that everything is still as it was, the present tense is often used. However, if one is referring to situations that happened some time ago then, prescriptively, the past tense should be used.

1. It was decided to include a count of verbs in texts relating to accounts of former teachers. It was found that many of the informants used the present rather than the past form of verbs. It could be that many of these teachers were still alive. However, prescriptively one can only use the present tense if

one sees or expects to see one's former teachers again. It was found that the norm for native speakers when asked about their former teachers was the use of the past tense rather than the present tense when describing events or characteristics related to the teacher in the school setting.

2. It was found throughout the whole continuum that many of the informants talked about their training or work routines at their previous place of work in the present tense. Again, as above, it could be that the informants thought the same situation obtained at the time of the interview. If we use SBrE as our yardstick, then when the pronouns *we* and *I* are used and if one talks about the past, the past tense should be used. Naturally, if the pronoun is *you*, one can use the present tense if one discusses generalities or makes comments. The following is part of a text by a speaker with secondary 2 education who had gone to a trade school. He discussed the training he received:

S2.3. Aah, for apprentice—normally we go ro—aah by rotation lah—maybe 6 mon(ths) in milling section ... During our—on the job training, er one supervisor will be dere ... But in my view ah, we apprentice, actually, we are not very well-treated lah you see (informant is no longer an apprentice), because the su(per)visor tings dat we are under bond. So most of de time dey can bully us you see ... and if we do someting wrong with our jobs or we spoil job y'see ... we do someting wrong to de dimension ... Let's say for examp(l)e de job we do—to a specific dimension. We do it undersize. Dat means we spoil a job you see. Instead of—supervisor—instead of console us, to do better—he scold us you see.

7.3.3 Classification of punctual verbs

The literature on aspect in English is quite extensive. The views of both linguists and philosophers, such as Kenny (1963), Vendler (1967), King (1969), Verkuyl (1971), Comrie (1976), and Dowty (1977), are often conflicting as to what constitutes punctual, non-punctual, and stative aspects.

It will be of interest to consider various definitions of aspect. Ho took into account a number of views before arriving at a set of criteria for classifying each of the past reference verbs in the corpus as punctual or non-punctual. The problem, in the case of verbs occurring in natural speech, is far from simple.

Comrie (1976:42) defines *punctuality* as being the opposite of durativity, where

the quality of a situation ... does not last in time (is not conceived of as lasting in time), one that takes place momentarily. It should be noted that the crucial point here is that punctual situations do not have any duration, not even duration of a very short period. Thus a punctual situation, by definition, has no internal structure ...

He gives *cough* as an example of a punctual verb, referring to a single cough and not a series of coughs. He continues:

the Progressive which has imperfective meaning, would be impossible with *cough* (on the interpretation when there is only one cough) i.e. *he was coughing* would be inappropriate in referring to a situation where he gave a single cough;...The only interpretation possible for such a sentence would be that the reference is to a series of coughs [Comrie refers to this as an iterative situation]...Thus the inherent punctuality of *cough* would restrict the range of interpretations that can be given to imperfective forms of this verb.

Bickerton's punctual aspect refers to a single event and his non-punctual aspect refers to iterative and durative events (Bickerton 1981:164–5). In general, his comments, reproduced below, are along the lines of Comrie above:

the punctual–nonpunctual opposition must also be marked in the semantic features of individual verbs. That is to say, some verbs are inherently punctual, while others are inherently nonpunctual. If you hit something for five minutes, it must be that you hit many times; similarly, if you jump for five minutes, you must jump many times; both *hit* and *jump* express inherently punctual actions. But on the other hand, if you push something for five minutes, you do not necessarily push it more than once, and if something rolls for five minutes, it does not necessarily roll more than once; both *push* and *roll* express inherently nonpunctual actions (although of course a compound verb like *roll over* is inherently punctual). (Bickerton 1981:170–1)

Although the particle *up* is often used with the meaning 'completely, to a finish', e.g. *break it up, cover it up, eat it up, twist it up, open it up* (Capell 1979:15), in other words they are inherently punctual compound verbs, it is always imperative to consider the context. As pointed out by Comrie (1976:47 n. 1) *eat up* is used in a non-punctual way in *some childern eat their food up*—'the addition of an indefinitely plural subject...means that the whole situation is not telic'.

One wonders if Bickerton has not wavered in his criteria—he sometimes looks only at the verb and sometimes at the situations. In analysing the conclusions reached by Antinucci and Miller (1976), Bickerton posits the hypothesis that change-of-state verbs such as *close, fall, give*, etc. which were well marked for past by the children could be looked at from the angle that these are all punctual verbs:

Now, it happens to be the case that change-of-state verbs are *all [our emphasis]* inherently punctual, the rare, apparent exceptions are often due to purely technological developments, as in *the abandoned astronaut fell toward the planet for several hours*. But even sentences like that can be seen to be underlyingly punctual if we apply another test for inherent punctuality: the question, 'If you stop halfway through *Ving*, have you *Ved*?' Thus, if you stop halfway through closing, you have not closed, and if you stop halfway through giving, you have not given; similarly, if the abandoned astronaut stopped halfway through falling, he would not have fallen, although he might have lost altitude. But with activity verbs, which are inherently nonpunctual, the converse applies: if you stop halfway through playing, you have played, if you stop halfway through writing, you have written and so on. (Bickerton 1981:173)

Le Page (1983:264) criticises Bickerton very strongly on this:

Bickerton's argument here rests, I believe, upon an absolutely fundamental linguistic and semantic fallacy: that units within predicates can be assigned absolute semantic values and functions regardless of specific contexts in which they may be used; that verbs can be classified as unchangingly and wholly active and stative, predication as punctual or non-punctual or habitual . . .

This controversy on what constitutes a punctual verb or situation has been going on for a long time. It all hinges on the degree of punctuality. As Comrie (1976:42) points out, a punctual verb is one which allows for no duration, not even for the slightest amount of time. Hence a verb like *reach* meaning 'to arrive' will be considered punctual in the strictest sense of the word. Another super-punctual verb is *slam*, e.g. *He slammed the door.* However, if we take verbs like *close* (which, inherently, is strictly not instantaneous like *reach* or *slam* or *punch*) it is possible to have a variation of the internal make-up of the verb, depending on the context. *He quickly closed the door* can be considered punctual. Certainly *He closed the door slowly* is non-punctual.

This brings us to the question of *telic* and *atelic*, if we wish to consider as punctual, situations with varying degrees of punctuality. King (1969:184) gives the following list of verbal expressions which exhibit [+ punctual] and [+ durative] features:

PUNCTUAL (= perfective, aorist, instantaneous)	DURATIVE (imperfective, descriptive, stative)
He *paints* a picture.	He *paints* like Rivera.
He *drinks* the glass of water.	He *drinks*.
He *reads* the first few lines.	He *reads* very well.
He *hits* a home run; appoints a captain.	He *bats* left-handed; *manages* the team.
She *wrote* that poem.	She *wrote* poetry.
She *said* something in French.	She *spoke* French fluently.
He *put on* a hat.	He *wore* a hat.
You'll *miss* the first act.	You'll *miss* your garden (= feel the lack of it.)

Even in the above exemplifications one cannot help but notice the varying degrees of punctuality. Thus *he put on a hat* is more punctual than *he reads the first few lines*, which is again more punctual than *he paints a picture*. All the sentences on the left of King's list are *telic* situations. King classifies these as punctual situations. All the situations on the right are *atelic* ones. They are classified as durative situations. In defining *telic* and *atelic*, Comrie (1976:44) gives the following exemplifications:

  (*a*) John is singing (atelic).
  (*b*) John is making a chair (telic).

The situation in (*a*) has no terminal point: that is, John can stop singing at any point and it can be said that John has sung. The situation in (*b*) has a terminal point, i.e. a point when the chair is completed. Hence if John breaks off at any point in the making of the chair, the chair has not been made (Comrie points out that the term *telic* corresponds to the use of 'accomplishment' in Vendler (1967:102)). What Comrie strongly stresses is that all situations must be viewed in context:

situations are not described by verbs alone, but rather by the verb together with its arguments (subject and objects). Thus although *John is singing* describes an atelic situation, the sentence *John is singing a song* describes a telic situation, since this situation has a well-defined terminal point . . . John is singing songs is again atelic, whereas *John is singing five songs* is again telic. (Comrie 1976:45)

In real-life situations it is often most difficult to tell whether a situation is telic or atelic. Comrie himself admits this (1976:46): 'However, although it is difficult to find sentences that are unambiguously telic or atelic, this does not affect the general semantic distinction made between telic and atelic situations.' Comrie underscores the importance of the telic-atelic distinction:

The particular importance of the telic/atelic distinction for the study of aspect is that, when combined with the perfective/imperfective opposition, the semantic range of telic verbs is restricted considerably so that certain logical deductions can be made from the aspect of a sentence referring to a telic situation that cannot be made from the aspect of a sentence referring to an atelic situation. For instance, a perfective form referring to a telic situation implies attainment of the terminal point of that situation . . . (Comrie 1976:46)

This distinction is important to a classification of verbs in SgE into the punctual-non-punctual semantic categories as, prior to the classification of the data, it was observed that in situations where a verb implied an attainment of a goal (i.e. [+telic]), the verb was more likely to be marked.

In defining *telic* and *atelic* situations, Comrie has not made a stand as to whether these are considered punctual or non-punctual situations. As mentioned before, he regards as punctual a situation which 'takes place momentarily' and which has no duration, 'not even duration of a very short period' (Comrie 1976:42).

Before the data were classified, Ho had to decide on criteria to define what would be considered punctual situations. There could be a class of clearly punctual verbs such as *die, marry, reach, buy*—i.e. verbs occurring at a point in time. The alternative would be a category of verbs with varying degrees of punctuality. However, the underlying or overt feature [+telic] or [+completive] should be present. Choosing the second classification would mean defining punctuality in a very broad way. As Dowty (1977: 49) remarks: 'the result-state of an accomplishment comes to be true at a single moment rather than over an interval of time'. He argues that in a sentence like 'John drew a circle', irrespective of the length of time taken for the activity, 'there is a single moment at which a circle came to exist'. It would thus be even more inconceivable to think of 'an instantaneous change of state ... for accomplishments such as building a house or crossing the desert'. Thus in a very strict sense (as defined by Comrie) only the point of accomplishment can be considered truly punctual.

However, Ho decided on the second classification for the following reasons:

1. The first classification was considered too restrictive. The data base would be a very small one as it was unlikely that there would be many strictly punctual situations.

2. Secondly, a classification similar to that adopted by Bickerton for Guyanese Creole (GC) and Hawaiian Creole English (HCE) was felt to be more beneficial since it would enable a comparison of the results of the SgE data with those of GC and HCE. Moreover, it was also clear that Bickerton used the terms *punctual* and *non-punctual* in a very broad sense (i.e. he referred to situations and did not restrict himself to considering only the verb). This can be seen in his analysis of the study undertaken by Antinucci and Miller (1976). The two exemplifications quoted by Bickerton are given below:

/22/ (Antinucci and Miller's 82)

  Mamma *e andato* (participial) al parco e io *stavo* (imperfect) a casa
  'Mommy *went* to the park and I *stayed* home'

/23/ (Antinucci and Miller's 90)

  Li *ha messi* (participial) nel saco e dopo gli altri bambini *piangevano* (imperfect)
  'He *put* them in a sack and then the other children *cried*'

(Bickerton 1981:174)

Bickerton comments, 'imperfects and participials are in complementary distribution, the first being used for punctual [*sic*, for non-punctual] verbs, the second for non-punctual [*sic*, for punctual] ones'. Thus if the above English sentences were used in GE or HCE, Bickerton, it was assumed, would have classified *went* [+telic] and *put* [+telic] as punctual. Conversely, *stayed* and *cried* being [+atelic] would have been put in the non-punctual category.

7.3.4 Classification of stative and non-stative verbs

To find out if a verb is stative, the following tests from Lakoff (1970:121) have been applied:

  (*a*) Imperative
    Look at the picture.
    *Know that Bill went there.
  (*b*) Do-something
    What I'm doing is *looking at* the picture.
    **What I'm doing is *knowing* that Bill went there.

(c) Progressive

  I'm *looking at* the picture.

  *I'm *knowing* that Bill went there.

Thus *know* has the feature [+stative] because the application of all the above three tests has failed.

In general, Ho has followed Joos's (1964:118) classification of 'status verbs', which are divided into two groups:

(1) *(psychic state*, including the specific perceptions (SEE, HEAR, etc.) and the intellectual and emotional attitudes (BELIEVE, UNDERSTAND, HATE, LIKE, REGARD, etc.);

(2) *relation*, such as the relations of representing, depending, excluding, and so on.

Quirk, Greenbaum, Leech, and Svartvik (1972:96) have two similar classes which they call stative verbs. They call the first class of stative verbs 'verbs of inert perception and cognition'. Examples of the second class, 'relational verbs', include *apply to* (everyone), *contain, cost, have, involve, remain (a bachelor), resemble*, etc. However, while the class 2 verbs cannot occur in the progressive, very often class 1 verbs can, e.g.

  I (can) smell perfume.

  I am smelling the perfume (activity verb).

                        (Quirk, Greenbaum, Leech and Svartvik 1972:96)

  I can hear it now.

  The Judge is *hearing* a case just now; you'll have to wait (process verb).

                                                        (Joos 1964:117)

The second example of each pair given above is of an action initiated or performed by the individual. Scheffer (1975) has compiled a list of verbs expressing 'static' ideas (cf. Zandvoort 1975:40). This is reproduced in Appendix B. Scheffer found that in his corpus there were 350 cases of verbs from this list which occurred in the progressive: '*apply, be* (23 times), *demonstrate*[+], *feel** (16) *fill* (3) *find*, forget, hang* (4), *hate* (3), *have* (25), *have to* (2), *hear** (7), *hold** (14), *hope* (3), *imagine* (3), *intend* (2), *lie* (14), *like, look** (31), *love, make** (37), *mean, plan* (2), *reach*[+], *refuse*[+], *represent*, see** (11), *show** (5), *sing* [*sic*, for *signify*] (6), *sit*[+] (38), *stand*[+] (33), *think** (53), *understand, want* (3), and *wish**' (Scheffer 1975:65). The verbs marked * appeared in Ho's corpus as both stative and non-stative verbs. Those marked + appeared only as non-stative verbs.

The list of verbs compiled by Scheffer is particularly useful as it gives us an idea of verbs which are most commonly thought of as stative, e.g. *see, hear, think, remember, understand, love, know, like, want*.

Verbs which are least discussed as verbs conveying 'static ideas' are either those which are of low frequency, e.g. *foresee* and *suffice*, or those which are often thought of as activity verbs, e.g. *reach, refuse, demonstrate, sit, stand, lie*, and *hang*. With the last category of verbs, it can be seen that there are situations where each of them can be used as a stative verb:

A picture of my grandmother *hangs* on the wall.
On the river bank *stands* the statue of X.
This jacket *refuses* to wear out.
The canals *reach* the sea.

However, Scheffer's investigation confirms that verbs such as *sit* and *stand* appear more frequently in the progressive. In the inceptive stage such verbs are activity verbs. They later have the feature [+stative]. In Ho's corpus such verbs are classified as non-punctual verbs as they have the element [+durative], e.g. when the verb *sit* refers to a state of being seated.

Aitchison criticises Bickerton for not being specific in his labelling of verbs such as *want, need, like*. According to her, Bickerton's term *state verbs* is too general:

if one looks more closely at the available child language data, there are a number of instances of *-ing* attached to verbs such as *sleeping, taking nap, sitting, holding, waiting, having*, (Bloom *et al.* 1980). Bloom *et al* classify all these as state verbs. So the verbs which tend to avoid *-ing* are not just state verbs, but a subcategory of these, internal state verbs, (i.e. those that express an internal state such as *want, need, like*). So one would have to assume that the bioprogram singled out internal state verbs, rather than state verbs alone. (Aitchison 1983:89)

Possibly Bickerton does make a distinction between the two categories because he uses the term *stative* rather than *state* in 'children never ever attach *-ing* to stative verbs' (Bickerton 1981:155).

However, earlier on, Bickerton's use of the word *state* does imply a broader semantic category:

We will now examine another distinction which is made even earlier and without, apparently, even a single reported case of error. This is the distinction between states and processes, including under the latter rubric verbs of experiencing as well as action verbs (hereafter referred to as the state–process distinction, or SPD). (Bickerton 1981:154)

In Ho's classification, a clear distinction has been made between statives (as defined by Joos (1964) and Quirk, Greenbaum, Leech and Svartvik (1972)) and non-statives which have the features [+duration, +activity].

It should be pointed out that there are many verbs which would, in a 'native' variety of English, be considered stative verbs. However, an examination of the context shows that certain verbs are used non-punctually; for example, verbs such as *hear* and *see* often mean *to listen to* and *to watch* respectively:

I *hear* the music.
I *see* my mother sew.

Such verbs are classified as non-punctual verbs and not stative verbs. Each verb in the corpus is assigned a semantic category according to the context. For example, *I accepted it* (i.e. 'my child's death') is a mental acceptance, showing resignation on the part of the informant. This is a stative verb. However, *I accepted the job* is certainly a punctual verb because it signifies a verbal or written acceptance.

7.4 Discussion of findings

7.4.1 Past tense marking in relation to semantic and phonetic types

There is no doubt that semantic factors do have an influence on past tense marking of verbs in SgE. The whole corpus of 8,725 verbs which would, prescriptively, be marked for past tense was divided into two categories, punctual and non-punctual, and as Fig. 7.1 shows, punctual verbs are better marked for past tense than non-punctual verbs: 56.2% as compared to 23.2% respectively.

A further breakdown of the broad non-punctual category of verbs into statives and non-punctual verbs shows that statives are better marked than non-punctuals (i.e. iteratives and habituals). Figure 7.2 gives a breakdown of the three semantic categories. The percentage marking of verbs in the corpus for past tense is in the following descending order: punctuals 56.2%, statives 36.9%, and non-punctuals 14.7%.

Obviously, phonetic factors play a part too as far as past tense marking is concerned. An examination of Fig. 7.3 shows that the verbs, when divided

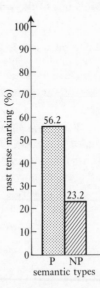

Fig. 7.1 Past tense marking, two semantic types: punctuals and non-punctuals

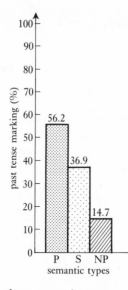

FIG. 7.2 Past tense marking, three semantic types: punctuals, non-punctuals, and statives

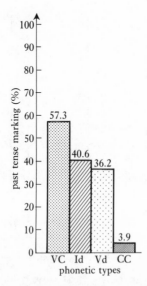

FIG. 7.3 Past tense marking, four phonetic types: VC, Id, Vd, and CC

into the four phonetic categories, display the following descending order in the degree of past tense marking:

VC type 57.3%
Id type 40.6%
Vd type 36.2%
CC type 3.9%

Figure 7.4 shows the interplay of the two linguistic factors: phonetic and semantic categories. That semantic factors have a very marked influence on past tense marking is shown by the fact that in all the four different phonetic categories, (VC, Id, Vd, and CC types), the degree of past tense marking is always in the following descending order: punctuals, statives, and non-punctuals. This is a very strong consistent trend. However, a comparison of percentage past tense marking of various phonetic categories for each semantic type does not show a fixed trend (see Fig. 7.5). The punctual category shows the following order: VC, Id, Vd, and CC. For the stative

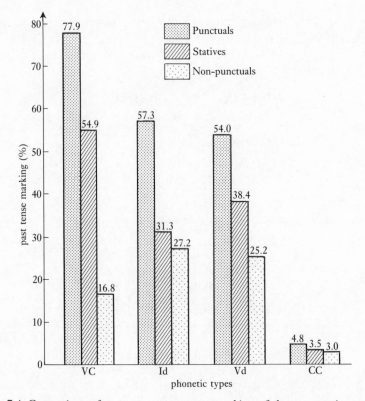

Fig. 7.4 Comparison of percentage past tense marking of three semantic categories for each phonetic type

category, the order for Id and Vd verbs is reversed. For the non-punctual category, VC verbs have a lower degree of marking than the Id and Vd verbs. This shows that the semantic factor is probably stronger than the phonetic one. A noticeable observation is the distinct difference in the degree of past tense marking between the punctual VC verbs (77.9%) and the non-punctual VC verbs (16.8%). Naturally, the results may have been affected by the fact that the number of VC punctual tokens is six times the number of VC non-punctual tokens. A comparison of the proportion of VC and Id tokens in the punctual and non-punctual categories shows that in both categories the number of VC tokens is one and a half times that of the Id tokens. One notices that in the punctual category past tense marking for VC verbs is higher than for Id verbs. However, the picture is reversed for the non-punctual category. Since the vowel change of VC verbs is phonetically easier for Singaporean learners of English, one can conclude that the semantic factor is a stronger one. An examination of the degree of past tense marking of individual VC verbs confirms this. Although in general the number of non-

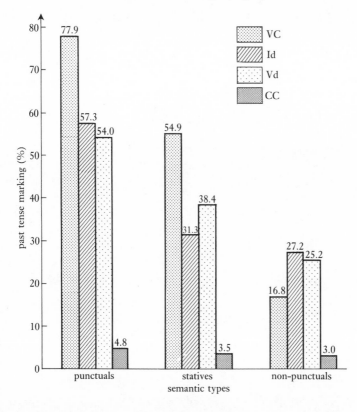

FIG. 7.5 Comparison of percentage past tense marking of four phonetic categories for each semantic type

punctual tokens is much lower than that of the punctual tokens, there are verbs such as *come, go, do* where there are more than a hundred non-punctual tokens. However, there is a marked contrast in the degree of marking between the punctual and non-punctual categories. For example, *come*: punctual (75.4%), non-punctual (9.4%); *go*: punctual (84.2%), non-punctual (15.3%); and *do*: punctual (94.3%), non-punctual (16.7%). As will be shown in the discussion later, the higher the proportion of punctual tokens for individual verbs, the higher the degree of marking for past. Conversely, the degree of marking for past is lower if the proportion of non-punctual tokens increases. It was found that of 38 VC verbs, 20 verbs had more than 50% of the tokens used punctually (Table 7.1). There were 12 verbs in the VC category with more than 50% of the tokens used non-punctually (Table 7.2), and 6 verbs with more than 50% used statively (Table 7.3).

Again, an examination of individual verbs shows that verbs where all tokens are used statively have a low marking for past. Five of the 15 Id verbs studied in detail have entirely stative tokens while only one of the 20 Vd verbs is used in this manner.

TABLE 7.1. *Class I verbs of which more than 50% of tokens are used punctually* (%)

Verb	Past tense marking	Proportion of punctual tokens
Begin	40.0	90.0
Break	57.1	78.6
Bring	56.6	75.0
Buy	62.1	75.9
Come	55.6	69.5
Do	59.6	55.3
Drive	58.3	62.5
Get	55.2	72.4
Give	23.2	67.6
Go	66.3	74.0
Leave	87.6	96.2
Lose	86.7	93.3
Meet	80.3	85.3
Ring	85.7	92.9
Run	57.1	60.7
Speak	72.0	60.0
Take	49.2	67.3
Tell	74.6	89.2
Throw	23.5	52.9
Write	59.0	66.7

The CC type stands out as a category that is markedly different from the other phonetic categories. It is the only category where the phonetic factor is dominant, being the least marked phonetic category. Out of a total of 2,262 CC verbs in the corpus, only 87 tokens (3.9%) were marked for past. Although the semantic factor may not be as significant as in the other phonetic categories, it cannot be totally disregarded, as one can still see a similar trend—the punctual verbs are slightly better marked than the stative and the non-punctual categories.

7.4.2 Correlation between educational levels and past tense marking

An examination of past tense marking according to educational levels and semantic types (see Fig. 7.6) and phonetic types (see Fig. 7.7) shows that the

TABLE 7.2. *Class II verbs of which more than 50% of tokens are used non-punctually* (%)

Verb	Past tense marking	Proportion of non-punctual tokens
Become	51.9	63.0
Catch	46.2	53.9
Eat	16.7	100.0
Grow	58.3	100.0
Keep	21.6	100.0
Read	35.7	78.6
Sell	12.5	66.7
Sing	41.2	88.2
Sit	39.4	54.5
Sleep	28.0	100.0
Teach	33.9	89.2
Wear	9.1	100.0

TABLE 7.3. *Class III verbs of which more than 50% of tokens are used statively* (%)

Verb	Past tense marking	Proportion of stative tokens
Feel	43.8	100.0
Find	58.3	65.9
Hear	87.3	90.5
Know	25.4	100.0
See	54.0	69.1
Think	75.2	92.8

acquisition of past tense marking is not a haphazard one. That there is a positive correlation between education and past tense marking is shown by the degree of past tense marking, which increases steadily from primary to tertiary level. The different rates of acquisition by informants with different levels of education according to phonetic and semantic types is in itself an interesting phenomenon, an area which requires further in-depth investigation, as it has important pedagogical significance.

7.4.3 *The Varbrul analysis versus the present analysis*

The data for past tense marking were also subjected to Varbrul analysis. However, there was a rather poor match between the predicted and observed frequencies.

As shown in Figs. 7.6 and 7.7, the rates of acquisition for the different phonetic and semantic types vary considerably. For example, there is a fairly constant steep rise according to educational level for the VC verbs but a very

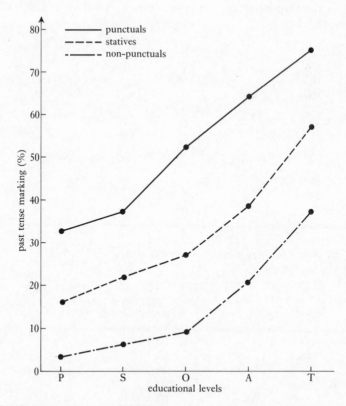

FIG. 7.6 Percentage past tense marking against educational levels for three semantic types

slight rise for the CC verbs, especially between the P and O levels. Again, there is a steep rise after the S level for verbs used punctually but with the two curves for stative verbs and verbs used non-punctually the change to a steeper rise is at the O level. The Varbrul analysis was therefore abandoned and individual verbs were analysed according to semantic and phonetic types in an attempt to determine whether there were different underlying phonological and semantic rules for speakers with different educational attainments.

Although a detailed analysis of the Id, Vd, and CC verbs has been undertaken by Ho, only the VC verbs will be focused on. This is because these verbs have the highest degree of past tense marking of all the four phonetic types and therefore the semantic influence may be more clearly observed. An analysis of 24 VC verbs is presented to show the importance of the semantic factor.

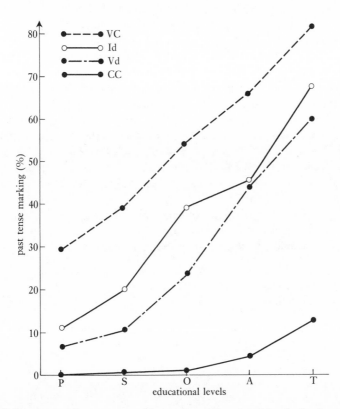

FIG. 7.7 Percentage past tense marking against educational levels for four phonetic types

7.5 Analysis of VC verbs

7.5.1 Preliminary discussion

Table 7.1 shows a list of verbs of which more than 50% of the tokens are used punctually. The overall past tense marking of this class of verbs, which Ho called Class I verbs, is 61.3%.

Class II verbs (see Table 7.2), consisting of verbs which are essentially non-punctual (i.e. where tokens of each individual verb are more than 50% non-punctual), has an overall past tense marking of 32.2%.

Class III verbs (see Table 7.3) are essentially stative. The overall past tense marking for this class of verbs is 55.1%. On the basis of Bickerton's (1981) discussion, one would expect statives (which are non-punctuals) to receive a low marking. However, as mentioned before, the overall past tense marking for statives is two and a half times higher than for non-punctuals. Two essentially stative verbs, *think* and *hear*, were very well marked for past, even at the basilectal end of the continuum. *Feel* and *know* (essentially mental verbs), the tokens of which were all stative, received the lowest marking for past tense among the Class III verbs. *Find* and *see* had a higher marking than *feel* and *know* because some of the tokens were used punctually.

We may now consider the Class I verbs in greater detail. If we single out verbs which have at least 30 tokens, we can see two distinct sub-classes. Table 7.4 shows a list of verbs with 85% and above of the tokens used punctually. The overall past tense marking for this class of verbs is 79.4%.

We notice that as the number of non-punctual tokens increases, the marking for past tense decreases. Table 7.5 shows a list of verbs which have between 55% and 75% of the tokens used punctually. The overall past tense marking decreases to 60.7%. An exception is the verb *give*, which has a particularly low marking and is therefore excluded from the table. Reasons for its low marking will be discussed later.

Among the Class II verbs are five which receive rather low marking (under 30%) for past. These verbs are listed in Table 7.6.

With the exception of *sell*, we note that the four verbs *keep*, *eat*, *sleep*, and

TABLE 7.4. *Class I verbs of which 85% and above of tokens are used punctually* (%)

Verbs	Past tense marking	Proportion of punctual tokens
Leave	87.6	96.2
Lose	86.7	93.3
Meet	80.3	85.3
Tell	74.6	89.2

wear are all used non-punctually. One major reason for the low marking of these five verbs is that more of the tokens are found at the lower end of the continuum, particularly for *eat*, *sell*, and *wear*. Another reason is that *keep*, *sleep*, and *wear* are basically inert verbs compared with the more active ones *sell* and *eat*. However, the latter two receive lower marking for other reasons. *Eat*, as can be seen below, is used 100% non-punctually. Moreover, in SgE the diphthong [eɪ] is not distinct. Hence the past form of *eat* which is pronounced in SgE as [eɪt] rather than [et] could have been heard by those at the lower end of the social scale as [i:t]. The same phenomenon occurs with the verb *give*, which receives a low marking. Strangely enough, the verb *sell*, which has some tokens used punctually, receives the second lowest marking among the five verbs. A possible reason is that the verb *sold* is not a high-frequency verb among those with lower levels of formal education. Most shop assistants seldom say something is *sold out*. A more common expression is *no more stock already*.

TABLE 7.5. *Class I verbs of which between 55% and 75% of tokens are used punctually* (%)

Verbs	Past tense marking	Proportion of punctual tokens
Buy	62.1	75.9
Bring	56.6	75.0
Come	55.6	69.5
Do	59.6	55.3
Get	55.2	72.4
Go	66.3	74.0
Take	49.2	67.3
Write	59.0	66.7

TABLE 7.6. *Class II verbs with a score of under 30% for past tense marking* (%)

Verbs	Past tense marking	Proportion of non-punctual tokens
Eat	16.7	100.0
Keep	21.6	100.0
Sell	12.5	66.7
Sleep	28.0	100.0
Wear	9.1	100.0

7.5.2 A detailed study of twenty-four VC verbs

7.5.2.1 Class I verbs: bring, buy, do, get, give, go, come, leave, lose, meet, sell, speak, take, tell, *and* write

Bring

It is noticeable that except for one non-punctual token each marked at the primary and tertiary levels, the rest of the non-punctual tokens are unmarked. An example of a non-punctual token marked for past is given below:

P20.21. I follow my friends. I douno where dey *brought* me. I went to the Huālián, and all dat. Where dey go, I follow dem, dat one lah.

'Wherever my friends went while we were in Taiwan, I just went along with them.'

The other unmarked non-punctuals are mostly habituals:

A10.5. dey *bring* us out sometimes (i.e. while he was in New Zealand, friends took them out sometimes).

S14.10. Everyday she brings her ten rulers.

Most of the punctual tokens marked for past are verbs of movement. Prescriptively *take* should have been used. An example is given below:

O6.20. Den he *brought* me up (the mountain).

Instances of verbs of movement unmarked for past include the following:

S20.4. X introduce me to Mrs Y. So Mrs Y *bring* me dere also.

Interestingly, a similar utterance to S20.4 by another informant is marked for past:

My mother *brought* me dere.

A possible reason for the variable marking of *bring* for past is that the telic–non-telic distinction is often not at all clear. If an informant were to focus on the journey itself, *bring* would be considered [+durative]. On the

TABLE 7.7. *Past tense marking of* bring

	NP		P		S		Total	
	Score	%	Score	%	Score	%	Score	%
Tertiary	1/1	100.0	15/17	88.2	—	—	16/18	88.9
A level	0/3	0.0	13/14	92.9	—	—	13/17	76.5
O level	0/5	0.0	4/5	80.0	—	—	4/10	40.0
Sec. 1–3	0/3	0.0	7/15	46.7	—	—	7/18	38.9
Primary	1/7	14.3	2/6	33.3	—	—	3/13	23.1
TOTAL	2/19	10.5	41/57	71.9	—	—	43/76	56.6

other hand, if the focus were on the completion of the journey, *bring* would be classified as [+telic]. It appears that an informant's perception of an event does affect past tense marking of *bring*.

Only two punctual tokens, marked by informants with primary level education, are not verbs of movement. The two tokens have a telic nature, with the meaning 'the children are now grown up':

P19.16. The first child I'm so happy. Then I get a ah—de first child is a son—quite happy lah—in my whole family all lah—mm—very happy and den I *brought* dem up when dey are small—baby *brought* dem up. Like baby know how to walk—like so cute like dat lah—*bring* dem *go* anywhere like go relatifs house—bring dem go—sometime go to my real mader (mother) dere—den dey grow up already, I have de second one (child).

Note that when she uses *bring* as a verb of movement, it is not marked. The other reasons why *bring* is not marked are that it is used with a serial verb *go* and also that in the above context *bring* is non-punctual. There were three tokens of *bring* used with a serial verb at primary level and one at O level, none of which was marked.

An interesting observation about non-punctuals is that when speakers are talking about their teachers, the present tense is often used:

A19.15. He *brings out* de mistakes.
'He used to point out our mistakes.'

Buy

We notice that all non-punctuals are unmarked at sec. 1–3 and O level. However, at primary level, two tokens of non-punctuals are marked. For some primary informants there is probably a rule whereby non-punctuals are marked if they have a [+anterior] element, which has the function of a pluperfect. An illustration is given in P19.17.

TABLE 7.8. *Past tense marking of* buy

	NP		P		S		Total	
	Score	%	Score	%	Score	%	Score	%
Tertiary	—	—	5/5	100.0	—	—	5/5	100.0
A level	—	—	6/7	85.7	—	—	6/7	85.7
O level	0/1	0.0	14/15	93.3	—	—	14/16	87.5
Sec. 1–3	0/7	0.0	8/11	72.7	—	—	8/18	44.4
Primary	2/6	33.3	1/6	16.7	—	—	3/12	25.0
TOTAL	2/14	14.3	34/44	77.3	—	—	36/58	62.1

P19.17. (Describing what her foster-mother used to do.) Den after dat he (she) come back to (from) de market. She put down de market baske(t) and den you must know to prepare everyting dat he (she) *bought* in—inside de basket dere.

In other words, what is happening is that she uses the present tense for habituals in the past, and the past tense instead of the pluperfect. Thus in the following token she uses the unmarked form of *buy* for habituals again.

P19.19. I see de comics when I was still chil(d)hood dat one—I like to see de comics. When my father every one, one mon(th)s one—everytime *buy* for me two comics boo(k) for me and my mother grumble.

Among the punctual tokens used by the primary-level informants, there is only one which is marked and this is an emphatic token:

P10.8. I *bought* one big bundle back—aah—and de rose and dose ah what—the Bali flowers—de small small white white one.

Notice that elsewhere he does not mark *buy* although they are punctuals:

P10.9. Singapore is selling ah, a dra: (branch) is fifty cen(t) 'know. So I buy back ah, not up to 10 cen(t) yet 'know. So I buy a few casket (baskets) from him ah, put ice an(d) I send dose ah grucose (lotus) and rose back.

As can be seen from Table 7.8, for speakers above primary level, punctual tokens of *buy* receive very high marking for past, but there are some unmarked cases. There are several possible explanations.

1. The *V and V* structures are not marked:

O15.16. He come and buy de carpet ah.

2. The occurrence of *since ever* (ever since) influences the use of the unmarked form of *buy*. There is possible confusion because *ever since* relates to present situations as well as a past event.

S4.24. I: Do you often go to the movies?

   J: Aah not very lah. Since ever I *buy* dis TV I don't feel like going out.

3. Sometimes *buy* is not marked because the informant discusses something in general and then switches to a particular case but retains the present tense. In the following text the informant is not working in the camera shop any more. Hence, prescriptively, even the general comments about customers should have been discussed in the past tense.

S3.14. Some of dem, dey know—some of the cameras and den sometimes dey ask your choice y'know. Then you all have to tell dem what you learn. I have a customer who's very nice er—he *buy* and den he bring his son along y'see. So after serving him must serve his son.

Do

On the evidence of the data, it would seem that for this verb, acquisition of past tense marking is very slow at primary and sec. 1–3 level. The primary-level group has a higher degree of marking than the sec. 1–3 group because in the latter group there are more non-punctual tokens. Notice too that marking for non-punctuals from primary to O level is very low, with zero marking for primary and sec. 1–3 levels and only one token marked by the O level group. There is a greater degree of marking at A and T levels. However, even at T level only 31% of the non-punctuals are marked for past.

Punctuals, on the other hand, receive very high marking. There is a lower marking by the sec. 1–3 level when compared with the primary level for punctuals but then there are only three tokens in the sec. 1–3 group. An examination of the marking of punctuals in the primary group shows that of the seven tokens, six were uttered by informant P20 and of these there were four tokens where she was merely echoing the interviewer.

Verbs which have the element of [+completion] have been classified as punctual, e.g. I *did* economics (meaning I completed a course in economics). It is probable that most informants had this meaning in mind. Tokens of *do* involving completion of courses and projects are often marked for past, e.g.

T5.16. I *did*—I *did* double maths.
O17.3. I *did* my (nursing) training dere.

However, it could be that for some informants *do* does not mean completion of a course. Rather, it means studying something over a period of time. Hence the following tokens are not marked for past:

A12.2. (Talking about the Chinese textbooks she used.) No I di(d)n'(t) do 'Ah Q Zhèng Zhuàn'. I *do* 'Jiǎ', 'Qū Yuán'.

As *do* in pseudo-cleft clauses is emphatic, it is often marked for past:

T4.2. So what we *did* was—I mean we *do* de normal ting lah—pay the supplier and all dat (this period is the time when the firm first started).

TABLE 7.9. *Past tense marking of* do

	NP		P		S		Total	
	Score	%	Score	%	Score	%	Score	%
Tertiary	9/29	31.0	69/69	100.0	—	—	78/98	79.6
A level	9/34	26.5	50/51	98.0	—	—	59/85	69.4
O level	1/14	7.1	8/11	72.7	—	—	9/25	36.0
Sec. 1–3	0/21	0.0	1/3	33.3	—	—	1/24	4.2
Primary	0/16	0.0	5/7	71.4	—	—	5/23	21.7
TOTAL	19/114	16.7	133/141	94.3	—	—	152/255	59.6

Notice that after the pseudo-cleft clause, *do* in the next clause is unmarked because it is a non-punctual token. Other examples include:

T6.14. So what he did—dey tried one hundred and one tricks.
T17.6. All we did was—design design design.

For the tertiary-level informants such structures are all marked, irrespective of whether they are punctual or non-punctual tokens. Punctual tokens refer to a particular occasion, e.g.

T16.13. What I did dat night . . .

Table 7.10 shows the marking of *do* for past in such structures.
The following is an example from a more basilectal speaker:

S5.5. What I *do* it. I just promote my product, dat—um what I hand it and what I *do* it, I just try my best to promote it and den whatever tings by step by step.

S5 had apparently not mastered the rules for such structures as she used 'it' after *do*.

We may now consider further reasons for the non-marking of do for past.

1. First, in SgE when generalities are discussed, the pronouns *I* and *we* are used. In SBrE *you* (unstressed) or *one* is used. As SBrE is being considered as the norm, the following tokens are treated as not marked for past:

T6.6. What happens is after *I* graduate, I *do* one year of housemanship first. Den I do two months of MO postings. And den I *do* another two months of army training. Dat's when I'm a Officer Cadet—den after we pass out as officers, we become Captain straightaway.

It is true that members of a certain class or profession, such as the military, can use the pronoun *we* and the present tense when talking about normal routines and training but the use of *I* would necessitate the use of past tense when discussing past events. The following are examples from a medical practitioner who gave an account of his undergraduate days. He used the pronouns *me* and *we* and it was probably because he was talking about the

TABLE 7.10. *Past tense marking of* do *in pseudo-cleft clauses according to two semantic types*

	Punctual	Non-punctual
Tertiary	3/3	4/4
A Level	1/1	0/2
O Level	2/2	0/1
Sec. 1–3	—	0/2
Primary	—	—

curriculum and the usual things any medical student would have to study that *do* was unmarked for past:

T3.3. During de first two years in de university for *me*—we just—*do* theoretical subjects.

T3.3. We *do* anatomy, physiology, and biochemistry.

T3.3. Like say for de third year, de first term ah, Group A to Group F we *do* medical and den medical posting.

Statements can often be made in the present tense if one is discussing things in general. This may be a possible reason why *do* is not marked. However, the fact that such a state of affairs does not exist in Singapore any more requires *do* to be marked for past:

T3.2. But at dat time dose in de Chinese school ah, dose from de Chinese school—want to do medicine ah, I ting—dey have to go through a compulsory firs(t) year in de Singapore U, where dey *do* all de Pre-U subjec(t)s 'know . . .

Notice that in the following example there is a switch of pronouns. The informant is referring to what she and her brothers and sisters did during their childhood days. The switch to *you* may occur because the informant wants to involve the listener in her past experience. Since it is about the past, *do* prescriptively ought to be marked for past.

A19.14. and dere was not much encouragement nah—so everybody—it was really relax( ) ah—*We* just (if) you want to do something you just *do*—want to study, just study. Is very relax( ).

2. Another reason why the above *do* tokens are all unmarked is that they all have the [+continuative] element. This is very clearly illustrated in the following text. Notice that the copula is marked—giving us the setting in the past. The punctual verbs in *came back*, *went to do*, and *went back* are marked for past, but not *do*. The informant, now a financial controller, is obviously using *do* in a [+continuative] way:

T2.2. Before I do my Chartered, I was ah programmer, system analys(t). Den I wen(t) to do my Chartered—came back, *do* auditing ah, auditor. Den I went back to de computer line again, for a while.

The following tokens where *do* is not marked all have the [+continuative] or [+iterative] element:

T6.14. So what he did—dey tried one hundred and one tricks just to get admitted—you won't believe it—dey swallow glass, dey swallow thermometers, dey—dey *do* every mad ting in de world just to get admitted (one of them is dead now).

A15.7. I *do* all de front line banking (she is not in that job now).

A very interesting [+iterative] utterance is given below. As *do* is used non-punctually it is not marked for past:

A2.20. (Recalling the forms of punishment during his schooldays.) Dey *do* something wrong only got to pull your ear (i.e. as soon as you did something wrong, well you had to pull your own ears). *Do* something wrong only—hit your head (or the other punishment was—as soon as you did something wrong he'd hit you on the head).

Get

The past form of this verb, *got*, is often used as an existential verb, e.g.

Here *got* one shop selling Chinese New Year cards.

It is used as a possessive verb too:

My family altogether I *got* ten brother( ) and sister( ). Girls I'm de eldes(t). So I *got* three eldest brother.

It is also used as a passive marker:

Yesterday I *got* scolded by the teacher.
(*Got* here substitutes for the Malay *kena* 'to suffer'.)

Get as used in the above examples is almost categorically realised as *got*. Hence such tokens have been excluded from the corpus. Most tokens of *get* have the meaning *to obtain, to receive, to become*. There are also a few pre-positional and to-infinitive phrases such as *get rid of, get into (an institution), get to know/learn*, etc.

It is noticed that structures with the to-infinitive are not well marked at all. Only 25% of *get* in this environment is marked for past. An example of an unmarked token is given below:

O6.15. so I stay dere for—one night. Stay with dem (the Dayaks)—sleep in the long house. I ate dere, everyting. I swam in de river so—I *get* to know de peop(l)e dere.

TABLE 7.11. *Past tense marking of* get

	NP		P		S		Total	
	Score	%	Score	%	Score	%	Score	%
Tertiary	1/8	12.5	23/23	100.0	—	—	24/31	77.4
A level	3/10	30.0	36/41	87.8	—	—	39/51	76.5
O level	0/3	0.0	10/19	52.6	—	—	10/22	45.5
Sec. 1–3	0/12	0.0	3/13	23.0	—	—	3/25	12.0
Primary	1/7	14.3	3/9	33.3	—	—	4/16	25.0
TOTAL	5/40	12.5	75/105	71.4	—	—	80/145	55.2

Note that here the two very obvious vowel-change non-punctuals *sleep* and *get to know* are not marked. In the latter token, *know* is also stative and this may contribute to the non-marking of *get* in *get to know*.

The scores for past tense marking of *get* for past in *get* + *to-infinitive* expressions are as follows:

Tertiary $\frac{1}{2}$
A level $\frac{2}{7}$
O level $\frac{0}{1}$
Sec. 1–3 $\frac{0}{1}$
Primary   —

It may be that *get to know* is a standard expression with *get* frequently heard in its unmarked form for past, and hence *get* is not well marked.

Get meaning 'to become' is used only three times and these tokens are all unmarked, e.g.

T13.9. And slowly I *get* use(d) to de place.

An interesting variation of *get to know* is seen in the following text:

A19.12. So our friends who are in Science—so we we *got to know* de people in Science and de guys' friends—dey were all in Science—so you know— dat's how we *get to know* more of de people in Science.

The last statement is a general summing up and, probably because it is not part of the narration, *get* is not marked. The same general summing up is also seen in the next text. The informant is no longer working there. Yet another reason for the non-marking of *get* is that the whole episode was recounted in a casual, conversational style. The present tense was used throughout and the informant seemed to relive the whole experience, as it were, again:

S18.13. Because some of dose people dere, dey really sweet-talk her and all dat . . . So long as I do my work right? Is my duty already. I'm paid to do dat and I'm not paid to sweet-talk you and all dat ah—so (I) ting maybe she like people to praise her—dat kind of tings. Well I don't like to do dat—so maybe dat's de result lah. I *get* dat kind of treatment.

The non-punctual tokens receive very low marking. Often with these tokens of *get*, habitual temporal expressions are used, e.g.

T2.4. Everytime we *get* a holiday (in England) . . .

In general *get* meaning *obtain* receives rather low marking, whether it is used punctually or non-punctually by speakers with primary to O level education. Examples of unmarked punctual tokens are:

S9.22. Den we get (the flat) dis old price fifty-one t(h)ousand (dollars).
O10.12. You know how much I bargain or not? How much I *get* de pan(t)s (for) lah?

Get in certain idiomatic expressions and prepositional phrases is often unmarked, e.g.

S19.24. . . . until I *get into* VI (Vocational Institute).

O6.8. Once you *get rid* of all dis (equipment) (a hypothetical situation).

Strangely enough *get in* is well marked. Again, in *V and V* structures, the second verb is seldom marked for past:

O10.11. My friend go and get the three-room flats quite fast. (This is non-standard. He meant his friend applied for a flat and obtained one quite quickly.)

Give

This verb receives very low marking for past. At primary level all punctuals and non-punctuals are unmarked for past. There is also no marking for non-punctuals for sec. 1–3, O, and A levels, while at tertiary level there is only one non-punctual token and this is marked. There are only three tokens of statives, two at T level and one at O level (used by a personnel manager). All three stative tokens begin with an *it* and are unmarked, e.g.

T2.5. And my wife was working—as an usherette in a theatre . . . She go to work in de night and when I come back—it *gives* me time to study ah—so de arrangement was very neat ah.

The following points give an idea of why *give* is sometimes marked while at other times unmarked for past.

1. First it should be mentioned that the fricative in final position is frequently realized as a voiceless one so that the past form is often heard as [ɡeɪf] rather than [ɡeɪv]. The unmarked form for past is often realized as [ɡɪ] or [ɡɪf], while the expression *give us* has variants such as [ɡɪʌs], [ɡɪfʌs], and [ɡɪvʌs]. There is no contraction such as [ɡɪvəs] as in SBrE. *Give me* is often pronounced as [ɡɪmɪ] or [ɡɪfmɪ].

A very strong reason for not marking *give* for past is the coalescence of *give*

TABLE 7.12. *Past tense marking of* give

	NP		P		S		Total	
	Score	%	Score	%	Score	%	Score	%
Tertiary	1/1	100.0	15/25	60.0	0/2	0.0	16/28	57.1
A level	0/4	0.0	13/14	54.2	—	—	13/28	46.4
O level	0/12	0.0	3/12	25.0	0/1	0.0	3/25	12.0
Sec. 1–3	0/12	0.0	1/22	4.6	—	—	1/34	2.9
Primary	0/14	0.0	0/13	0.0	—	—	0/27	0.0
TOTAL	1/43	2.3	32/96	33.3	0/3	0	33/142	23.2

with *me*, possibly an influence from American films and TV shows. It occurs at all levels, e.g.

A7.12. And he *gimme* de title ah 'Public Nuisance number two' or someting like dat. Dere was a 'Public Nuisance number one!' So he *gimme* a second title lah—de number two lah.

Slightly over a fifth of the *give* tokens occur in the environment *give + me*, of which 71.9% are not marked for past. Table 7.14 shows the marking of *give* followed by *me*, according to different educational levels.

2. Another very strong reason why *give* is unmarked is that the diphthong [eɪ] is not very distinct in SgE, so many informants could have heard past forms of *give* with [ɪ].

3. In idiomatic expressions *give* is often unmarked, e.g.

T7.12. I mean de two of us (on a scholarship) really *gif* dem a go.
'We made them sit up! Singaporeans are not duffers!'

4. As with other verbs, the use of temporal habitual expressions co-occurs with the unmarked form of the verb.

5. Another reason for the non-marking of *give* is that sometimes the informant is making a general statement and at the same time referring to a particular period in the past. In the following example, the informant is saying 'It was the policy (and probably still is) of the company to train its employees' yet in using the pronoun *us* he is referring to the period when he received training. As he is no longer with that company, *give* would, prescriptively, be marked for past:

O5.2. So I applied for de apprenticeship lah—so dere dey *gif* us training y'see.

6. Some tokens may have an implied stative meaning and are unmarked. For example, *to give credit for t(h)irty days* may refer to a state where credit is allowed for thirty days:

O6.13. Every(thing) OK so we *gif* t(h)irty days credit. So we deliver de goods. Only two t(h)ousand dollar plus we deliver . . .

However it is sometimes difficult to explain the variation in marking, as in the text O6.10.

TABLE 7.13. *Past tense marking of* give *in the environment preceding* me

	Score	%
Tertiary	3/9	33.3
A level	3/10	30.0
O level	2/4	50.0
Sec. 1–3	1/7	14.3
Primary	0/2	0.0

O6.10. (Talking about a trickster trying to secure credit.) He told me, he say, 'Oh! I know your Peter (an employee working in the informant's company) ah I know him very well' and all dat y'know. Den he will show me, 'You see dis one, I just purchase from so and so—de invoices. She *gave* me thirty days. Dat company *gimme* thirty days'—to gain your confidence.

A possible explanation for the variable use of *give* is that the first token is an emphatic one whereas the second token is unmarked probably because it is meant to be iterative—i.e. one company after another allowed him credit. Also, as mentioned earlier, *gimme* is a common set phrase in colloquial SgE.

7. Sometimes certain verbs are unmarked because the informant makes a switch in tense. A general comment can trigger off a switch to the present:

T13.14. One interviewer ask me 'So you know what is a credit analyst job?' So I mean the name itself tells you what (particle expressing disapproval) analysing de credit worthiness of de company y'see. So I *gif* him a brief history.

Go

Go has the highest number of tokens which should, prescriptively, be marked for past. There were 1,029 tokens, of which 682 (66.3%) were marked for past. The degree of marking of punctual tokens (84.2%) is five and a half times that of the non-punctual ones (15.3%).

A few noticeable features are found in the speech of basilectal informants. First, a high proportion of the examples of the *V and V* structure is used by the basilectal informants. Thirty-one tokens were found in the primary group. This forms 19.4% of the tokens used by informants with primary level education. Twenty-two tokens were found in the non-punctual category. All these were unmarked for past. There were 16 tokens of this structure used by informants with sec. 1–3 education. With increasing levels of education, the use of this structure decreases. There were only 6 tokens at the A level and

TABLE 7.14. *Past tense marking of* go

	NP		P		S		Total	
	Score	%	Score	%	Score	%	Score	%
Tertiary	15/46	32.6	217/219	99.1	—	—	232/265	87.5
A level	7/47	14.9	189/206	91.7	—	—	196/253	77.5
O level	7/39	17.9	76/87	87.4	—	—	83/126	65.9
Sec. 1–3	10/58	17.2	113/167	67.7	—	—	123/225	54.7
Primary	2/78	2.6	46/82	56.1	—	—	48/160	30.0
TOTAL	41/268	15.3	641/761	84.2	—	—	682/1029	66.3

2 at tertiary level. Marking for past of *go* in such structures is very low indeed. Only 2 punctual tokens, one at A and one at sec. 1–3 level, were marked out of a total of 59 tokens, in other words only 3.4% of *go* was marked in this type of structure. For example,

P12.17. Den—he was in hospital we everyday *go and visit* him.

Secondly, it is found that in the two lower basilectal groups, there are unmarked tokens such as the following where two time periods, the past and the present, have been collapsed into one. Such structures reflect Chinese syntax.

P4.19. (Saying that he can't remember what Haw Par Villa, a tourist spot, looks like.) Because now very long not very sure already ah. Because the small time I *go* up to now ah.
'I *went* when I was a little boy and have not been there since.'

Thirdly, speakers even in these more basilectal groups, are inclined to use the past tense form when referring to events in the past with a terminal point, as in the following example when *went* is followed by *there*.

S5.8. J: Once, once I'm. I travel once.
    I: Where did you go?
    J: I go um, Taipei.
    I: Uh huh
    J: Yah, dat's all only lah, Taipei I wen(t).
    I: Did you like Taipei?
    J: The place there is quite um, a lot of people lah.
    I: Uh huh.
    J: An(d) then, when the time I *wen(t)* dere—is very cool lah. Very cool at all and (th)en some more the place that—the the people dere is quite friendly at all also lah. But they are lot of people den—dat time we *wen(t)* dere is very cool and (th)en some more—the place dere ah is very crowded at all also lah. Then—we jus(t) *wen(t)* dere for—I *wen(t)* dere not really very long what—jus(t) um—fi(ve) day only what.

Note, however, that the unmarked *go* is used when [+durative] is implied— the imformant was touring Taiwan, going from one place to another:

S5.23. .... we *go* by ourselves—after dat we *wen(t)* dere—we reach to Taipei ah—so just *go* ourse(lves) lah. We never join tour at all lah. We just *go* ourse(lves) (*never* meaning 'we did not join any tours').

Fourthly, it is found that the use of temporal markers by basilectal informants is high, particularly with habituals rather than non-habituals. An exemplification is given below:

P2.16. Like *last time* we go school.
'For instance, in the past when we went to school.'

In the primary group, 15 tokens (19.2%) of the non-punctual *go* had a temporal marker, and were all unmarked. The temporal markers used include *last time, everytime, sometime,* and *everyday*. One possible reason why the verbs are unmarked is that the use of these markers for the habitual may make the informants forget that they are talking about the past—hence the verbs are uninflected. In Chinese, verbs are not inflected for past. Temporal phrases such as *yǐqián* 'last time', *shàng cì* 'before', may be used when reference is made to the past. Habitual phrases such as *měi cì* 'everytime', *cháng cháng* 'usually, always', *yǒu shí* 'sometimes', convey the habitual aspect. Interestingly, *used to* is not used at all with past reference at the lower end of the continuum. It is, however, used frequently as a present habitual marker. Only one token of *used to* + *go* was used by a tertiary informant:

T12.8. I use(d) to go swimming regularly in de weekend (referring to the past).

Probably the most important reason for the non-marking of habituals for past is that the Chinese perfective marker *-le*, which shows that an event is past, is incompatible with habituals. A full discussion of this is provided in Section 7.4.

An environment where *go* is categorically unmarked is the hypothetical situation. It is also noticed that *if* is sometimes omitted at all educational levels.

P1.5. Last time (if) you go Bras Basah Road, you got a lot of dose cheap (books) ah, so just grab and read lah. (There used to be many bookshops on Bras Basah Road selling second-hand books. Note the missing pronouns in *grab and read*.)

P19.19. If you go home by bus—late a late litt(l)e bit lah, you have to wait because bus everytime queue up. (Talking about the past.)

Another environment where *go* is not marked for past is when semi-idiomatic expressions are used, e.g.

O8.11. My daughters are being brought up by my sister-in-law. As soon as dey are one month old, *dere dey go* . . . (the daughters are now teenagers).

When a verb phrase is a serial verb construction, as in the exemplification below, *go* is unmarked:

T2.5. And den we have a total of half year study leave—which is about—two, t(h)ree weeks . . . so we go—*go attend* lah course full time . . .

Naturally, the very fact that all the above examples are non-punctual tokens is a strong factor influencing the non-marking of *go* for past.

It is also noticed that non-punctual tokens are often marked for third person singular, particularly at the acrolectal level, e.g.

T2.5. She *goes* to work (in London, in the past).

T11.15. Like we have to kiss our dad goodbye when he *goes* off to work y'know (about childhood).

As mentioned before, punctual tokens receive a much higher marking for past than non-punctual tokens. Many of the punctual tokens are of the structure *go + preposition*, or are phrasal verbs. The use of prepositions and particles gives an element of [+completion]—a possible reason for the higher degree of marking for past. Other frequently marked punctual tokens include locative and purpose phrases. For instance, informant O6 had categorical marking for all 17 punctual tokens: *go + preposition* (6 tokens), *go + locative* (11 tokens), e.g.

O6.20. I went up to volcano dere.

He had categorical non-marking of *go* used non-punctually.

O6.12. When you *go* dere, dey will make coffee (about the past).
O6.18. But normally we *go* by taxi (when he was in Brunei).

Come

Come has the second highest number of tokens that would, prescriptively, be marked for past. There were 403 tokens, of which 224 tokens (55.6%) were marked. Of the punctual tokens, 75.4% were marked for past as against 9.4% of the non-punctual tokens. There were very few stative tokens, which appeared only at the sec. 1–3 level and above. Stative tokens were marked for past only by the tertiary informants.

It can be seen from Tables 7.15 and 7.16 that for both *go* and *come*, the punctual tokens receive a higher marking than the non-punctual tokens, right through the five educational levels. The degree of marking for *go*, both for the punctual and non-punctual categories, is always higher than for *come* at all educational levels except for the non-punctual category at primary level, where for both verbs, only two tokens were marked. One possible reason is

TABLE 7.15. *Past tense marking of* come

	NP		P		S		Total	
	Score	%	Score	%	Score	%	Score	%
Tertiary	2/19	10.5	69/72	95.8	2/3	66.7	73/94	77.7
A level	0/12	0.0	70/82	85.4	0/1	0.0	70/95	73.7
O level	3/36	8.3	29/41	70.7	0/1	0.0	32/78	41.0
Sec. 1–3	4/29	13.8	30/55	54.6	0/1	0.0	34/85	40.0
Primary	2/21	9.5	13/30	43.3	—	—	15/51	29.4
TOTAL	11/117	9.4	211/280	75.4	2/6	33.3	224/403	55.6

that *go* is probably a higher-frequency verb than *come* (even in this corpus the number of tokens for *go* is more than two and a half times that of *come*) and is probably often used punctually in its marked form, especially in locative expressions such as *I went home/to X*, etc.

With *come*, as with *go*, there are structures of the kind *V and V*. Again, it is found that there are more of this kind of structure at the bottom end of the continuum (nine at primary level) than at the upper end (two at tertiary level). Out of the fifteen tokens with this structure, only one token was marked for past.

If is often omitted in hypothetical clauses, particularly by basilectal informants, and in such clauses as well as in non-punctual clauses with the connectives *if* and *when*, *come* is freqently unmarked for past:

P14.26. When raining come ah . . .
P14.27. If the wind come ah . . .
P19.17. (If) (I) come back school . . .

What is most striking is that many informants have categorical marking for punctual tokens of *come* and categorical non-marking for non-punctual tokens of *come*. This happens particularly with acrolectal speakers who, in addition, mark the non-punctual tokens with third person singular. This trend is shown in Table 7.17.

For illustration, only examples from informant T6 will be given. Note the categorical past tense marking of T6's punctual tokens and the third person singular marking of his non-punctual token:

T6.8. So when we *came* at—when recruit training.
T6.14. So one day dis chap actually *came* to hospital complaining of . . .
T6.15. So when he *came* to hospital . . .
T6.15. Because he always *comes* in half-drunk anyway and always complaining
   (talking about a patient who was already dead at the time of the interview).

TABLE 7.16. *Categorical marking of punctual tokens and categorical non-marking of non-punctual tokens of* come *for past*

Informants	Punctual	Non-punctual	Total
T6	3/3	0/1[a]	3/4
T13	6/7	0/1[a]	6/8
T11	6/6	0/4[a]	6/10
T14	—	0/2[a]	0/2
T5	6/6	0/2[b]	6/8
T15	6/6	0/1	6/8

[a] All tokens were marked for third person singular.
[b] One token was marked for third person singular.

T13 did not mark a punctual token of *come*, probably because of the influence of the use of an unmarked stative token which appeared in close proximity to this token:

T13.14. During de interview he told me y'know, 'I like you when you first *come* in.'

It is likely that the same influence could have affected the non-marking of T12's punctual token of *come* below:

T12.11. And so I ting dey waited about ah two to t(h)ree weeks for me to come home. And it seems when once I *come* home I'm suppose to ring dem up, but again once (referring to the past) ...

Two informants, one each at A and O levels, marked their non-punctual tokens with third person singular. A number of informants had categorical marking of punctual tokens for past and categorical non-marking of non-punctual tokens.

However, the picture begins to change at sec. 1–3 level. Only one informant, S1, had a score of 3/3 for punctual tokens and 0/1 for non-punctual tokens. Many informants like S6 and S10 had categorical non-marking for both categories. There was one token marked for third person singular by S6 and a hypercorrect form was used by S3. These examples are given below:

S3.8. And den after dat when I *comes* to secona—secon(d)ary two, I was then ...

S6.14. I: Did your classmates come to see you?

J: Yah my classmate *comes* and see me.

Naturally, right at the lower end of the continuum, where the syntax used by the primary informants shows a strong influence from Chinese, there is no categorical marking of *come* for punctual tokens. Neither is there any use of the third person singular affixation.

Leave

There are certain intrinsically punctual verbs such as *leave* and *lose*, which, unless used in a habitual manner, e.g. *I always leave/left home at seven in the morning*, are naturally associated with a point in time. Except for only four non-punctual tokens in the whole corpus of 105 tokens of *leave*, the rest are all used punctually. The overall marking for this verb is 87.6%. It is noticed, too, all the four non-punctual tokens at three different levels are unmarked, e.g.

P19.11. (If) I can't do, leave out.

'If I couldn't do any of the maths problems, I just left them out.'

A18.11. (Talking about a colleague at her former place of work. He treated the casting machine as if it were his own.) He take it as i(f) his 'know— so—whenever he *leaves* his place he'll switch off de switch. (Note the third person singular marking.)

Most of the punctual tokens of *leave* involve departure from a location at a point in time in the past:

P10.1. Actually I left school for around twenty years already.

'It is 20 years since I left school.'

S18.6. I left for Hong Kong.

O14.1. When I left ah secretarial course ah . . .

Lose

Except for two tokens in the primary level which are used non-punctually, all the other tokens are used in a punctual way. The following are exemplifications of *lose* used non-punctually:

P6.20. (The informant used to play billiards with his friends before he went into the army.) If who *lose* ah, who pay de tab(l)e money ah. 'The person who lost would have to foot the bill for the game.'

P6.20. Starting I play, I *lose* ah. Then the so long I win ah.

'In the beginning I used to lose. After that I had been winning all the time—in fact for a long period.'

TABLE 7.17. *Past tense marking of* leave

	NP		P		S		Total	
	Score	%	Score	%	Score	%	Score	%
Tertiary	—	—	26/27	96.3	—	—	26/27	96.3
A level	0/2	0	18/19	94.7	—	—	18/21	85.7
O level	—	—	22/23	95.7	—	—	22/23	95.7
Sec. 1–3	0/1	0	16/21	76.2	—	—	16/22	72.7
Primary	0/1	0	10/11	90.9	—	—	10/12	83.3
TOTAL	0/4	0	92/101	91.1	—	—	92/105	87.6

TABLE 7.18. *Past tense marking of* lose

	NP		P		S		Total	
	Score	%	Score	%	Score	%	Score	%
Tertiary	—	—	2/2	100.0	—	—	2/2	100.0
A level	—	—	9/10	90.0	—	—	9/10	90.0
O level	—	—	1/1	100.0	—	—	1/1	100.0
Sec. 1–3	—	—	7/8	87.5	—	—	7/8	87.5
Primary	0/2	0.0	7/7	100.0	—	—	7/9	77.8
TOTAL	0/2	0.0	26/28	92.9	—	—	26/30	86.7

The following are examples of punctual tokens of *lose* marked for past:

P2.19. When you *los(t)* confidence.
P3.19. Dat time I *los(t)* my temper lah.

Apart from the fact that *lose* and *leave* are used punctually more often than non-punctually, another reason for the high marking of these verbs for past is that the past participle forms of these verbs are the same as the past forms. Hence one often hears these verbs being used adjectivally as well, as for example 'the *lost* and found section' in the newspaper and expressions such as *left-over food* and *there are only two eggs left*. This may reinforce the use of these forms. In SgE *left* is frequently heard in expressions where the existential *there is/are* is omitted. This clearly shows the influence of Chinese syntax where the object follows *shèng xia lai* (translated as *left* in SgE). An exemplification is given below:

A15.2. Den um—my dad pass away. Den only *left* my mum. So only *left* de girl—de t(h)ree younger one( ) lah, de younger brother—my eldes(t) sis, me.

Interestingly, *leave* and *lose* are verbs which are among those that are frequently marked for past in Guyanese Creole. Bickerton explains:

> The stem form of the verb is identical with the stem form of its English cognate (phonological representation apart, and where such cognates exist) apart from a handful of exceptions. Three of these exceptions have stem forms derived from English strong past forms: *lef* 'to leave', *los* 'to lose', *brok* 'to break'. One has a stem form derived from an English weak past: *marid* 'to marry'. (Bickerton 1975:28)

Meet

Meet is one of the verbs with a high percentage of marking for past tense: 80.3%. It is also a verb where the proportion of punctual tokens is very high—85.3%. As shown in Table 7.19, there are very few non-punctual tokens. The non-punctuals always receive a lower marking than the punctuals. Examples of punctual tokens marked for past are given in S18.11 and T6.15.

TABLE 7.19. *Past tense marking of* meet

	NP		P		S		Total	
	Score	%	Score	%	Score	%	Score	%
Tertiary	—	—	23/23	100.0	—	—	23/23	100.0
A level	0/4	0.0	3/6	50.0	—	—	3/10	30.0
O level	0/1	0.0	6/6	100.0	—	—	6/7	85.7
Sec. 1–3	2/3	66.7	15/17	88.2	—	—	17/20	85.0
Primary	0/1	0.0	—	—	—	—	0/1	0.0
TOTAL	2/9	22.2	47/52	90.4	—	—	49/61	80.3

S18.11. In Hong Kong I *met*—on de roadside, I *met* some of dem lah (i.e. bumped into some actresses).

T6.15. No, finally what happen( ) was he actually *met* an acciden(t)—he *met* a genuine acciden(t). Someone actually ran him down.

Some possible reasons for the non-marking of punctual tokens of *meet* are the following.

1. The word *meet* often appears in the stem form in religious language, e.g. 'The Lord will meet your needs', and this probably accounts for the following unmarked token:

S18.11. So I really prayed hard and the Lord really *meet* my prayers. And I have one copy (she received a free copy of the Bible).

2. One often comes across the expression:

'I'll come and meet you at the airport.'

This use of *meet* is less punctual than bumping into someone suddenly. This is a possible reason for *meet* not being marked below:

S18.13. Relatives yah. Not in fact not said very close lah. Dey *meet* us. Dey bring us roun(d). (Note the common negative SgE expression *not said* in 'not said very close lah' meaning 'I wouldn't say we are close relatives').

3. The present form is often used in vivid narratives where informants seem to relive their experiences in the past.

A17.16. Dat's why! We din expec(t). Because dat is not a station—next stop at Kanchanaburi actually but dis peop(l)e for visitors want to look—jus(t) mus(t) alight very quickly. An(d) we din know dis de firs(t) time. And he din know either. Aiyah! like adventure—we *meet* and den left me in de train! And den for one momen(t) I din fear. (In SBrE the pronoun *you* would have been used: 'Fancy that! You meet and go together as a group and suddenly you find that they've left you behind . . .'.)

We may now consider some non-punctual tokens. The following are not marked because they are used non-punctually and often temporal adverbials such as *seldom* are used. Sometimes informants can be carried away when talking about general things in the past and hence they tend to use the unmarked form of *meet*:

S7.18. (Commenting on rude motorists during the time when the old parking system was in operation.) If you willing to pay the forty cen( ) he grumble ah. Some peop(l)e very rude 'know. Some we *meet* ah 'know some dirty rascal outside, very naughty, scold you bad word even 'know.

A12.8. Since after I have left Ministry of Labour I went to Postal, Post Office . . . as postal clerk. So—I *meet*—I *meet* clients, I mean customers— over the counter.

A14.3. (Relating her experiences in England.) Normally goes on our way—den we *meet* dis people—talk to dem lah.

Sometimes, as very often happens in SgE, a non-punctual token is marked because of specific occasions in the past when something happened, e.g.

S15.15. (Commenting on some rude salesgirls and salesmen when asked if he had come across any rude ones.) . . . salesman and salesgirl—sometimes only. Sometime we *met*—some are rude but some are very good. (Notice here the informant wavers between two tenses—trying to recall the times when he actually met rude ones and trying to give a general comment—i.e. 'there are times when we meet rude sales assistants.')

Sell

Sell is a rather low-frequency verb in the corpus and therefore the figures for past tense marking cannot be considered as statistically significant. However, it has been included because the distinction between the degree of marking of punctual and non-punctual tokens is still evident. Only three tokens are marked. The following token is from an informant with primary-level education, who lived and worked in the house of a European pastor for a number of years:

P12.4b. So dey—dey *sold* it to X Company.

This is a definite transaction and may be a reason why it is marked. One of the other two tokens which is marked is a very emphatic token:

O15.10. I *sold* one big piece of carpe(t).

In the following text, there are three tokens of *sell*, of which only two are counted:

S9.20. Last time we bought de old house ah, twenty-fi(ve) t(h)ousand (dollars) (informant is referring to her HDB flat; In SgE there is often no distiction between the use of 'houses' and 'flats'). Then we *sold* it forty-one

TABLE 7.20. *Past tense marking of* sell

	NP		P		S		Total	
	Score	%	Score	%	Score	%	Score	%
Tertiary	0/1	0.0	0/1	0.0	—	—	0/2	0.0
A level	0/1	0.0	—	—	—	—	0/1	0.0
O level	0/1	0.0	1/1	100.0	—	—	1/2	50.0
Sec. 1–3	0/4	0.0	1/5	20.0	—	—	1/9	11.1
Primary	0/9	0.0	1/1	100.0	—	—	1/10	10.0
TOTAL	0/16	0.0	3/8	37.5	—	—	3/24	12.5

t(h)ousand fi(ve) hundred (dollars). We renovate it also. So after selling dat one a few mon(th)s ah, waah! dey recently dose people ah, dey say we all *sell* already den dey start to sell also (i.e. 'They said we had sold ours—so there was a spate of selling—one after another'). About sixty over t(h)ousand, seventy over t(h)ousand y'know. Dat's why we lost a lot 'know. We renovate it also, we *sell* forty-one t(h)ousand.

Observe the variable use of *sell* here. The first token of *sell* is marked because it is a definite transaction. The selling of HDB flats one after another by her neighbours shows an iterative use of *sell*. This iterative use is not counted because of the use of the aspect marker 'already' which means that prescriptively a pluperfect should have been used there. The third unmarked token of *sell* could have been influenced by the stem form of *sell* in *we all sell already* and *we start to sell*.

There are other reasons why punctual tokens may not be marked. In the following text both *sell* and the particle *lah* are said with much emphasis. The use of the particle *lah* and the omission of the objective pronoun *it* is typical of colloquial SgE, where verbs are less frequently marked for past:

T4.10. So she (the house-agent) talk to dem and true enough, dey say 'OK'. So dey *sell* lah. And de price two fifty ($250,000). Asking for two fifty y'know, which was y'know . . . reasonable.

All non-punctual tokens were unmarked. Most of them were either [+habitual] or [+durative] tokens:

P10.3. So I *sell* for two, t(h)ree hours.

P14.27. Dat time my brother-in-law *sell* in de night market.

All tokens of *sell* in *V and V* structures were not marked for past:

S20.12. She like dat go and *sell* (she used to sell guava in two baskets attached to a bamboo pole which she carried over her shoulder).

The very fact that informant T19 believes that a stall is still at a certain place could have influenced the non-marking of *sell*:

T19.8. We liked one—one porridge stall very much—y'know—dey *sell* chicken and meat porridge in de morning. Dat was very very delicious and I don't ting you could find such—dis type of ah quality ah in Singapore at dat price (talking about a stall in Hong Kong).

Speak

Most of the punctual tokens which were marked for past fall into two categories. The past form of *speak* is often used with reference to a particular single occasion:

T13.8. So I *spoke* to my dad.

A16.14. He sort of *spoke* to me.

S1.25. I *spoke* to my manageress.

TABLE 7.21. *Past tense marking of* speak

	NP		P		S		Total	
	Score	%	Score	%	Score	%	Score	%
Tertiary	4/4	100.0	5/5	100.0	—	—	9/9	100.0
A level	1/3	33.3	5/7	71.4	—	—	6/10	60.0
O level	—	—	1/1	100.0	—	—	1/1	100.0
Sec. 1–3	0/1	0.0	1/1	100.0	0/1	0.0	1/3	33.3
Primary	—	—	1/1	100.0	0/1	0.0	1/2	50.0
TOTAL	5/8	62.5	13/15	86.7	0/2	0.0	18/25	72.0

Secondly, the past form of *speak* forms part of religious terminology, often heard in sermons:

A16.4. He (God) *spoke*. He *spoke* through a speaker. 'God gave me a message through a sermon I heard.'

A basilectal informant used the past form of *speak* too, again in a religious context:

P12.18. I was afraid to fear away from God 'know to be backslided also. I was tingking myse(lf) I was tingking myself and someting dat *spoke* to me 'know dat.

The informant had been living with the family of her pastor. Such uses of *speak* as in 'God *spoke*' to Abraham, Isaac, and other Old and New Testament characters must be familiar to the informant, who related the loss of her first child and how God spoke/gave her a message or comforted her when she read a verse in the Bible.

Examples of non-punctual tokens include iterative tokens such as the following:

S12.6. (When she was in school she had an illness.) sometime I—I *speak* y'know—I find myself is—in a difficulty in speaking.

Higher up the continuum, more acrolectal speakers, such as A2, begin to mark habitual tokens with the third person singular:

A2.19. And my dad is basically English-educated and he *speaks* more English dan Hokkien ah (his father is dead).

Speak, as a stative verb, was used by two informants with primary and sec. 1–3 education. In the following text, informant P3 talked about his former employer whom he referred to as 'a Hong Kong boy':

P3.1. He *speak* English very well lah but sometime, sometime I can't understand what . . .

The following token of *speak* by S20 is also unmarked for past:

S20.16. 'cause I *tot* (since) she speak Engrish ah, her Engrish is no ploblem. 'At that time I felt that she should not have any problem with English since she spoke English.'

As P3's former employer and S20's daughter spoke English at the time of the interview, it might have been difficult for the informants to orient themselves to a past time. This is a possible reason for the non-marking of *speak* for past.

Take

In English *take* is a verb often used statively in general statements such as:

It takes three days to get from Perth to Melbourne by train.

Take is often used in its stem or present tense forms, e.g. adjectivally as in *takeaway food*, as a noun in *to buy something from the takeaway*, and in expressions such as *she takes after her father, to take photographs, to take in boarders*, and *to take makan* (in SgE meaning 'to eat'). As a result it is not surprising that in a narrative about the past, most Singaporeans tend to use the stem form of *take*, especially when it is used statively or non-punctually. In the following written narrative by a Singaporean student, *take*, a stative token was unmarked for past.

We *drove* to X to see my relatives. My baby sister *went* too. She *takes* the long drive well. A girlfriend of ours from Singapore *met* us in X and she *came* back to Y with us for a few days.

In the corpus, only one stative token, by a tertiary level informant, was marked for past:

T12.13. It took altogether about two mon(th)s (to complete the project).

The other stative tokens used by P1, O1, O18, and A13 were all unmarked for past but were marked for third person singular instead.

TABLE 7.22. *Past tense marking of* take

	NP		P		S		Total	
	Score	%	Score	%	Score	%	Score	%
Tertiary	1/7	14.3	35/36	97.2	1/2	50.0	37/45	82.2
A level	0/9	0.0	42/56	75.0	0/2	0.0	42/67	62.7
O level	0/14	0.0	24/31	77.4	0/1	0.0	24/46	52.2
Sec. 1–3	5/22	22.7	15/32	46.9	—	—	20/54	37.0
Primary	1/25	4.0	1/16	6.3	0/1	0.0	2/42	4.8
TOTAL	7/77	9.1	117/171	68.4	1/6	16.7	125/254	49.2

P1.27. (It) takes two t(h)ree days' job some more 'know. (What's more it took two or three days to complete the job.)

O18.5. And jus(t) preparing jus(t) t(h)ree subjecs—'cause—already *takes* up a lot of time.

A13.6. It (playing the piano) *takes* up a lot of my time.

Looking at individual variation, one notices that the punctual tokens receive a higher marking than non-punctual tokens. For example, A18 marked all her punctual tokens of *take* but did not mark her non-punctual tokens:

A18.7. Mrs X *took over* (the teaching of geography).

A18.11. He *take* it as if his 'know—so—whenever he leaves his place, he'll switch off de switch (of the casting machine).

What is interesting about the non-punctual tokens at the basilectal level is the frequent use of temporal markers such as *sometimes, everytime, seldom*, e.g.

P6.8. We all *everytime take* seventy.

'We used to get $70 as salary.'

S6.31. I *seldom take* part (in sports, referring to schooldays).

This is a possible reason why *take* is unmarked. In using these markers to denote the habitual, it is possible that the informant often forgets that he is talking about the past. In fact, in some instances the verb *take* even receives third person singular marking instead:

P16.2. Sometimes teacher *takes* us (out).

T7.5. Because she *takes* certain tes(t) you see.

The following token shows non-standard marking where 's' is attached to *care* instead of *take*.

P8.29. She *take cares* of us so big. (The informant was talking about his deceased grandmother.)

It is noticed that semi-idiomatic set expressions such as *take care of, take turns* are rarely marked for past, e.g.

T6.7. No I don't *take care of* dem. I only *take care of* dem for emergencies. What I *take care of* is army, army population there. (The informant, a medical doctor is not stationed there any more.)

T9.7. Ah professionals *take it as a snub* in the face lah.

It is noticed that *take* is frequently marked for past when the element [+completion] is present, e.g.

T1.8. I *took* about a year to finish it.

The same informant, however, did not mark the following token of *take* for past:

T1.6. Yah *take turns* to cook lah.

The Acquisition of Past Tense

The following tokens used by informant A17 show variable marking of *take* for past.

A17.9. . . . but from Bangkok itself is not worth driving up y'see . . . so we *take* a—we din take a train—we *took* a coach up.

The same tendency of not marking *take* for past in set phrases is also seen in the following token used by informant O6:

O6.10. my account manager *take* a look . . .

However, the punctual token below is marked for past:

O6.19. In de hotel he *took* de money, quickly ran off.

Naturally, in very colloquial speech, such as when *take* means 'to seize (an opportunity)' in SgE, and the subject and object pronouns are omitted, *take* is unmarked for past:

A10.8. And well from de fun of it I applied and I got in ah—So *take* lah! Try to learn what I can. (The informant was successful in getting into the Singapore Polytechnic.)

In the environment *V and V*, *take* is not marked for past either:

S17.16. Go and *take* courses (talking about the past).
A15.1. Just go and *take* pictures (about a past wedding).

Tell

What is interesting about the verb *tell* is that it receives extremely high past tense marking at the primary level, in fact almost as high as the marking at A level. We see that marking at sec. 1–3 is only 52.3% but the marking increases as one moves up the educational ladder with *tell* receiving 72.4% marking at O level, 83% at A level, and 91.3% at tertiary level.

A comparison of punctual and non-punctual tokens shows that overall, verbs used punctually are always better marked than those used non-

TABLE 7.23. *Past tense marking of* tell

	NP		P		S		Total	
	Score	%	Score	%	Score	%	Score	%
Tertiary	—	—	42/46	91.3	—	—	42/46	91.3
A level	1/6	16.7	43/47	91.5	—	—	44/53	83.0
O level	0/5	0.0	21/24	87.5	—	—	21/29	72.4
Sec. 1–3	3/6	50.0	31/59	52.5	—	—	34/65	52.3
Primary	4/8	50.0	28/31	90.3	—	—	32/39	82.1
TOTAL	8/25	32.0	165/207	79.7	—	—	173/232	74.6

punctually. Other factors in various contexts which appear to influence the marking or non-marking of *tell* for past are given below.

1. *Tell* is often unmarked for past when used in the context of giving someone instructions or advice. The following is an example from an A level informant:

A19.9. (Talking about how courteous the bus conductors were while she and her friends were on a tour of the States.) And dey were very courteous— dey says 'Good morning' y'know 'Where you going?' Dey really taught us so forth y'know—tell us where to go and so forth.

One often asks directions with the set phrase '*Tell* me how to get there' and this may be a possible reason why *tell* is not marked for past.

2. *Tell* is often used in certain specific contexts, e.g. *to tell a lie, to tell a story*, etc. These contexts may certainly account for the following two tokens which are unmarked:

S20.4. I *tell* (a) lie lah.
T13.4. An(d) den he (she—the landlady) *tell* me a story 'know, she is actually a mistress of de guy lah y'know and de guy jus(t) pass away two weeks ago.

Another reason for the non-marking of the token in T13.4 is that it is part of a section where the informant suddenly switched from the past to the present, triggered off, as it were, by a verb like *start* (an inchoative which does not receive very high marking for past especially when it occurs with an -*ing*) and a general statement:

> When he left ah, my tears *start* dropping. And suddenly you realize dat you are alone y'see . . . I just cannot get use(d) to it you see. An(d) den he tell me a story . . .

3. When talking about generalities the pronoun *one* or *you* is used in SBrE. If *we* or *I* is used, then a particular situation is referred to and this necessitates the use of the past form for any verbs used. In the following token, the informant is combining a general statement as well as trying to recall her experience with the police, reliving the whole episode, as it were, and hence using the present form of *tell*.

A14.4. All gone! (Passports, money, and all their belongings. Thieves had broken into their motel room while she and her mother were fast asleep.) Dat's why dat's de worst experience we had. And den dis Americans—not helpful at all—we tell dem (they told the police)—dey just take it as another case—dat kind of ting.

4. Yet another reason for the non-marking of *tell* for past is that in SgE *tell* often replaces *ask* at the upper end of the continuum. Lower down the social scale *call* is used instead. *Tell* is heard so often in its unmarked imperative

form in such situations that it may be one of the reasons why the informants did not mark *tell* for past.

5. At the lower end of the continuum the use of temporal adjuncts such as *usually*, *sometimes*, *all the time*, is very noticeable for non-punctuals and this too has influenced the non-marking of *tell*. At school, it is emphasized that the simple present tense should be used with adverbial adjuncts expressing habitual activities such as *usually*, *generally*, *sometimes*. This could be a reason for the use of non-past forms of verbs when informants recount past habitual events. Or it could be a linguistic universal as claimed by Bickerton (1981). The following are examples of non-punctuals with habitual expressions, where *tell* is unmarked for past:

P20.15. Now she OK (i.e. her daughter has changed a lot). She say, 'OK mummy everything your wish.' Last time no. Sometime, I *tell* her say 'Bring water OK?' She se' she want Ribena.

6. It is noticed that where direct speech is used, *tell*, as the verb introducing direct speech, is often unmarked. The following are some exemplifications:

O15.10. She *tell* me, 'The light, I don(t) wan(t) already!'
S20.7. So one day I bring ou(t) her work. I—just *tell* her—she douno how to read. I say, 'Douno how to read, you ask.' (*Tell* may be unmarked because it is in the context of advising her daughter.)
S13.7. . . . de customer keep on complain 'Where are de carrier boy?' Might as well I do it. Den I *tell* de cashier 'You hold (on)'.

7. Among those with primary-level education there are structures of the *V and V* kind involving *tell*, which are categorically unmarked:

P16.21. (Talking about the boys in her class who were mischievous.) But sometime we *go and tell* teacher lah. Den teacher will tell us (them—the boys) not to be so rude to us ah.

8. What is most interesting about the use of *tell* in the primary level group is that when it is marked for past, it has a [+anterior] meaning. Prescriptively, in SBrE the pluperfect should be used. The contrastive use of the marked and unmarked forms of *tell* is illustrated in the following examples. The non-past form is used to describe past events occurring in an ordered sequence. The past form is used for [+anterior] events.

P14.15. At firs(t) he don't like lah. So I *tell* dem (him—her father) de idea lah . . .
'Initially my father did not like the idea at all. I then told him why I had arranged for him to be put in an old folks' home.'
P17.5. Mrs X *told* me you are Hokkien.
(Prior to the interview, the informant had been given this piece of information.)

One notices that past tense marking for *tell* by informants with primary level education is very high. One reason is that *tell* may be so well learnt by the primary informants that, as in the speech of informant P19, it is marked all the time, except for one token when she echoed the interviewer:

P19.12. I: What did the teacher *tell* you to do?

  J: Dey *tell* me to read story book a lots—den you can improofs— improof your English. Dat's all only.

Thus it can perhaps be argued that for informant P19, the stem form of *tell* is *told*.

Another point which should be mentioned regarding *tell* is that when it is used to refer to habitual events, either the unmarked form is used or else *will* + *tell* is used. In SBrE *would* or *-'d* + *tell* is used. Sometimes the simple past can be used as well. The expression *used to* often occurs in the speech of speakers of native varieties of English, too. The following are some examples of *tell* used in a habitual way:

O12.4. He (the shorthand teacher) always *tell* us to write out (recalling the time when she did a secretarial course).

O18.2. So—tsch—well—people like dis people ah, mostly if dey ask prices ah, sometimes we got so frustrated y'know. We just *tell* dem below cost. So when dey come back ah, we won't sell dat price ah (recalling the time when she worked in a goldsmith's shop).

Write

It is noticeable that all the non-punctual tokens are unmarked from primary to A level. Most of the non-punctuals involve reference to habitual events, e.g.

A19.14. usually when we *write* an essay y'know we *write* ah every week once—den he will tell us de mistakes.

T9.9 and T13.7 contain iterative tokens used by tertiary informants.

TABLE 7.24. *Past tense marking of* write

	NP		P		S		Total	
	Score	%	Score	%	Score	%	Score	%
Tertiary	1/3	33.3	15/16	93.8	—	—	16/19	84.2
A level	0/3	0.0	3/5	60.0	—	—	3/8	37.5
O level	0/4	0.0	3/3	100.0	—	—	3/7	42.9
Sec. 1–3	0/1	0.0	—	—	—	—	0/1	0.0
Primary	0/2	0.0	1/2	50.0	—	—	1/4	25.0
TOTAL	1/13	7.7	22/26	84.6	—	—	23/39	59.0

T9.9. I *wrote* to him a few times.

T13.7. So on Sunday—I jus(t) stayed in my room lah—an(d) *write* letters—doing not(h)ing but *write* letters, waiting for Monday to come y'see.

A possible reason why the first token is marked while the second is not is that the first token is more definite whereas the second is vague and also has the element of [+durative] because the passage of time is evident from the context.

Most of the punctual tokens are about writing to someone on a single occasion, writing a message and writing a program (in the telic sense of completing writing up a program). They receive very high marking for past. Examples are as follows:

O14.25. He *wrote* me once ah.

T20.10. She *wrote* back to say . . .

The following are some interesting variable uses of *write*. At the primary level, informant P7 wavered between the use of the marked and the unmarked form:

P7.1. Den my sister [raɪt] (read) a newspaper, [i:] see go(t) boys' school lah, SAF Boys' School. Den my sister *wrote* (wrote a letter, or wrote on my behalf) for me ah, *write* for me. Den—de [gɑ:mən] (government) service letter came ah. Den I go for interview.

A possible reason for the unmarked form is that there is really no clear demarcation as to whether *write a letter for me* is punctual or non-punctual. Because of the telic nature of the situation, the token has been classified as punctual. However, *write* does have a [+durative] element, unlike very punctual verbs such as *bump* or *meet* (on a single occasion).

At tertiary level there is also a variable use of *write* by informant T7:

T7.5. I still recall one of de topic was de underground y'see, right? As you know in de British context—de underground means the tube system and she *wrote* a fanciful essays on ah on I ting de undertakers y'see, that surprise me . . . you know *underground* means y'know going under ground but does not mean death or what er associated with undertakers. So she *write* a essay on de undertakers.

At the A level, an informant marked one token in:

A9.7. I *wrote* something for him and his wife y'see.

but did not mark *write* for past in:

A9.7. No I din *write* (down the name of this company) I just *write* 'Check with another company'.

The unmarked token could have been influenced by the negative token *din write*. Moreover, while the first token has the element of [+completion]—he completed writing something—the second token is more stative in the sense that he is saying 'I just have this message on the card'.

Among the other punctual tokens used by A level informants, it is found that the expression *write in* is not well marked, which is strange because it is punctual. The following are illustrations:

A18.1. I just *write in*—in fact dere was no advertisement at all.

A16.5. I din want to write in 'know—I leave aside—until de second last day before it closes—application closes—I just *write in* ah and within two, t(h)ree weeks I got de interview.

The last text is reminiscent of what one often reads in advertisement columns: *Application closes on . . . Please write in for more details.* This certainly could have influenced the non-marking of *write* for past. Another factor, of course, could be the influence of the 'to-infinitive' in the expression *din want to write.*

7.5.2.2 Class II Verbs: keep, sleep, and teach

Keep

Keep, being an inherently non-punctual verb, receives very low marking for past. At the sec. 1–3 level, there were two tokens that were marked:

S2.19. I: You kept some chickens there or what?

J: Formerly we *kept* chickens (the informant echoed the interviewer).

S11.31. Then he pull him up ah, all dose bubbles ah, *ke(pt)* flowing ah—I really dunno what to do. I just faint.

At the A level there were three tokens that were marked for past, two tokens with the structure *keep + Adj.*, and one with *what + keep . . . + V-ing* as illustrated below:

A2.10. What *kept* me going dere was . . .

TABLE 7.25. *Past tense marking of* keep

	NP		P		S		Total	
	Score	%	Score	%	Score	%	Score	%
Tertiary	6/11	54.5	—	—	—	—	6/11	54.5
A level	3/11	27.3	—	—	—	—	3/11	27.3
O level	0/13	0.0	—	—	—	—	0/13	0.0
Sec. 1–3	2/15	13.3	—	—	—	—	2/15	13.3
Primary	0/1	0.0	—	—	—	—	0/1	0.0
TOTAL	11/51	21.6	—	—	—	—	11/51	21.6

A7.12. Quite angry with him lah. (I) jus(t) *kep(t)* quiet and he laugh a bit lah.
A19.17. Yah when I *kept* quiet and so forth you see. Yah he still persist to de very end y'know.

At the tertiary level, there were six tokens which were marked for past. The following [+iterative, +durative] token was marked for past:

T11.13. She *kept* telling me.

The others were all [+continuative] tokens:

T4.9. I *kept* a dog.
T18.4. called a friend of mine . . . 'know *kept* me who *kept* me company.
T19.4. and he *kept* in touch.
T20.5. She wanted a transfer . . . de principal *kept* her back.

Notice that *kept back* in T20.5 also has a rather punctual element in that it means the principal stopped her from leaving. At the same time it also has the element of [+ continuative] in that she was retained in the school.

A very noticeable feature about the tokens that are not marked is that a large proportion of these are of the structure *keep + V-ing*. In fact at the tertiary level all the unmarked tokens are of this structure:

T12.10. So I was unwilling lah. But y'know—again de ting *keep* coming into my head.
T15.7. I throw up. I feel very nauseated. I *keep* on retching. So my father send me dere.
T16.6. My colleagues dere were very surprise why I left . . . I find myself very unsettled y'know—at the end of three and a half years . . . And I *keep* on looking for more challenges—someting dat is new you see.

The *keep + V-ing* structure received, on the whole, very low marking for past. Only 10% (2/20) of this structure was marked for past. Likewise, it was found that the verb *start* in a parallel structure *start + V-ing*, was frequently unmarked for past. A breakdown of the scores for past tense marking of *keep* in *keep + V-ing* structures is given below:

Tertiary	1/6
A level	0/4
O level	0/7
Sec. 1–3	1/3
Primary	—

Two tokens of *keep* in the structure *keep + serial verb* which should, prescriptively, be *keep + V-ing* were also not marked for past:

S13.7. The customer *keep* on *complain( )* 'Where are the carrier boy?'
O18.3. But she *keeps* 'know *say( )* ah 'two plus two plus' y'know—is already below our cos(t) y'see.

The tokens other than the *keep* + *V-ing* structure received a marking for past tense of 31% (9/29).

As commented on before with regard to the marking for past of other verbs, the contracted modal *'d* is often used to mark the habitual in SBrE. However, in SgE either the full uncontracted modal *would* is used or else only the simple present is used as illustrated below:

A10.3. Den de whole class *would* say 'Yah Yah Yah!' (We) follow him. So you always [kɪʔ] (keep) disturbing him in dat way.

The use of the pronoun *you* above is unusual. One would have expected *we* to be used as it conveys a sense of personal involvement.

Sleep

This is an inherently non-punctual verb and, as can be seen from Table 7.28, it received very low marking for past. Most of the tokens refer to habitual *sleeping* in the past.

P8.28. She die in de end . . . until de final few year( ) den, he really cannot help herself. Everyday have to . . . sit down dere only. And *sleep* everyday like dis (describing his deceased grandmother).

O16.28. (Talking about the Lunar New Year when she was a child before firecrackers were banned.) Because last time you know, you can—at night when you *sleep* dat time ah you can hear a lot of dose fire crackers sound y'know.

Many of the tokens that were marked for past occurred in the environment *just* + verb.

A17.11. So er we had seats lah. So he—he knew we coun sleep so he gave up his seats. Den de other boy who came with us—so gave up so we *sleep* lah. Like dat—dat means we *jus(t) slep(t)* in seat in case . . .

O18.19. . . . So we *just slep(t)*—slep(t) for—de next morning.

TABLE 7.26. *Past tense marking of* sleep

	NP		P		S		Total	
	Score	%	Score	%	Score	%	Score	%
Tertiary	—	—	—	—	—	—	—	—
A level	4/9	44.4	—	—	—	—	4/9	44.4
O level	3/10	30.0	—	—	—	—	3/10	30.0
Sec. 1–3	0/2	0.0	—	—	—	—	0/2	0.0
Primary	0/4	0.0	—	—	—	—	0/4	0.0
TOTAL	7/25	28.0	—	—	—	—	7/25	28.0

Teach

Most of the tokens of *teach* fall into the non-punctual category. It is noticeable that marking of this verb for past by informants with primary to O level education is low. Most of the tokens are habitual ones. In the examples given below, the informants talk about their teachers:

P8.5. [i:] (he) *teach* about me jus(t) a few mon(th). 'He taught me for a few months.'

O13.1. Because we have de nuns teaching us ah, so dey *teach* us etiquette and . . .

When *teach* is used in a durative manner, there is repetition of the verb, which is not marked for past:

O16.18. Den—one geography teacher you know [i:] (she) *teach* us geog(r)aphy you know, *teach teach teach*, and den she as(k) write on de blackboard.

There were two instances where *teach* was marked for third person singular although reference was to the past:

A19.13. She *teaches* physical science you see.
S12.11. He *teaches* me.

There were two environments where non-punctual tokens were marked for past. Firstly there were a few instances where the informants were merely echoing the interviewer, who asked a question using the past form of *teach*. Secondly, when an informant used a more formal style, as seen in S2.9, where the relativiser *which* was introduced, *teach* was marked for past:

S2.9. Secondary school—I ting is my form teacher lah, which he *taught* us in English and mathematics.

In contrast, habitual tokens of *teach* were unmarked. In the following text, S3 used a very colloquial style:

S3.4a. . . . just *teach* her (him) what sty(l)e to play—or what adult style I *teach* him—we(ll) he straight away—he can show me already . . .

TABLE 7.27. *Past tense marking of* teach

	NP		P		S		Total	
	Score	%	Score	%	Score	%	Score	%
Tertiary	6/7	85.7	—	—	—	—	6/7	85.7
A level	6/12	50.0	2/3	66.7	—	—	8/15	53.3
O level	1/13	7.7	—	—	—	—	1/13	7.7
Sec. 1–3	4/14	28.6	1/1	100.0	—	—	5/15	33.3
Primary	0/12	0.0	2/3	66.7	—	—	2/15	13.3
TOTAL	17/58	29.3	5/7	71.4	—	—	22/65	33.9

The same informant marked the following token of *teach* for past:

S3.4b. I *taught* him ah when he was in kindergarten—y'see—so now he's in Primary Two.

Note that *teach* in S3.4b has the element [+anterior]. The juxtaposition of two time periods, the past and present (signalled by *now*), may be a possible factor which aids the marking of *teach* for past.

The following is an unmarked token by a primary informant:

P19.17. She (my mother) *teach* me one time—'Like come back you see got prawns, you peel the prawns' skin.' (Here *teach* is considered punctual because of the single occasion 'One time'.)

Teach is basically an inherently [+durative] verb and in spite of the use of *one time* in P19.7 the informant did not mark the verb for past. In fact when a verb is inherently a [+ durative] one, the distinction between whether it is punctual or non-punctual is very blurred. We can see this in the following two sentences. The first one is considered telic and therefore punctual; the second, because of the use of the preposition *towards*, is considered 'un-bounded' and therefore non-punctual:

He *drove* home.

He *drove* towards the city.

Nevertheless, vague as the distinction is, it is interesting to note that on the few occasions when the verb *teach* is used punctually by the informants in the other levels, it receives a higher marking than when it is used in a non-punctual way.

Interestingly, it is noticed that at the basilectal end of the continuum, the verbs *think* and *teach* in their past forms are both phonetically realised as [tʊt]. Yet the verb *think* received a higher past tense marking than *teach*. The duration element of the verb is an important factor in deciding whether a verb is marked for past or not. Most tokens of *think* are used statively and, as will be discussed later, [+momentary] tokens such as *thought of* receive a higher marking for past.

7.5.2.3 *Class III verbs:* feel, know, hear, think, find, *and* see
Feel and know

As mentioned before, all tokens of *feel* and *know* are used statively, and receive lower marking for past than the rest of the Class III essentially stative verbs. However, *feel* has a higher marking for past than *know*—43.8% for the former as against 25.4% for the latter. This trend is consistent right through the five educational levels: *know* always has a lower degree of marking than *feel*. One possible reason is that the Chinese postverb *dào* 'arrive' can be used with the verb *gǎnjué* 'feel' to indicate that an action has been realized and hence is a past action.

TABLE 7.28. *Past tense marking of* feel

	NP		P		S		Total	
	Score	%	Score	%	Score	%	Score	%
Tertiary	—	—	—	—	35/41	85.4	35/41	85.4
A level	—	—	—	—	17/35	48.6	17/35	48.6
O level	—	—	—	—	2/8	25.0	2/8	25.0
Sec. 1–3	—	—	—	—	1/37	2.7	1/37	2.7
Primary	—	—	—	—	1/7	14.3	1/7	14.3
TOTAL	—	—	—	—	56/128	43.8	56/128	43.8

TABLE 7.29. *Past tense marking of* know

	NP		P		S		Total	
	Score	%	Score	%	Score	%	Score	%
Tertiary	—	—	—	—	16/41	51.6	16/31	51.6
A level	—	—	—	—	11/37	29.7	11/37	29.7
O level	—	—	—	—	2/17	11.8	2/17	11.8
Sec. 1–3	—	—	—	—	0/17	0.0	0/17	0.0
Primary	—	—	—	—	0/12	0.0	0/12	0.0
TOTAL	—	—	—	—	29/114	25.4	29/114	25.4

Dào 'arrive' is, however, incompatible with *zhīdao* 'know'. Although it is possible to say:

    wǒ zhīdao-le
    I   know-PFV

meaning 'I'm now in the know' as in 'I now know who did it', most informants used *know* in a stative way. The stative equivalent of *know* in Chinese is just *zhīdao*.

Another expression for *feel* in Chinese is *juéde* 'feel', which is a stative expression, without the postverb *dào*. The non-past use of *feel* in SgE referring to past situations could have been influenced by *juéde* in Chinese. This may explain why *feel* has a lower marking for past than *hear, see, think*, and *find*.

Feel
Marking of this verb for past is very low at the lower end of the continuum. Only one token each was marked for past at the primary and sec. 1–3 levels and two at the O level.

Three tokens of *feel* were marked for third person singular, one by an O level informant and two by tertiary informants. Informant O14 probably feels that her brother still thinks that the educational system in Australia is better than the local one, hence the use of the non-past *feel*:

O14.2. (Talking about why her brother wanted to go to Australia to do a degree.) And ah he *feels* dat over (there), the system of study ha, will be much better. Since my father agree to his going ah, so he jus(t) wen(t) off lah.

That informants have a tendency not to mark *feel* and to mark other statives such as *see* and *hear* (note that the Chinese verbs *kàn* 'see' and *tīng* 'hear' may co-occur with the postverb *dào*) is shown in the following texts:

S20.10. My sickness a bit cure—a bit stronger, so—somebori (somebody) recommend me to go a chur(ch). So I fo—I *went* to a chur(ch)—I I *met* the peop(l)e dere—ah—everyone—very nice to me—dey greet me—ah—dey as(k) me any problem dey pray for me—An(d) from dere—dat nigh(t) I really *heard* some—know—like—'know whenever—they pray for me I close my eyes—I *saw* dem crose—I also crose my eyes . . . I just *feel* dat— when I crose my eye I just—an(d) I touch a sister han(d). I just know *feel* dat someting . . . OK I *feel* a bit OK—at times ah, I *saw* dose ah—dose like—you know—ah—dose cow and horse head . . . I *feels* there's someting ha—dere's a cow head or the horse head.

Note that in the above text, four tokens of *feel* were unmarked for past (one token was a hyper-correct form, marked for third person singular), while two tokens of *see*, one of *hear*, and the punctual verbs *meet* and *go* were all marked for past.

The same trend is observed in O18.6:

O18.6. . . . Den maybe she *feel* dat is quite correct lah—den later on she change her attitude lah. Dat's what I *heard* from dose younger classmates lah (school friends).

Know

There was categorical non-marking of *know* with the lowest two groups, while at the O level, only two tokens were marked for past.

As with the verb *feel*, the same trend is observed for the verb *know*. Although informants such as S1 marked statives such as *see* for past, *know* is categorically unmarked for past. Note that the punctual tokens *come* and *speak* are also marked for past:

S1.25. Then coinciden(ce) one of my manageress *came* down. I *spoke* to my manageress . . . So she was dere y'know. She *knows* that I was speaking to my manageress, but when she *saw* my manageress, she just walk out of the entrance. And (th)en I'm just on longing [lɒŋgɪŋ] for her letter to come

you see . . . Because I *know* what I'm doing is correct. So I'm not afraid . . .
But I *know* what I ha(ve) satisfy her.

S1 also had one token of third person singular marking. This phenomenon
is quite common with statives and non-punctuals in general. There were six
tokens of third person singular marking by the T and A level informants as
against three tokens used by those with O and sec. 1–3 level education. No
third person singular marking occurred at the primary level. There were two
instances of hypercorrect forms used by sec. 1–3 informants:

S11.3. I don't ting dey *knows* also.
S14.10. But so far er—all de students very co-operative lah. *Know—knows*
her character lah. Don't bring all the rulers ah.

In general when *know* implies a state lasting over a period of time it is not
marked for past. However, when *know* has the element [+anterior], it is
marked for past. This is clearly shown in the variable use of *know* by
informant O17:

O17.12. He live by himself but y'know—he had a stroke an(d) he wen(t)
unconscious—nobody *knows*.
O17.1. Oh I op(t) to come to Melbourne—because I *knew* a couple of girls
here (Melbourne). So—yah I came to Melbourne.

Likewise, the following token of *know* which has the element [+anterior] is
also marked for past:

A11.11. I was elected by de class. Because de de main ting was . . . I was from
X school when I was in Secondary . . . so most of dem—dey *knew* me—
y'see—so dey elected me.

Know is also frequently not marked for past when it is used as an
inchoative:

O5.2. So—from dere lah—I *know* (got to know)—I learn someting of
electronic( ).
P18.26. I first I *know* you ah.
'When I first came or got to know you.'
P3.25. I *know* him during army time lah.
'I came to know him during the time I was in the army.'

In SBrE the past form of *know* is used if it has relevance to the situation at a
time in the past, e.g.

We found difficulty in getting accommodation but fortunately X *knew* the
manager of the hotel and we managed to get a room.

However, in SgE, as shown in the following exemplifications, the non-past
form is used. The fact that *know* is also relevant to the present may have had
an influence on the non-marking of this verb for past. Thus if X knew Y in
the past, he may still know him at present (if Y is still living).

S11.13. Because it happen dat the principal *know* my mother y'know. So I *went* to school ah.

O6.11. Dat company call upon us—so he said, '. . . and I'm de broder-in-law of so and so of your company.' So I counter-check. And it is true y'know— di fella *knows* him.

Hear

Among the Class III verbs, *hear* received the highest marking for past— 87.3%. If we consider only stative tokens of *hear*, the degree of marking for past is 94.7%. There is categorical marking of stative tokens in three groups of informants from sec. 1–3 to A level. There is a wide contrast between the degree of past tense marking for stative as against non-punctual tokens, the latter category receiving very low marking indeed. For instance informant S10 has categorical marking of the stative tokens of *hear* and categorical non-marking of non-punctual tokens for past. Very often in SgE *hear* means 'to listen to', e.g.

S10.4. I douno he scold behind of me 'know. He, she *heard* lah.
S10.11. Then the boss only *hear* one side ah.

Likewise informants A1 and A2 make a similar distinction between stative and non-punctual tokens, marking the former tokens for past and not the latter tokens:

A1.8. (Why he enjoyed reading Chinese comics.) But mainly because of the story that I I—*hear* through the Rediffusion.
A1.17. I *heard* that there is a tunnel, is a tunnel lah.
A2.12. I ting I *heard*—*heard* of it lah. I *heard* (from) some friends and so I tot (thought)—so we approach her.
A2.10. So when we *hear*—I became receptive to de idea lah.

One reason for the high marking of *hear* for past is that it is often used to

TABLE 7.30. *Past tense marking of* hear

	NP		P		S		Total	
	Score	%	Score	%	Score	%	Score	%
Tertiary	—	—	—	—	11/12	91.7	11/12	91.7
A level	0/2	0.0	—	—	17/17	100.0	17/19	89.5
O level	—	—	—	—	7/7	100.0	7/7	100.0
Sec. 1–3	1/3	33.3	—	—	11/11	100.0	12/14	85.7
Primary	0/1	0.0	—	—	8/10	80.0	8/11	72.7
TOTAL	1/6	16.7	—	—	54/57	94.7	55/63	87.3

refer to hearing in the past about something, as shown in the following examples:

A14.4. I *heard* is a very lovely place.
P17.17. I *heard* dem said Queenstown.

In SBrE *hear* and *heard* are both used when stating that one has received information. In SgE, a sentence such as

I *hear* you are being considered for promotion.

would be used only by acrolectal speakers. The norm is *heard* for most situations. Apart from *hear* meaning 'to listen to', another non-standard use is found in the primary group:

I: How did you get this job?
J: Aah—I *hear* of the vacancy from the newspaper.

Think

Think ranks second in the degree of marking for past among the Class III verbs. Apart from *hear*, it is the second verb where tokens are found only in the stative and non-punctual categories. As with the verb *hear*, there is a stark contrast between the degree of marking for past of stative (80.2%) as against non-punctual tokens (11.1%).

Non-punctual tokens of *think* are those which have either of the elements [+iterative] or [+durative]:

P8.11. I *ting*—many time.
T4.10. So she's—*ting ting*—'Yah!' she says 'I got a client y'see.'

Note that the repetition of verbs shows active thinking. It is a dramatic device often used in colloquial Singaporean English and verbs used in this way are categorically unmarked for past. There is only one [+durative] token of *think* used in a standard way, where *think* is not repeated:

T19.10. So a few of us sat down and *thought over* it.

TABLE 7.31. *Past tense marking of* think

	NP		P		S		Total	
	Score	%	Score	%	Score	%	Score	%
Tertiary	1/2	50.0	—	—	30/32	93.8	31/34	91.2
A level	0/1	0.0	—	—	25/31	80.7	25/32	78.1
O level	0/1	0.0	—	—	15/21	71.4	15/22	68.2
Sec. 1–3	—	—	—	—	15/21	71.4	15/21	71.4
Primary	0/5	0.0	—	—	8/11	72.7	8/16	50.0
TOTAL	1/9	11.1	—	—	93/116	80.2	94/125	75.2

When *think* is used statively as an opinion verb meaning 'to feel that' it is almost categorically unmarked for past. The Chinese equivalent for *think* used in this way is *juéde* which is the same verb used for *feel*. As discussed before, the resultative postverb *dào* cannot be used with *juéde*. This may be a reason why *think* used in this way is almost categorically unmarked for past. Exemplifications are given below:

O1.9. And den eventually I—I already have a strong interes(t) in music, I *ting* I better join de NS (National Service) and try my luck in de army band.

A15.5. at dat time dere's a—dere's a small crisis—den I *ting*—is wise—is better not lah (i.e. not to repeat that year but to start working instead).

Sometimes *think* is unmarked for past when followed by so:

P19.9. Sometime dey *ting* so.

Very often, as with most statives, *think* as an opinion verb receives third person singular marking. There were four tokens altogether of *think* marked for third person singular by informants from O, A, and T levels, e.g.

T14.12. (About her teacher.) I *ting* she *tings* dat you are suppose to read more den what is your basic tex(t).

An interesting case of variable use of *think* is by informant O11. Her two tokens of *think* as an opinion verb are unmarked for past, e.g.

O11.12. My mum pamper me a lot. Whatever tings I wan(t) she sometime jus er let me have it. Then sometime she she *ting* er er I shoulden get it den she don't give it to me.

However, in her next piece of text *think* is marked for past because the time factor has the element [+anterior].

O11.13. I was crying—then she *tot* what happen—den she saw—she was touching my head. Then she found de needle head was dere.

In SgE, the set phrase *I tot (so) what happen(ed)* is a common expression, meaning 'I was wondering what had happened. Is that all?' In the following episode, we notice that all the verbs are uninflected except for *think*, used in the same set phrase:

S10.21. Then sekali (Malay—here meaning 'suddenly' or 'unexpectedly') the teacher come in. We all chabot (Malay meaning 'to run away') off ah. Then when de Sir (teacher) want to sit down den she shout you know. She shout you know. Den de Sir *tot* what happen 'know. Den he se, 'Got kum—dose pin ah, kum (thumb) tacks ah.' So den de Sir as(k) who lah.

The Chinese equivalent for *think* used in this way is *yǐ wéi*, meaning 'to be under the impression of'. When *think* has this meaning, it is frequently marked for past, e.g.

O10.5. Dey *tot* I'm the one.

S10.21. Den de Sir *tot* what.

Another use of *think* which is frequently marked for past is when it has the element of [+momentary]. The following tokens of *think* were marked for past by a basilectal informant:

P10.3. So I *tot* of going down for sailing.
P10.3. So I *tot* of going off dat place.

Here the informant was not actively thinking. Rather a thought flashed across his mind (most probably on a certain occasion) and therefore this is a rather momentary verb. If we compare the use of *think* with the use of *know* for instance, in the primary group we realize that the latter verb is often used in a way which implies duration or a state. Although it is possible to say 'Suddenly I *knew* the answer', where the verb is momentary, most informants would not have used it that way. Thus in the following *know* implies [+duration] of a state, i.e. they had this knowledge all the time. It does not have the connotation of [+momentary] as in 'I *tot* of'.

P01.10. (Be)cau(se) dey *know* dat I won't expected to have a dis school y'see, (be)cau(se) dey *know* my background very very well y'see.

However, *think of* as used here cannot be considered a punctual verb because the informant received an impression or idea, i.e. *think of* is non-volitional.

One reason why *think* used in this manner is marked for past is because in such contexts, resultative postverbs such as *dào* 'arrive' can occur with *xiǎng* 'think' in Chinese:

Wǒ xiǎng dào   bànfǎ   le
I   think arrive solution CRS
'I have thought of a solution.'

It could well be that *tot* is a fossilized form. A16 used a past form of *think* which, prescriptively, should not have been marked for past:

A16.9. Dey tell you certain tings about mental patiens ah, an(d) from dere you *tot* you—you are one of dem y'know . . . and firs(t) t(h)ree days was mental torture. 'When you work in a mental hospital, and people tell you certain things about mental patients, you soon begin to have doubts about your own sanity. I remember my first three days were a real mental torture.'

It may well be that A16 is confused in trying to combine generalizations (when she used the pronoun *you*) and a particular situation, based on her actual experience working in a mental hospital. It is found that in many cases, informants tend to switch too abruptly from the general to the particular without giving enough context that they are switching to a particular case. This has often caused confusion in the use of the sequence of tenses.

Find

The punctual tokens of *find* received very high marking for past: 81.1%. The non-punctuals on the other hand, were categorically unmarked for past. Many

TABLE 7.32. *Past tense marking of* find

	NP		P		S		Total	
	Score	%	Score	%	Score	%	Score	%
Tertiary	—	—	17/17	100.0	19/29	65.5	36/46	78.3
A level	0/1	0.0	5/8	62.5	9/28	32.1	14/37	37.8
O level	0/1	0.0	6/9	66.7	8/11	72.7	14/21	66.7
Sec. 1–3	0/2	0.0	1/2	50.0	8/15	53.3	9/19	47.4
Primary	0/4	0.0	1/1	100.0	3/4	75.0	4/9	44.4
TOTAL	0/8	0.0	30/37	81.1	47/87	54.0	77/132	58.3

of the non-punctual tokens were used in a non-standard way, where *find* meant 'to look for'. Exemplifications are given below:

P10.9. Everyday just *find* for mah-jong.

'Everyday I just looked for friends who wanted to play mah-jong (i.e. to gamble).'

S11.33. I asked I go up and *find* for dem (looked for them).

Examples of punctual tokens include the following which were marked for past:

S14.24. Den later my mother—mean—*found out* lah.

P1.11. and dey *found* dat *out*.

The non-standard use of the non-punctual *find* and its low marking for past compared to *find* used punctually can be traced to the background language, Chinese. In Chinese the verb *zhǎo* is used for both 'to look for' and 'find'. When *zhǎo* includes the successful realization of a goal, it is followed by a resultative postverb, e.g. *dào* 'arrive' or *chū lai* 'out come', as in *zhǎo dao* 'find arrive' and *zhǎo chu lai* 'find out come'. Thus the Chinese verbs *zhǎo chu lai* 'find out come' or *chá chu lai* 'investigate out come' can be substituted for *found out* in the above examples, S14.24 and P1.11. The fact that in Chinese the postverb acts as a completive marker may be one reason why punctual tokens which bear such markers receive a higher marking for past. Non-punctual tokens of *zhǎo* in Chinese do not co-occur with a resultative postverb.

The Chinese equivalent for *find* used statively is *juéde*. *Juéde* substitutes for two verbs in English: *feel* and *find*. However, when one compares the percentage marking of *find* and *feel* used statively, the former has a higher marking than the latter. One possible reason is that *find* is an opinion verb based on one's actual experiences. In fact, it is sometimes very difficult to tell if *find* is used statively or punctually.

While informants in the O level had a score of 72.7% for *find* used statively, the score for A level informants fell to 32.1%. A possible explanation is that these speakers may have used the non-past form of *find* very frequently to express their opinions. This has resulted in the use of a fossilized non-past form which is used even when informants are referring to past situations, e.g.

A14.5. for us is first experience (losing our money)—we *find* it—really sad, very disappointing.

A2.15. I *find* my dad (deceased) was quite innovative.

Two other O level informants used the non-past form. It could be that they have picked up this form because of their frequent contact with more acrolectal speakers during the course of their work. Exemplifications from O3 and O6 are given below:

O3.5. so when I heard dat dere is a shortage of terrazzo, well—I were—I start looking around and I *find dat* ah Malaysia is supplying terrazzo quite cheaply.

O6.9. he offered me tea y'know. Wah! make for me, everything. So I *find it* quite doubtful y'know—dubious y'know.

It is found that for the basilectal speakers and a few O level speakers the past form of *find* is a fossilized stative. As shown in the following example, prescriptively the non-past form should be used:

O1.6. especially nowaday I *found* ah, dis Singaporean . . . part of dem ah, are really irresponsib(l)e everyting . . .

The next example clearly shows that past experience has an influence on the use of the past form of *find*.

O12.5. But if you so used to this electric one, next time you so used to this, you can't—you know—you *found* it so hard y'know. (From past experience the informant had found difficulty when she went back to the manual typewriter after she had got used to working on her electric one.)

When informants discuss habitual situations in the past, the non-past form of *find* is used, e.g.

S1.5. So far I *find dat* my teachers—majority are all very nice (talking about the past).

In the discussions about the past in texts involving *find*, informants often switch very abruptly from the use of the pronouns *I* and *we* to *you*. This is exemplified in the text below:

A1.4. . . . so well, I got in. When I got in well, I was—at firs(t) I din realize the the standard was tha(t) tha(t) high ah. An(d) you *find* that you are being pressurize 'know. You *find* everybody is working very har(d) 'know. So— you jus(t) go along and you *find* that as you go along you pick up the momentum 'know an(d) the spi(r)it is there y'know, you jus(t) wor(k) wor(k) and wor(k) harder and harder—tha(t)'s all 'know.

In SBrE, the pronoun *I* would have been used to describe a personal experience. However, if one were to generalize and switch to the pronoun *you*, one would need to add some introductory comments such as 'you know when you are put into a good school, you face tremendous pressure . . .'.

The next piece of text, which involves one token of *find*, shows the confusion most speakers face in their choice between the past and non-past forms of verbs when they try to generalize about certain situations and describe a personal experience as well.

A19.8. (Asked if the people she met in the USA were friendly.)

J: Depends on where we go y'see. Because when we went to LA to Disneyland and so forth de people dere were frien(d)ly y'know. It gives you ah—a different kin(d) of outlook y'know. Dey—dey er so open, . . . Den when you went to SF

I: What's SF?

J: San Francisco ah—den you *find* dat everybody is so aloof.

See

In the overall marking for past, there is a stark contrast in the marking of the stative tokens (65.6%) and the non-punctual tokens (17.9%). In addition, the stative tokens have, overall, a higher degree of marking than the punctual tokens (46.7%).

The way *see* is used punctually, non-punctually and statively is shown in the following examples:

See used in a punctual way:

T9.1. We just *saw* him as a friend (we consulted him, a medical practitioner, as a friend and asked him for advice).

See used in a non-punctual way:

P6.7. (Talking about his student days.)

At home, I never do my homework. I just back then aah the bag put—put i(t) aah put beside asi(de) lah. Then I go already . . . play ah, *see* picture.

TABLE 7.33. *Past tense marking of* see

	NP		P		S		Total	
	Score	%	Score	%	Score	%	Score	%
Tertiary	5/10	50.0	4/4	100.0	13/19	68.4	22/33	66.7
A level	—	—	1/1	100.0	19/25	76.0	20/26	76.9
O level	0/3	0.0	1/1	100.0	13/18	72.2	14/22	63.6
Sec. 1–3	0/7	0.0	0/5	0.0	17/26	65.4	17/38	44.7
Primary	0/8	0.0	1/4	25.0	1/8	12.5	2/20	10.0
TOTAL	5/28	17.9	7/15	46.7	63/96	65.6	75/139	54.0

See used in a stative manner—i.e. it is non-volitional:

P7.29. I *saw* got puppy ah, I jus(t) pi(ck) dem out (up) lah. 'When I noticed a stray puppy on the road I always picked it up and took it home'.

The non-punctual category was unmarked from primary to O level. This is not surprising as at the basilectal end of the continuum the verb *see* often shows the semantics of the Chinese verb *kàn*, which can mean *read, look at, watch,* and *see.* That informants at the lower end of the continuum often have difficulty with these distinctions is shown in the following text where O18 wavered between the use of *watch* (she meant 'looked at') and *saw*:

O18.11. Jus(t) er a day ago, I wen(t) to Lucky Plaza. I jus(t) *watch* a—jus(t) *saw* a blouse 'know—and is georgette only 'know—an(d) it cos(t) about . . .

The various uses of *see* in SgE are shown below:

P7.25. You *see* all de story book( ) lah.
'You *read* all the story books' (referring to exercises in school).
P7.25. See book write.
'We *looked at* the book and wrote.'
O12.12. den later er you *see* (watched) de doctor doing de stitching.

All the above tokens were used non-punctually and were not marked for past. As these are habituals, the equivalent of *see* in Chinese *kàn* cannot co-occur with a postverb. This may be a possible reason for the low degree of marking of the non-punctual tokens of *see* for past. All punctual tokens from O level to tertiary received categorical marking for past. However, punctual tokens were categorically unmarked at sec. 1–3 level, and at the primary level only one token was marked. One reason is that many of the tokens are of the structure *V and V*, an environment which is often categorically unmarked for past.

A possible reason for the very high degree of marking of stative tokens of *see* is that in Chinese the stative non-volitional use of *kàn* is followed by the postverb *dào* 'arrive' or *jiàn* 'perceive'. The stative use of *see* in SgE may have been influenced by Chinese. What is interesting is that for many informants distinction is often made between a momentary stative and a habitual stative, with the latter frequently not marked for past. Thus for informants such as T11 and O16, only their habitual statives were unmarked for past:

T11.15. She's always—aah—maybe we *see* her so often—we begin to take her for granted. (In the past, they did not show their affection openly for their mother.)
O16.17. Den when people—[i:] *see* people shirt ah, wear not so nice, he'll pull dem out, and den scold dem, for not(h)ing.

All the momentary statives referring to a single occasion, received categorical marking, e.g.

T11.16. She *saw* dis man.

O16.28. Because I'm very scared of lion dance. I one day I ting I *saw* one in my house you know—as dey was coming.

Another environment where *see* used statively is unmarked for past is when the nominative pronoun used is *you*, i.e. when an informant switches from the pronoun *we*, which signifies personal involvement, and moves into the general. T19 had near categorical marking for *see* except for the token where *see* is preceded by the pronoun *you*:

T19.3. (When she visited Saigon.)
　　We *saw* dose people who had no decent accommodation . . . y'know all over de place, you *see* signs of war, y'know—you have all dose—ah—lockages (lock-ups) and at night you hear bombs and firing and curfews.
T19.2. Then we went back and we *saw* de ticket.
T19.3. We really *saw* a lot.
T19.3. and we *saw* a lot of tings.

8

Substratum or Bioprogram?

8.1 The interplay of factors influencing past tense marking

The figures given in Chapter 7, based on Ho's careful analysis of her data, certainly do not give the impression of random variation and suggest that Bickerton's bioprogram cannot be totally ignored when looking at the acquisition of a second language. A comparison of the findings for past tense marking with Bickerton's results is given in Table 8.1. Ho's investigation is based on a corpus of 8,725 past-reference verbs. Bickerton's survey is based on 1,000 verbs each in a decreolizing situation in Guyana and Hawaii (cf. Bickerton 1981:164–5).

What can be clearly seen here is that past tense marking is higher for verbs used punctually than non-punctually—for GC 3.2 times higher, for HCE 7.6 times, and for SgE 2.4 times higher.

Bickerton's recasting of Bronckart and Sinclair's (1973) data is interesting. The six goal-oriented actions used in their investigation are as follows:

1. (P10−) A truck slowly pushes a car toward a garage.
2. (P1+)   A car hits a marble which very rapidly rolls into a pocket.
3. (JX10+) The farmer jumps over ten fences and reaches the farm.
4. (J2+)   The farmer's wife jumps in one big jump over ten fences and reaches the farm.
5. (JX5−) The cow jumps over five fences and does not reach the stable.
6. (J1−)   The horse jumps over one fence and does not reach the stable.

Bickerton (1981:167) has coded these actions according to type of action, duration, and iteration (where applicable), as shown in parentheses. P and J represent pushing and jumping movements respectively, while X indicates iterative actions. The numbers following P and J show the number of seconds taken for the actions. Two new symbols have now been added to represent the achievement of the goal: + indicates the successful realization of the goal, while − indicates the unsuccessful accomplishment of the goal. The results of only age-groups 3.7 and 6.6 are reproduced in Table 8.2. Bickerton comments, 'From the first column, it would appear that children in the lowest age group do indeed discriminate between events on the basis of pure length' (Bickerton 1981:170). This comment is particularly relevant to Ho's data. The more punctual the verb, the higher the degree of marking for past tense it receives.

However, the successful achievement of a goal seems important too, apart

TABLE 8.1. *Past tense marking in Guyanese Creole, Hawaiian Creole English, and Singaporean English* (%)

	Punctual	Non-punctual
Guyanese Creole	38	12
Hawaiian Creole English	53	7
Singaporean English	56	23

TABLE 8.2. *Rank orders for past-marking frequency*

Rank	Age-group	
	3.7	6.6
1	P1+	J1−
2	J2+	JX5−
3	J1−	J2+
4	JX5−	JX10+
5	JX10+	P1+
6	P10−	P10−

X = iterative actions.
Numbers following J and P indicate seconds taken for the actions.
+ = goal successfully achieved.
− = goal not achieved.
Source: Adapted from Bickerton 1981:169, Table 3.3.

from the length of time taken to complete an action. This is perhaps why J2 ranks second after P1 in the first column. Note that J1 takes only one second but is placed after J2. The action J1 is considered [+telic] as there is a goal (a pocket) and the marble successfully rolls into the pocket. Bickerton (1981:171) comments that it is only at a later age (6.6) that the children are able to distinguish between inherently punctual actions and the non-punctual ones. Hence the iterative jumping actions are classified as a series of individual punctual actions. Nevertheless, it is observed that the faster actions are still placed right at the top. J1 is ranked first because the action takes only one second. However, it is apparent that at this stage the children are also able to classify the type of goal. Hence JX5 and not J2 is ranked second, as both JX5 and J1 have similar goals.

Most of Bickerton's observations are pertinent to Ho's investigation of SgE as the following trends have been observed.

1. Inherently non-punctual verbs receive a low degree of marking for past.
2. Inherently punctual verbs receive a high degree of marking for past.

3. The attainment of a goal is important as it shows that a situation is both punctual as well as telic. Goal-oriented verbs receive a higher degree of marking for past.

When tokens of inherently non-punctual verbs are categorically used non-punctually, the degree of marking is lower still. In the following list all tokens of *need* and *enjoy* were used statively while all tokens of the other verbs were used non-punctually:

keep	21.6%
eat	16.7%
cry	16.7%
enjoy	16.7%
need	10.8%
wear	9.1%
scold	3.6%

Verbs which are inherently punctual receive the highest degree of marking for past. Some of the verbs in the list below can be used punctually, non-punctually, and statively. However, the following figures for past tense marking are based on only the tokens used punctually:

lose	92.9%
leave	91.1%
meet	90.4%
speak	86.7%
marry	80.0%
accept	80.0%
tell	79.7%
apply	77.8%

The degree of marking for punctual tokens is higher compared to the overall marking of each verb. Furthermore, 'superpunctual' verbs, e.g. *lose*, *leave*, and *meet*, which show actions pertaining to definite points in time on particular occasions, receive a higher marking than verbs which are less punctual, e.g. *speak* and *tell*, which certainly entail some degree of non-punctuality.

The lexical aspect of *tell* used punctually can be quite ambiguous. This may be a reason for the variable marking of two punctual tokens of *tell* used by informant T13. The story in T13.4 certainly takes a longer time to tell than uttering the line used by the interviewer in T13.14:

T13.4. An(d) den he *tell* me a story 'know . . .

T13.14. During de interview he *tol(d)* me y'know 'I like you when you first come in.'

An interesting study on the emergence of *-ing*, *-s*, and *-ed*/IRREG in the speech of children was conducted by Bloom, Lifter, and Hafitz (1980). The semantics of verb aspect was one of the factors discussed in relation to the use of the three morphemes. They looked at two semantic oppositions basic to analyses of verb aspect: durative–non-durative and completive–non-completive (cf. Bloom, Lifter, and Hafitz 1980:398). They found that there were certain verbs whose lexical aspect was ambiguous. 'Thus *find* and *break* were clear in their reference to completive/non-durative actions, whereas *comb* and *write* named events that were only approximately completive/non-durative; indeed they occurred in non-completive/durative events as well. There is a clear sense in which verbs like *eat, take, write* could name events that were either completive/non-durative or non-completive/durative' (Bloom, Lifter, and Hafitz 1980:399). The overall score for the punctual tokens of *tell* in Ho's investigation is affected because its lexical aspect is often not clear-cut. As shown in the discussion of the verb *write*, the ambiguity of its lexical aspect is evidenced in the variable use of *write* by informant P7 as he wavered between the use of the marked and unmarked form:

P7.1. Den my sister [raɪt] (read) a newspaper, [iː] (she) see go(t) boys' school lah, SAF (Singapore Armed Forces) Boys' School. Den my sister *wrote* (a letter) for me ah, write for me.

Bring and *take* are two other verbs whose punctual tokens receive a lower marking than very punctual verbs. The scores are 71.9% for *bring* and 68.4% for *take*. As these verbs contain many tokens which are mainly durative-terminal verbs (used in the SgE way—with no distinction according to whether the direction is away from or towards the speaker), the lexical aspect is again ambiguous, i.e. it cannot really be determined whether the informant is focusing on the terminal point or the [+durative] period. Likewise, the lexical ambiguity of the verb *fight* could have led to T13's unmarked token:

T13.13. So he took a ris(k) and *fight* for my case y'see.

Another punctual verb whose lexical aspect is ambiguous is the verb *start*. Whereas *he started at 8 o'clock in the morning* is clearly punctual, *he started to sing* has an inceptive-durative aspect if we consider the whole verbal aspect. Hence the punctual tokens of *start* receive a score of only 46.3% for past. The same phenomenon occurs in GC, as the following comments by Bickerton show:

It is also worth noting that *start* is, almost by definition, [+punctual]. However, in its patterns of behaviour it is very like a modal, and all modals are [−punctual]. It may be for this reason, rather than for any phonological cause, that some speakers systematically omit *-ed* when *start* is followed by *to*.
(Bickerton 1975:109)

It is noticed too that verbs like *die, forget*, and *break*, which have a built-in end-point, also receive very high marking for past. In Chinese such verbs co-occur with the perfective aspect marker *-le*. Li and Thompson (1981) make an interesting point regarding the verbs *die* and *forget*. Whereas it is possible in English to say *he is dying* and *he is forgetting his French*, it is not possible in Chinese to use the durative aspect with *die* and *forget* because of 'the inclusion of the end point in the meaning of such verbs' (Li and Thompson 1981:196). The strong influence from Chinese is reflected in the frequent use of *already* (aspect marker representing *-le* in Chinese) with *die* or *pass away* and *forget* or the marking of these verbs for past when prescriptively the present perfect should have been used:

P6.4. I: You had to work?
     J: Douno, *forget already*.
P13.27. I: Did you do that?
     J: I *forgot already*.
O13.4. We can tell whether they really *forgot* to pay or they have de intention of taking (talking about shoplifters—a present state of affairs).
P18.18. Pass away already. My parents all *pass away already*.
P20.36. (Referring to her grandparents) *pass away already* ah.

Even in the face of very strong phonological constraints, which would restrict the marking of *pass away* (the past form of this verb ends in a double consonant cluster), this verb has quite a number of tokens marked for past in the speech of A- and tertiary-level informants:

A4.10. Both my paren(t)s *passed away* ah.
A15.5. dat is de year when my dad *passed away* y'see, *passed away* y'see.

The terminal point of a verb is often marked in English by verb particles, as in *turn off the tap*, *the car broke down*. In Chinese such terminal points are shown by the use of resultative endings, e.g. *jiàn* 'perceive' in *kànjiàn* 'see perceive'. The resultative ending *jiàn* shows the successful realization of an action. The use of verbal particles in L2 and the use of postverbs and the perfective aspect marker *-le*, reinforce the meaning of [+completive], at a single point in time. Such verbs can be said to be 'super-punctual' and receive very high marking for past. If such verbs are not marked for past, e.g. in the speech of basilectal informants, then the aspect marker *already* is used:

P19.16. The first chil(d). I'm so happy. Den I get a ah—de first child is a son—quite happy lah—in my whole family all lah—m—very happy and den I *brought* dem up when dey small—baby *brought dem up*. Bring dem go anywhere like go relatifs house—bring dem go—den dey *grow up already*— I have de second one . . .

8.2 Some unresolved problems

There have been instances where verbs have been marked for past when the non-past form should have been used. This is an interesting phenomenon which merits further investigation. For instance, it has been found in Ho's corpus that in the midst of a narration of present habituals, informants often switch to the past forms because they are illustrating the general situation with

[+realis] events which occurred in the past, as seen in the following examples from more basilectal informants:

S20.18. Every Sunday dey sure want to go one. (*One* is an emphatic marker. The children insist on attending Sunday school every Sunday.) Heavy rain also, dey *wanted* to go. (Even if it rains, they'd still want to go.)

P10.14. But Saturday Sunday mostly dey (his children) went to my mum place (they still go there).

S7.25. J: (Talking about Bugis Street, a famous night spot for tourists.) Aah, European a lots 'know. Every touris(t) dey will send by cart, buses, some dey go by demself; a lot of Navy (seamen) *wen(t)* dere. I see dem, some of dem wearing caps, Navy, New Zealand. Some are Navy . . . Even Japanese also *went* dere. Mmm.

I: You know the place very well!

J: Oh! I always *went* dere y'see. (She still does.) At night I not(h)ing to do—I *went* dere.

I: Always?

J: Aah majority (frequently) because ah, always I *go* from work—aroun(d) t(h)ree—one week two times.

It could be that the verb *go* in its past form is one of high frequency; hence S7's use of *went* four times. However, when she related a current habitual situation she used *go* in *always I go from work*. The use of the past form in the habitual *I always went dere y'see* is related to [+anterior] actions.

The same phenomenon is observed in the speech of informants with tertiary education:

T11.9. My husband is in marketing so he travels a lot—quite used to it ah being independent myself. When he's away, I stay at home—except that I have to conform to my mother's ideas and she will say, 'How come you don't come back and stay?' So I go back and *stayed* two nights or five nights, isn't it? My mother is worried dat I stay by myself and tings like dat.

It is likely that T11 used the past form because such events have occurred in the past even though they can be expected to continue in the future.

In English one uses the non-past form for a discussion of generalities and current habituals. If one wishes to switch to the past and refer to particular events in the past, some form of an introductory comment has to be used, e.g.

For instance the other day . . .

The insertion of past forms in a piece of narrative referring to a current situation is an influence from the target language, where the use of the past form is obligatory for past events.

It is also noticed that certain past forms are used for particularly punctual verbs, e.g. *landed* in the following exemplification, even though prescriptively the non-past should have been used:

S16.29. I mean, I belief dat way lah, rather than forcing a child to learn where he shoulden be force. He can be a very good learner—you can force a person to learn but reach to certain age, what happen, he *landed* Woodbridge! (a mental hospital).

'One can't really put too much pressure on a child to study. The pressure mounts up over the years and one day he might just land up in Woodbridge.'

Landed is also used in the following utterance:

S8.15. Now he was, *landed* in jail.

'Now he is in jail.'

This seems to suggest that *landed* is part of a 'learned' list of lexical words (cf. Bickerton's (1975:107) Guyanese Creole examples: *populated, accommodated, admitted, inoculated, excited*). There are many verbs in basilectal SgE which are marked for past but seem overly formal in the context used:

P2.8. I: Why did you put him (your son) in that school?

J: . . . because last time you *selected* becau(se) (it was) near our place lah!

These 'learned' stabilized forms are often used with negatives and modals:

S6.14. I: They didn't give you any injection?

J: Yah dey give injection, but I din *admitted* lah (i.e. admitted to hospital).

S8.22. De [gɑ:mən] (government) *don't allowed* de hawkers dere.

S9.13. Yah I *won't allowed* dem to go—go down.

The use of the past/past participle forms could be the result of exposure to similar forms present in adjectival and passive structures, e.g.

'Dogs are not allowed in here.'

'I am worried' or 'a worried look'.

Many adjectives are formed by adding *-ed* to verbs, e.g. *an annoyed look, a selected number of participants*. These words begin to appear as a learned vocabulary. The *-ed* suffix is attached to both the verb and adjective:

O3.5. So we—went in—and den we manage to—secured ah about twenty to t(h)irty t(h)ousand pieces—

O4.3. you feel very *secured*.

8.3 Is the punctual–non-punctual distinction a language universal?

Evidence from Bickerton's data for HCE and GC, as well as data from BEV and SgE, seems to suggest that the punctual–non-punctual distinction is a language universal.

From Black English Vernacular. As pointed out by Bickerton (1975:159–60), in the following narrative which he quoted from Loman (1967:24–5) the verbs which are italicized are non-punctual verbs and are unmarked—'their referents are not single-point actions, but series of actions which were repeated on frequent occasions in the past—in other words are marked [−punctual]':

/4.97/ Anita, you remember when we—it was a long time ago. We used to—when somebody used to be crying in our house we used to do just like this. We used to do our fingers—all like that—do like this to 'em—...and sometimes we *make* then laughy. They—we *make* somebody laugh when we be doing that you know. Whoever it be crying, we *make* them laugh so hard—...And then we say—and then we used to say—when they *do* that—we used to say: 'Crying when you laughing!'

Bickerton also points out that in the following text, from Loman (1967:21), the [+punctual] causative verb *scare* is marked for past while the [−punctual] token is not:

/4.95/ And the ghost *scared* him out [twice repeated]...So the coloured man went in there, and he say—and he *scare*.

In the first half of a narrative of a fight recounted by a black teenager in Wolfson (1982) before a switch to the conversational historical present (CHP), it is noticed that all verbs are marked for past. However, the strongly non-punctual verb *stand* is unmarked for past:

the Snyder boy started to hit Benny and Benny pushed him back and he fell on the ground. And the dude from Lincoln just *stand* there and looked at him because he know how Benny is. (Wolfson 1982:37; our italics)

From Guyanese Creole. The following is an example from Bickerton (1975) of the habitual use of verbs, all of which are unmarked for past. As observed in Ho's data on SgE, so too in Guyanese Creole English, non-punctual verbs are sometimes marked with third person singular, e.g. *rings* in the following text:

/4.93/ His name was Bell, we *call* him Bell. Holding the bell he *rings* his bell, *say*, 'well, you have dance tonight, dance tomorrow night and dance the other nights,' and he *give* you the place where they have the dance. (Bickerton 1975:150–1)

In contrast, verbs which are [+punctual] and occurring in non-temporal clauses are often marked for past:

/4.86/ I can't tell you the year that I *came* here.
/4.85/ And another time again they going in the bush, you know, they *went* through tramping, they see a little one [sc. jaguar] lie down. (Bickerton 1975:149)

From Singaporean English. The many examples from the data show that the punctual–non-punctual distinction is crucial to past tense marking. However, does Chinese, the background language, have some influence on past tense marking?

It would seem that for SgE, the semantic space around habituals is like 'the Guyanese (majority creole) analysis' as set out by Bickerton (1981:258, 260),

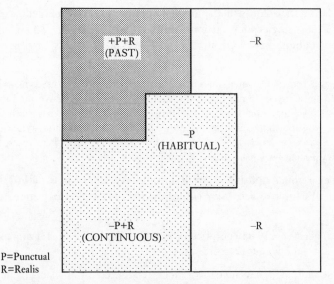

F<small>IG</small>. 8.1 Semantic space around habituals found in the Guyanese (majority Creole) analysis. (Based on Bickerton 1981:260, Fig. 4.9*a*)

with the past–non-past distinction superimposed upon it (see Fig. 8.1).

Using Spanish as an example, Bickerton shows that the Romance languages follow this pattern:

yo trabajo means 'I am working' or 'I work'.
yo trabajaba means 'I was working' or 'I worked' (habitually)
yo trabajé is limited to 'I worked' (punctually, on a particular occasion).

(see Bickerton 1981:258)

It is noticed that Chinese fits this pattern too, as may be seen from an examination of the situations where the completive or perfective aspect marker *-le* can be used. *-Le* can be used only in the '+P +R' area but not in the '−P' (habitual) and '−P +R' (continuative) areas, e.g.

1. tā   zuótiān wèi-le   gǒu
   3 sg yesterday feed-PFV dog
   'Yesterday s/he fed the dog.'
2. *qùnián tā   měitiān wèi-le   gǒu
   last year 3 sg everyday feed-PFV dog
   'Last year s/he fed the dog every day.'
3. *tā   zuótiān bā   diǎn zhōng zài   wèi-le   gǒu
   3 sg yesterday eight time   DUR feed-PFV dog
   'S/He was feeding the dog at 8 o'clock.'

4. *qùnián tā   xǐhuān-le wèi gǒu
   last year 3 sg like-PFV feed dog
   'Last year s/he liked to feed the dog.'

Examples 1 to 4 show that *-le* , being a perfective aspect marker, cannot co-occur with habituals, duratives, and statives. SgE, especially at the more basilectal levels, shows the strong influence of the Chinese aspectual system. In situations where the features [+completion, +event] are present, the degree of marking of verbs for past increases. Vice versa, verbs found in contexts showing such features as [+durative], [+habitual] and [+stative], receive a lower marking for past.

It is therefore not surprising that when situations are habitual ones, for example when Singaporeans discuss their former employers, teachers, or work routines in previous places of work, verbs are often not marked for past. Naturally, there is also a possible L2 influence in that in SBrE, one can often have asides and make certain comments about one's past:

> We worked in the coal mines—it's tough work down there. (Speaker feels that it's still tough to be a coal miner, hence the use of the non-past form.)

However, habituals can be viewed differently (cf. Bickerton 1981:255–6) if we focus our attention on each individual event, which will now have the label [+punctual] as it has the feature [+completion]. Thus in Chinese *-le* can be added to events with the features [+completion, +anterior], even though they take place habitually:

> qùnián, wǒ méitiān wèi-le   gǒu, jiù   chōngliáng[1]
> last year, I   everyday feed-PFV dog, then pour cool
> 'Last year, everyday, after I had fed the dog, I took a bath.'

In SgE, habitual events with the features [+completion, +anterior] are often marked for past:

P19.17. (Talking about habitual events in her childhood.) Den my mother quite stric(t) too lah. Like se' she wan you early in the morning get up six o'clock, cannot late. Must early in the morning get up six o'clock, follow her go to market. Den after dat he (she) come back (from) to de market, she put down de market baske(t). An(d) den you must know to prepare everyting dat he (she) *bought* in—inside de basket dere.

Note that *bought* is marked because it is [+anterior]. As Bickerton remarks 'the anterior–nonanterior contrasts, not events at all, but the relative timing of events' (Bickerton 1981:284). Further on he adds: 'Anterior marking is

---

[1] *Chōngliáng* is used in Singapore Mandarin, which is heavily influenced by the Southern dialects. In Standard Mandarin *xǐzǎo* is used instead.

primarily a device which alerts the listener to backward shifts of time in a narrative or a conversation, thus enabling him to preserve the correct sequence of reported events...' (Bickerton 1981:286)

What is extremely interesting is that the same speaker above who marked *buy* because it has the element of [+anterior] did not mark the same verb when all the habitual actions in her narrative are in an ordered sequence:

P19.19. I see the comics when I was still chil(d)hood dat one—I like to see de comics. When my father everyone, one mon(th) one—everytime *buy* for me two comics boo(k) for me and my mother grumble.

In the following text, informant S7 is referring to a habitual situation in the past (the car-park ticketing system which has since been superseded by a new coupon system).

S7.16. (Talking about rude motorists whom she had to deal with.) Sometime over five minute like nine o'clock dey *came* in, and ten o fi(ve) (10.05) he (they) *came* out; eighty cen(ts) we *charge* dem, dey *scold* you know.

Note that the two non-punctual verbs *come*, being [+anterior] are marked for past, while the other non-punctual verbs *charge* and *scold* are not.

Very often in SgE, the simple past tense is also used for [+anterior] single events. Exemplifications from Ho's corpus are given below:

T12.3. I always *wanted* (had wanted) to see the reflection of de mountains.
A17.18. I brought a slipper—a pair of slippers almost broken. I was in—I *intended* (had intended) to throw it away... So lucky I was in slacks.
A18.4. I was stuck in the hotel for five days. So I intend (story-line)—actually I *intended* (had intended) to stay for three days.
S9.8. After (she) *came back* (had come back from)—carry the purse put here. Reach her house already—she din know...

From the evidence discussed one can say, too, that for habitual [+anterior] situations, SgE sometimes follows the Jamaican Creole pattern (as shown by Bickerton 1981:258, 260) where iteratives merge with the past punctuals (see Fig. 8.2).

8.4 The use of *already* to show [+anterior] in SgE

In SBrE, use of the perfective forms is one way of showing anteriority. In basilectal SgE, the use of *already* shows the influence of the Chinese perfective aspect marker, *-le*. For current events, (both for habitual and single events) *the simple present + already* is used to mark anteriority:

S20.17. (Talking about her daughter.) I cannot teach more—teach her more. I go(t) to prepare for dinner lah... So I just tell her some (help her with

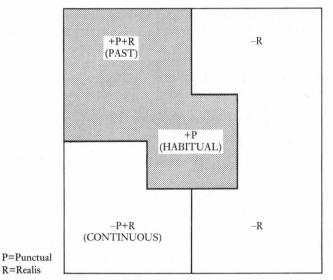

FIG. 8.2 Semantic space around habituals found in the Jamaican Creole analysis. (Based on Bickerton 1981:260, Fig. 4.9*b*)

some of her school work). Den she do. *Do 'ready* (already), she douno, she come to de kitchen an(d) as(k) me.

P6.8. Den we all go *already*, we all douno pass or fail ah. 'After going for the language test, we were not informed if we had passed or failed.'

For past situations, [+anteriority] is shown not only by the use of the simple past, but the completive aspect marker *already* is often used as well:

S1.27. he *bought already*, when he was going off—den—you know what I tell him?
'When the customer was going off after he *had bought* something from the store, do you know what I told him?'

8.5 Why are habituals, iteratives, and statives in SgE often marked with the third person singular even though the reference is clearly to the past?

It has been shown in many of Ho's examples that verbs which are used in a non-punctual or stative manner are not only frequently unmarked for past, but are sometimes even marked for third person singular.

The data show that non-punctuals and statives are always [+continuative] irrespective of whether the time is past or non-past. Punctual tokens in SgE always have the element [+completive].

As Bickerton (1981:167) points out, 'semantically, the categories of past and punctual overlap. While all pasts need not be punctuals, all punctuals must be pasts—if they were not, they would still be happening, and if they were still happening now, they would be non-punctual by definition.' Hence in SgE the punctuals or [+completive] verbs are often marked for past. The non-punctual and stative past reference verbs are treated as still happening, i.e. having the feature [+continuative]. As mentioned before, in Chinese, the -*le* perfective aspect marker is incompatible with [+continuative] situations. Since SgE shows very strong influence from Chinese, [+continuative], non-punctual, and stative verbs are therefore not marked for past. Sometimes third person singular forms are used instead. A few examples are given below:

A2.16. And I thin(k) he *worries* about his business and all that lah (talking about his deceased father).

T5.18. He *makes* it a point actually to to—to come down to de level (talking about his former principal).

P12.16. But you know, day and day we pray and pray and pray y'know. It *seems* that nothing happen and it *seems* that he is suffering more 'know (talking about her deceased baby).

Marking of non-punctual past reference verbs for third person singular shows the possible influence of the target language. Morphologically, the verb form in Chinese does not show any change with respect to the subject (e.g. first, second, and third person pronouns). Since the teaching of the use of the third person singular is given heavy emphasis in English instructional programmes in schools, this may be a possible reason for its use in habitual and stative contexts even though the reference is past.

Ho's findings are also substantiated by evidence from interviews reported in the newspapers. Here a mother talks about her deceased child:

> 'He *likes* to play chess and was good at music, passing his grade I piano forte with distinction.'
>
> *(Sunday Monitor,* 22 July 1984)

However, it seems that the crucial factor for the use of the third person singular with habituals, continuatives, and statives is a purely semantic one: such situations are often thought of as happening in the present. The same phenomenon occurs with past reference verbs in GC:

/4.57/ My mother was poor—lives in trash house.
/4.58/ No steamer *takes* you from this [sc. there] straight over to town—there were no trains in those days.
/4.59/ We have two steamer, one *goes* in the morning and one come in the afternoon— one was 'Sproston Wood' and one was 'Lady London'.

> (Bickerton 1975:135)

As is expected in second-language learning, hypercorrection occurs but it is noticeable too that third person singular hypercorrect forms are often used in non-punctual past situations, e.g.

P19.18. (Referring to her mother.) Very happy, told me, 'Can learn everyting!' Then I *learns*, step by step—den she teach me how to coo(k), teach me how to cook rice firs(t).

8.6 To what extent is the non-marking of habituals for past a phonological factor?

Levin (1985:46) quotes the following HCE text from Bickerton, showing that non-punctual verbs are not marked while punctual ones are:

'O, abat fiftin yia, ai *statid* [=started] tu work. ... espeshli jaepanis, dei kam [=come] in da mawnin taim go skul, bai da taim pau ['over' in Hawaiian] skul, abaut faiv aklak, den die *stat* [=start] tu go hom'

Levin remarks: 'Typically a creole drops any distinction that is neither phonetically conspicuous nor sharp semantically' (1985:46). Phonetically, the standard forms *they'd come*, *they'd start* are very close to the simple present forms *they come*, *they start*. Hence the contracted modal *'d* has been deleted. This seems to imply that the HCE speakers have underlying past forms for habituals. However, they are not realized because of a phonetic problem.

  Like HCE, in SgE, the contracted modal *'d* is often omitted for past non-punctuals, as the following text shows:

A1.8. I mean—you used to buy it (spiders) from friends ah—dis schoolmates ah. You (you'd) *buy* it from dem and den 'know—you just *keep* (you'd put it away) it in a box like dat lah.

However, the omission of *'d* does not mean that the verbs *buy* and *keep* have an underlying past form and that *'d* is deleted because of phonological constraints. Moreover, other texts such as the ones below show that for habituals the non-past modal *will* instead of *would* may be used by speakers from all educational levels. This shows that the semantic rather than the phonetic factor is more dominant as far as past tense marking is concerned:

T11.13. ... I remember—aah—when I was—before I wen(t) to school—my mother would use to er—'Oh! kiss dad y'know before he goes to wor(k)!' And all of us *will* run towards him ... then he *will go* to work.

O12.12. Very fun. we—we—we—y'know de doctor *will* train us himself lah ... So he *will* tell us how to take—ah—temperature, how to give injection, den how to do dressing ... he *will* teach us ah, but is very fun working in de clinic. (The informant is no longer working at the clinic.)

It is frequently the case that after the expression *used to* is introduced into a piece of narrative, most verbs are in the stem form, as shown in text A5.4

below. Where *used to* is absent as an introductory marker, *will* + *V* is used for most habituals, as shown in Text A1.8.

A5.4. J: No during my Sec one days. We use to go up to—

I: Oh what school was that?

J: School—we *used to go* up to er a sort of flats ah, in de las(t) storey of de flat and we *sit* in de staircase dere and *start*. And after dat we *get* started lah.

What is most noticeable in SgE is that for habituals, there is the constant reliance on a habitual aspect marker. For current habituals the habitual aspect markers are *use to* and the modal *will*. It could well be that as the past habitual marker *used to* is heard so frequently, its use has, over the years of development of SgE, been extended to present habitual events.

The following texts show the use of *will/'ll* + *V* for habitual events. It is true that such forms are used in SBrE for habitual activities, but these are rather outdated forms. They are probably 'fossilized' forms remaining from earlier textbook usage.

S9.24. Yes, same time eight fi(f)teen we—we go English Section lah, (we attend the English service in my church) with my husband and den my children *will go* Sunday School up to ten someting finish. After finis(h), sometimes my youngest one (son) and de second one (son) *will go* to de Chinese section. Sometimes he he—dey dey I mean don't feel—if dey got friend den dey *will attend* Chinese (service) also.

S7.7. When I beat her (her daughter) I *will call* her 'XX come here! Why mummy beat you?' *I'll tell* her 'know.

The use of *will* + *V* can also be traced to the source language. The following exemplification shows a sequence of events:

wǒ měitiān, wèi-le   gǒu, chōng-le liáng, jiù   kàn bàozhǐ,
I   everyday feed-PFV dog pour-PFV cool   then see newspaper

ránhòu jiù   chū qu sànsanbù
after   then out go walk walk step

'Everyday, after feeding my dog and having a shower, I read the newspapers. Then I go out for a stroll.'

The word *jiù* (then) has the element of [+future]. In the target language there are structures where *will* is used to show a sequence of events:

After he has fed the dog, he will go out.

It is probably these two factors that have contributed to the stabilized use of *will* + *V* for habituals in SgE. Interestingly, one of Bickerton's (1975:132) examples shows a habitual use of *will* + *V*:

That man will walk house house and give people. (The informant was talking about a Catholic priest.)

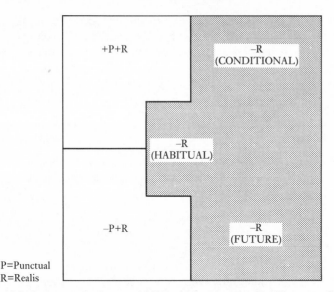

FIG. 8.3 Semantic space around habituals found in the São Tomense Creole analysis. (Based on Bickerton 1981:260, Fig. 4.9*c*)

As *jiù* is also used in Chinese for past events in a habitual context, the same modal *will* is used for past habituals. *Would + V* is sometimes used by informants with higher levels of education, while the number of occurrences of the contracted form *'d* as in *Then he'd go to the park* is negligible. Interestingly, the contraction *'ll* is more frequently used, e.g.

A5.8. (Talking about the brass band practices in school.) So everytime we had, we we'll take some time off lah, say fifteen minutes to warm up my instruments y'know . . .

As anything which takes place in the future is [−realis], we can say that the semantic space for such habituals corresponds to the picture given by Bickerton for languages such as São Tomense Creole, where iteratives are treated in the same way as futures and therefore put in the irrealis category (Bickerton 1981:256). This is shown in Fig. 8.3.

It is noticeable that [−realis] or −R verbs receive lower marking for past tense. Ho's previous exemplifications have shown that habituals which are treated as −R have a low degree of marking for past.

The second category of verbs which are −R are verbs such as *want, prefer, expect*. In Chinese, such verbs cannot be followed by the perfective aspect marker *-le*. Such verbs receive a lower marking for past. An example of a token of *want* unmarked for past is given below:

T3.1. Den at dat time I got no ambition yet y'know what I *want* to become—in my future life y'know.

The third class of verbs which belong to the −R category is the conditionals. Verbs occurring in the *if* clause and the main clause receive very low marking indeed for hypotheticals. Some examples of such verbs are given below:

T15.3. (Talking about someone now deceased.) Oh! So wicked! If you *know* how she *looks* like—dat's really wicked.

P14.27. (Referring to a past habitual situation.) Waah if the wind *come* ah, more worse ah.

The non-marking of verbs for past is almost categorical in hypothetical situations if the verbs involved are those with the elements [+future] or [+stative], e.g. verbs like *want* and *intend*:

P11.1. (If) you *want* to (be) di(s)charge you must pay him money like dat lah.

P2.17. Last time you say—where go(t) bus—(If) (you) *want* to take bus—ting about fi(v)e cen(ts). You better walk lah.

A15.12. If normally like ah—tsch—if de principal *want* you to . . .

A18.8. In Hong Kong I join tour. When I reach a place, if I *intend* to go for sight-seeing, den I join a tour.

The conjunctives *when* and *if* are interchangeable in the following exemplifications. The utterances with *when* and *whenever* below can thus be considered [+hypothetical] too—an environment which favours the non-marking of verbs for past. The following habitual situations refer to the past:

P14.27. When we want to keep everyting dat time ah.

A2.19. Whenever my mum—tsch—want to see a Chinese show ah, she very—she very impatient in teaching us y'know.

A3.11. When a boy makes too much noise, he *canes* him.

Probably the strongest reason for the non-marking of hypotheticals for past is that they belong to the realm of the irrealis. Naturally, if an event has not been realized, it is difficult to conceive why it should have a [+past] form.

Secondly, in SBrE there are conditionals which express two propositions in the real world, e.g.

If you walk to the end of the road, you will see the post-office on the left.
If he works hard, he will pass.

Such conditionals express the likelihood of certain events taking place. They are more likely to be of a higher frequency than hypotheticals and consequently have an influence on the form in which the latter is expressed.

Thirdly, in Chinese there are no overt markers on the verb to show the difference between the two types of conditionals (cf. Li and Thompson 646 ff.). Meaning is derived from the context. The following is an exemplification in Chinese where both the reality and hypothetical interpretations are possible:

Rúguǒ wǒ jiàn-dào   Zhāng xiānsheng, wǒ huì bǎ zhè-běn shū   gěi   tā
if   I   see-arrive Zhang Mister   I   will BA this-CL book give 3sg

Reality: 'If I see Mr Zhang, I will give him this book.'
Imaginative hypothetical: 'If I saw Mr Zhang, I would give him this book.'

The first intepretation can occur in a context when the speaker is likely to meet Mr Zhang, e.g. at a board meeting. The hypothetical example can occur in a situation such as when Mr Zhang is abroad and is unlikely to return in time for the meeting.

9

Verbs of Movement: *Come/Go, Bring/Take, Send, Follow*, and *Fetch*

9.1 Introduction

These verbs are discusssed in the above order according to their degree of frequency. It would not have been feasible to make a quantitative investigation of the use of *come* and *go* as the number of tokens is extremely high.

With the other verbs of movement, non-standard usage is pervasive and is found in the speech of informants in all the five educational groups. As shown in Table 9.1, the number of tokens of non-standard usage is much higher at the basilectal end of the continuum. However, with verbs such as *bring* and *send*, particularly with *bring*, the almost equal number of informants with different levels of education who use these verbs in a non-standard way shows how widespread and entrenched such variant usage has become.

Non-standard use of *bring* where, prescriptively speaking, *take* should have been used, is very high—84.7%. This figure can be broken down as follows:

Tertiary	87.9%
A level	69.7%
O level	86.4%
Sec. 1–3	82.3%
Primary	95.5%

Interestingly the speech of informants with A level education often shows more standard usage than the speech of those with tertiary level education. The verb *take* has been excluded from Table 9.1 as the number of tokens is rather small.

9.2 The use of *come* and *go*

In SBrE, the use of these two words depends on the place from which the action is viewed. This place forms the point of reference and either the addressee A or the speaker S must be or intend to be at this place P. In SgE the action is frequently viewed from the position of the person who will initiate movement. The following two sentences show that this is the case:

1. *I'll *go* over to your office in five minutes and have a talk with you.
2. *We will be *going* to your house at six o'clock so please wait for us.

(Crewe 1977*b*:77)

TABLE 9.1. *Non-standard use of bring, send, follow, and fetch in Singaporean English*

	Bring		Send		Follow		Fetch	
	Tokens[a]	Informants[b]	Tokens	Informants	Tokens	Informants	Tokens	Informants
Tertiary	29	13	5	3	1	1	1	1
A level	23	12	5	4	3	2	7	2
O level	38	14	20	6	7	3	1	1
Sec. 1–3	51	15	16	5	7	6	5	5
Primary	42	13	27	6	19	8	5	1
TOTAL	183	67	73	24	37	20	19	10

[a] Number of non-standard tokens used.
[b] Number of informants who used these verbs in a non-standard way.

The actions in these sentences are viewed from the position of the speaker or the person referred to by the speaker. The first two sentences are deviant because in SBrE, the action is viewed from the position of the place relevant to the discussion which, in the above sentences, is the place where the addressee is.

Let us take a case in SBrE where S intends to be at a particular place:

3. S to A: We're thinking of *going* to the opera next week. Would you like to *come* with us?

We note that P has already been established and this forms the point of reference. Viewed from this position, the second verb should therefore be *come*, as the addressee is accompanying the speaker. In SgE, both *come* and *go* are used interchangeably although the use of *go* is of higher frequency, e.g.

4. S to A: We are *going* to the opera next week. You want to *go* with us or not?

In SBrE, when the addressee intends *not* to be at the place discussed, *go* is used:

5. S to A: We'll *go* to your house every week to water your plants while you are away in Hong Kong.

The action has now to be viewed from the position of the speaker.

Other exemplifications showing the use of *come* and *go* which depend on the position or intended position of S or A, are given below.

If S makes a phone call to London where A is, he will probably say:

6. I'm *coming* to London next week.

This is because the message is of relevance to the addressee. However if S were to tell a friend elsewhere about this coming trip to London, he would probably say:

7. I'm *going* to London next week.

Going is used because the addressee will *not* be in London. In SgE *go* is frequently used in 6 instead of *come*.

Other examples (based on Platt and Weber 1980:93–4) are:

8. S to A: Mary will be *coming* home at 6 o'clock.

Here the speaker forecasts his position at P, his home. If S does not intend to go to a particular party, he'll say to A:

9. Are you *going*[1] to Fred's party?

This is because S will not be at P. However, if S intends to be at P, his question will be rephrased:

---

[1] Platt and Weber (1980:101, 106) claim that sentence 9 'may not exactly imply with some speakers of SBrE that they will not be there'. However, sentence 10 shows more certainty of the speaker's expectations to be there than in 9.

10. Are you *coming* to the party?

Utterances 1, 2, and 4 where *go* is used in SgE clearly show the influence of Chinese deictics:

11. jīnwǎn   liù diǎn zhōng wǒ huì qù[2] nǐ   jiā
     this evening six time   I   will go   you house
     'I shall go to your house at 6 o'clock this evening.'

The use of *qù* 'go' is independent of the position of the addressee at reference time. *Qù* is used irrespective of whether the addressee intends to be at home or not at 6 o'clock.

12. jīnwǎn   wǒ yào   qù kàn diànyǐng
     this evening I   want go see movie
     nǐ   yào   bu yào   gēn wǒ yìqǐ   qù?
     you want not want with I   together go?

     'I'm going to a movie tonight. Would you like to come with me?'

In 12, when the addressee is asked to accompany the speaker, *qù* 'go' is obligatory. One can see from the above examples that the choice of *lái* 'come' and *qù* 'go' does not seem to depend on the intended position of the addressee.

9.3 The use of *bring* and *take*

Webster's Dictionary (1976) gives the following definitions:

BRING: to convey, lead, carry or cause to come along from one place to another, the direction of movement being toward the place from which the action is being regarded.

TAKE: to convey, lead, carry, remove or cause to go along to another place, the direction of movement being away from the place from which the action is regarded.

In SBrE, the position A or S intends to be at (represented by **A** and **S** respectively) is of particular importance in a discussion of *bring* and *take*. If S̄ knows that A intends to go to the party, S will probably say to A (e.g. over the phone):

1.   P **A**   I'll *bring* a bowl of curry to the party.
     ↗
   S . . . A

And S can also say to A (since S intends to be at P):

2.   **S** P   Please *bring* a plate of satay to the party.
       ↖
   S . . . A

---

[2] In some of the Chinese dialects e.g. Hokkien, Cantonese, and Hainanese, *qù* 'go' and *lái* 'come' are used interchangeably here.

S can also say to A:

3.   <u>S</u> <u>A</u> P   He'll *bring* a plate of mee siam to the party.

        S . . . A H

Bring is used because S or A or both of them intend to be at the party. Other examples include the following. Schoolboy A to schoolboy B, over the phone:

4. Don't forget to *bring* your atlas with you or Mr X will make you stand outside the class.

Bring is used because both A and B intend to be at school the next day. But the mother of B will probably say to B:

5. Don't forget to *take* your atlas with you to school.

She obviously will not be in school with him.

In SBrE, another factor has to be taken into consideration when one chooses whether to use *bring* or *take*—that is whether something is of relevance or of concern to the speaker or not, as in the following example. S and A are both going to England. A is helping S with his excess luggage. S will probably say to A:

6. Don't forget to *bring* my winter coat with you.

However, if S were merely giving A a piece of advice, he would probably say:

7. Don't forget to *take* your winter coat with you. (In other words, taking your winter coat with you is of relevance to you.)

Thus it means that although both are going to the same place, whether A takes along his winter coat with him or not is of no relevance to S. A is going to shiver in the cold, not S!

Other sentences show that when something is of concern to the speaker, i.e. when the speaker is involved in the project, *bring* is used. For instance, if both the speaker and the addressee are conducting a joint workshop in Canberra and the addressee has all the hand-outs with him, S will probably say to A:

8. Don't forget to *bring* the hand-outs with you.

Or if the success of the party depends on everybody bringing a plate, then S will say to A:

9. Don't forget to bring a plate.

Whether one is focusing on the point of arrival or departure of an entity is just as important in SBrE, for example in a situation where it has been agreed that the function will be held at X's place. Various people will bring certain foods to the party.

10. A: What about drinks?
    B: I've got some whisky. I'll *take* a bottle of whisky.

Here the speaker B had her cellar as the focus and the point of departure from the cellar was important to her. She was probably not focusing on her arrival at the party. But if the party were the focus of attention, then *bring* would have been used:

11. S to A: I gather that Jack *brought* a bottle of wine to the party?

Here the speaker is viewing the action from the setting, which is the party.

In the following illustrations from the Bible (RSV) where *bring* and *come* are used, the focus is on the temple in Jerusalem:

12. And ... they *brought* him (Jesus) up to Jerusalem to present him to the Lord. (Luke 2:22)
13. And inspired by the Spirit he (Simeon) came into the temple; and when the parents brought in the child Jesus, ... (Luke 2:27)

Given the situation mentioned earlier, it is possible for S to say to A in SgE (cf. utterances 1, 2, and 3)

15. I'll *take* a bowl of curry to the party.
16. Please *take* a plate of satay to the party.
17. He'll *take* a plate of mee siam to the party.

Other examples include:

18. We were lucky, Kok Fai's father *took* us here this morning.
19. The NTUC bus *takes* me here every day.

A possible explanation for the use of *take* in 15–19 is that the action is viewed from the position from which movement commences.

9.4 The influence of Chinese on the use of *bring* and *take* in SgE

Take and *bring* are often used interchangeably by most Singaporeans, possibly because of the influence from Chinese.

The Chinese words 拿 and 帶 (in Mandarin *ná* and *dài*, and in Hokkien *gîa/thẻh* and *tòa/chhōa*) can be used for the actions of *bringing/taking* and *bringing/taking along with*. The direction of movement in relation to the speaker and addressee is indicated by the addition of the obligatory [post]verbs *qù* in Mandarin or *khì* in Hokkien for an action away from the speaker and *lái* in Mandarin or *lâi* in Hokkien for an action towards the speaker, e.g.

拿　去 ná　qu [Mandarin] gîa/thẻh khì [Hokkien]	Take (an object) away! or Take it there! (literally Bring/take go →)
拿　來 ná　lai [Mandarin] gîa/thẻh lâi [Hokkien]	Bring (an object) here! (literally Bring/take come ←)
帶　去 dài　qu [Mandarin] tòa/chhōa khì [Hokkien]	Take (an object/a person) along with you there (literally Bring/take along with go →)

帶　來   Bring (an object/a person) along with you there (literally
dài　lai [Mandarin]   Bring/take along with come ←)
tòa/chhōa lâi [Hokkien][3]

Structures like these sometimes appear in Singaporean English, e.g.
That book on the TV, take come here.
(Father and son are sitting on the sofa and the latter is sent to fetch the book.)
Where's your drawing book? Bring come here. Let Aunty see.
(Father to five-year-old daughter, telling her to fetch her drawing book so that her
aunt can have a look at it.)
Give him bring go la!
(A nurse is speaking to the clerk who is to hand over a file to the 'tamby', the office
messenger, who is to take it to the doctor.)
We still have a lot. Take go la!
(A housewife urging a friend to take some mangoes home. There are still a lot more
ripe ones on the trees in her backyard.) (Platt, Weber, and Ho 1983*b*:159–60)

Structures with directional postverbs *go* and *come* are particularly frequent at
the basilectal end of the continuum. Educated Singaporeans use them too in
informal stituations such as in the family, with friends, at the hawker centres,
on public transport, and when talking to someone lower down the educational
scale, for example a tamby (messenger boy) or amah (maid). One token each
of such structures with *take* and *bring* was found in the speech of informants
with tertiary and A level education. Two tokens were used by informants
with O level education, while those with sec. 1–3 and primary-level education
used seven and nine tokens of such structures, respectively.

In Hokkien, the verb *chhōa* and not *gîa/thèh* must be used for an entity
which is [+animate]. This distinction is clearly seen in SgE as in the following
example:

Everyday I *bring* my son up at seven a.m. and then at six p. m. I *bring* him
down.

Mr and Mrs Ng, who live on the second floor, have fostered their two-year-
old son out to the family living on the tenth floor as both the Ngs are working.
This is the Hokkien equivalent of the above sentence:

tåk   jit chhit tiám   góa chhōa góa ê   kia^n khì lâu-téng ê-hng
everyday seven o'clock I   lead   I   GEN son go upstairs evening

låk tiám   góa chhōa i   lòh   lâi
six o'clock I   lead   he down come

The verb *chhōa* is translated into *bring* in SgE. Thus in Hokkien one can *chhōa*
'lead' one's dog for a walk. In basilectal SgE, it is unlikely that someone will
take a dog for a walk. The following two examples show that with [+animate,
−human] entities, the verb *bring* rather than *take* is used:

---

[3] The Hokkien morpheme equivalents have been added to the four examples.

TABLE 9.2. *The use of* bring *in Singaporean English*

	[+human]		[−animate]	
	Standard use	Non-standard use	Standard use	Non-standard use
Tertiary	4	22	—	7
A level	5	20	5	3
O level	—	25[a]	6	13
Sec. 1–3	1	34	10	17
Primary	—	36	2	6
TOTAL	10	137	23	46
Percentage	6.8	93.2	33.3	66.7

[a] Includes one [+animate, −human] token.

O16.22. Sometime dey *bring* deir dogs come down (from the flat).

She even *brought* their big Alsatian dog and parrot in her taxi to a vet. (*Straits Times*, 10 July 1984)

Other examples below exemplify the influence of *chhōa* used for [+animate], usually [+human] entities:

T13.4. So he *brought* me to de landlady's place.

A12.15. I'll *bring* him there.

O2.6. Dey *brought* you to dis places and let you have a look.

In Ho's corpus, the verb *bring* (216 tokens) has a far higher frequency than *take* (24 tokens). That *bring* is influenced by the verb *dài* (*chhōa* in Hokkien) is shown in the high percentage (93.2%) of non-standard use of *bring* with [+animate] entities (particularly with [+human] entities) as against 66.7% when it occurs with [−animate] entities (see Table 9.2). Table 9.3 shows the infrequent co-occurrence of *take* with [+human] entities.

Another reason for the high frequency in the use of *bring* is that many actions have the element of [+distance] which is inherent in the Chinese verb *dài* but is missing in the verb *ná*. The semantic difference in these two verbs is illustrated in the following sentences:

1. Qǐnq bǎ wǒ de zìdiǎn dài guo lai
   please BA I GEN dictionary bring over come
   'Would you please bring my dictionary over (e.g. to Australia).'
2. qǐng bǎ wǒ de zìdiǎn ná guo lai
   please BA my GEN dictionary take over come
   'Would you please pass me my dictionary.'

TABLE 9.3. *The use of* take *in Singaporean English*

	[+human]		[−animate]	
	Standard use	Non-standard use	Standard use	Non-standard use
Tertiary	2	—	—	—
A level	2	—	2	—
O level	4	—	2	1
Sec. 1–3	3	—	1	1
Primary	4	—	2	—
TOTAL	15	—	7	2
Percentage	100	—	77.8	22.2

In sentence 2, if students A and B were sitting at the same table, and student A wanted student B to hand him the dictionary, he would not use *dài* but *ná*.

The following three examples (*a*–*c*) in SgE show that the use of *take*, which is influenced by *ná*, is restricted in terms of distance:

(*a*) Teacher enters the school office:
   Can give me some batteries?
   (Please let me have some batteries)
   Girl in the office, who is very busy:
   OK, OK I take for you, I take for you
   (meaning 'I'll get them for you in a minute').

(Platt, Weber, and Ho 1983b:157)

In Chinese, the verb *ná* would have been used for *take* above. In the next illustration, a basilectal speaker expresses her dislike of having to live in an HDB flat because she has to shut the door when she leaves the flat. In the kampong (village) where she previously lived, she didn't need to do so because her neighbours would keep an eye on her house:

(*b*) *P16.10.* Then we must go inside and *take*—difficult lah! (She is referring to leaving her keys behind in the flat and the nuisance of having to break into the flat to get her keys.)

The third example:

(*c*) I must go home and *take* the present first.
   (The speaker wanted to go home and get the present before attending the birthday party.)

In contrast, the following examples show the element of distance when the verb *bring* is used with [−animate] entities:[4]

T20.14. So (she) *brought* (took along) a beautiful rug (to China).

O8.3. We usually *bring* our books along (i.e. when he is sent on an assignment overseas).

S20.13. I ask my hubby to *bring* (the food) over to my grandmother and unc(le)—uncle (i.e. to their flat).

Examples (*a*), (*b*), and (*c*) above show that the Chinese verb *ná* has rather similar features to the verb *get* in English. Sometimes the lack of distinction between *get* and *take* can lead to confusion, as seen in the example below:

A to B: I'll *take* the milk for you.

In SgE this means 'I'll get it for you'. In SBrE, since *take* indicates an action away from the speaker, it means that A will do B a favour by taking the milk away to another place. Similarly,

A20.7. We ask back. We have to *take* dem *back*. (Referring to some passengers on the plane who had taken some spoons and forks.)

This can be interpreted in SBrE as 'to take the cutlery away to another destination', when in fact the informant meant that she had to *get* the cutlery *back* from the passengers.

In addition to the meaning 'direction away from a place', the verb *take* in SBrE has the meaning 'to borrow or use without asking permission or by mistake', as in the following examples:

Someone *took* my hat by mistake so I had to wear theirs home.
If you *take* things without asking the owner's permission you're a thief. (*LDOCE*)

In fact informant T20 in

T20.7. If dey (the passengers) take one teaspoon or so . . .

used *take* meaning 'to steal'. However, the following examples do not have the same connotation of taking things without permission:

S6.32. I *take*, I *take* the books from my brothers and sister (I get the books from them).

S8.24. I just *take* (choose the vegetables) and den dey (the vendors) will weigh it.

P9.10. You can help yourself ah, *take take*.
'You should go and get yourself a plaster.'

P19.1. *take* soft roll(s) (get the soft rolls and lay them on the trays).

---

[4] In the whole corpus there are only two tokens with [−animate] entities where distance is not involved and *bring* is used.

Besides interference from Chinese, the use of *take* may be the result of overgeneralization from the target language as shown in the examples below:

'Please *take* a handout on your way out of the lecture theatre.'

'*Take* one' (e.g. a sign over a box of leaflets telling passers-by to help themselves to the leaflets).

9.5 The use of *send* in SgE

Send has been defined as 'to cause to go or be taken to a place' (*LDOCE*), i.e. the movement is away from the speaker. This semantic feature is common to both SBrE and SgE. However, the sender does not accompany the entity X. If the entity is [+human], the sender must always be in a higher role relationship, and the verb *send* has the meaning of instructing somebody to go somewhere (Platt, Weber, and Ho 1983*b*:158). The following examples illustrate this:

I'll *send* you to bed if you don't stop crying.

Could you *send* Miss Brown to the bank to cash the cheques?

As the role relationship is not important in SgE, the following utterance is possible:

Grandson to grandpa: 'I'll *send* you home now.'

This is considered very polite in SgE as the grandson has kindly offered to give grandpa a lift home in his car. Other examples to show that the sender can be on an equal relationship with the persons *sent* include:

I'm passing that way so I'll send you home. (Friend to friend, meaning 'I'll give you a lift home.')

I can *send* you to church in my car tomorrow morning if you like. (Host to guest: 'I'll give you a lift to church.')

As previously mentioned, in SgE when *send* is used it implies accompaniment by the sender. The following are examples where the entity is [+human]:

T4.4. But if when de school starts, I'm force(d) to *send* my children to school early (to take my children to school).

A15.1. You have some ah—friends—I mean—so call(ed) sisters to go—to go *send* you *off* (i.e. her friends will accompany her in other cars to the bridegroom's place).

In SgE, the sender can also accompany a [−animate] entity back:

O6.3. (If) the tools break down dey want you to go down—collect *send* back for repair (i.e. take the tools back for repair).

The influence of the Chinese verb *sòng* in Mandarin or *sàng* in Hokkien is very strong. The use of *sòng* includes accompaniment by the sender or another person. The role relationship when *sòng* is used is also unimportant. *Sòng* can also mean *deliver*. Hence in the examples given below when goods are referred to, *send* is used instead of *deliver*:

S6.26. Some Indian sho(ps) lah, we *send—send* to dem lah. (We deliver potatoes and onions to the shops.)

P6.13. We all—go—go to PSA then load the tongkang (bumboat) then we all go, go and *sang* (send) one. (We deliver the goods to various places.)

The fact that the pronunciation of *sàng* is fairly close to *send* may have influenced the widespread use of *send* as a substitute for *sàng*. In the example cited above, informant P6 actually used the velar instead of the alveolar nasal in final position. The verb *deliver* does occur in SgE but *send* is used more frequently to replace *deliver*. There were 13 tokens of *send* (all of which were found in the primary and sec. 1–3 groups) where *deliver* would have been used in SBrE.

The verbs *send, fetch, take,* and *bring* can all have an inanimate subject. In SBrE only the latter two verbs can have an inanimate subject:

The bus will *take* you there or the bus will *bring* you here.

One cannot say in SBrE:

The ferry will fetch you there (to the island)

or

O18.9. De boat *send* us back to Singapore (the boat took us back from Pulau Tekong to the main island of Singapore).

The use of an inanimate noun as the subject of *send* is also found in written SgE:

It was learnt that the buses were *sending* the workers to the factory when the mishap occurred. (From *Straits Times*, quoted in Leslie 1981:80)

In SBrE, these sentences can be intepreted, absurdly, as the boat instructing the informant and her friends to go back to Singapore and, likewise, the buses telling the workers to go to the factories.

Where all the features of a Chinese verb are the same as those of the English verb *send*, the use of *send* in SgE is similar to that in SBrE. The Chinese verbs are *sòng* (used in expressions like *sending* children to certain schools), *jì* (used for *sending* letters and parcels), and *pài* (used by persons in authority, e.g. the government of a country, a school, a government department such as the Ministry of Education, a company, for *sending* someone somewhere).

9.6 The use of *follow* in SgE

In SBrE the verb *follow* means 'to move behind in the same direction'. In SgE the verb *follow* can mean 'to accompany someone or to go along with someone'. The examples given below show this semantic difference between SBrE and SgE. Besides *following* a person, e.g.

S1.10. I *follow* her to de police station.
　　'I went with her to the police station.'

one can also *follow* a coach in SgE:

T12.4. I *followed* a coach tour.
　　'I went on a conducted tour by coach.'

Such constructions show a close resemblance to the local Chinese dialects, for example, Hokkien:

　　góa tè　　i　　khì (Hokkien)
　　I　follow 3sg go
　　'I went along with him/her.'

Another possible influence for such usage is the extended meaning of *follow* in SBrE, where *follow* can mean 'to go in the same direction as or continue along' (*LDOCE*):

　　The railway line *follows* the river for several miles.
　　Follow the road until you come to the hotel.

Informant P7 has a token which is similar to SBrE usage:

P7.7. You just *follow* de track and run lah.

There is also the biblical use of *follow*, which is another possible influence; the follower in Luke 9:57 (RSV) decided to go along with Jesus when he said:

　　'I will *follow* you wherever you go.'

Thus in educated SgE, there are utterances like

　　My husband is going to Canada for further studies so I'll resign from my job and *follow* him.

This does not mean that she is walking behind her husband or is joining him later, as the SBrE interpretation of this sentence would suggest, but that she is accompanying him.

9.7 The use of *fetch* in SgE

In SBrE there seems to be a sliding scale and 'fetch' co-occurs in the following manner with:

　　1. *Inanimates*
　　　　Master to dog:
　　　　Fetch the bone!
　　2. *Non-humans*
　　　　He has to *fetch* the cows in for milking.

3. *Humans in a lower role relationship*
   Mother to daughter:
   Go and *fetch* little Aggie for me.
   Boss to a junior clerk:
   Go to the second floor and *fetch* Mr Smith (the accountant) for me.
4. *Humans of similar role relationship*
   I've to *fetch* Doris from the airport.
5. *Humans of higher role relationship*
   Branch manager to chauffeur:
   Please go and *fetch* Mr Wong (the Director) who is arriving this afternoon
   from Hong Kong.

In SgE fetching [+animate] entities is more common than fetching
[−animate] entities. In Ho's corpus all tokens of *fetch* co-occur with
[+human] entities. This is not surprising as *fetch* is another substitute for the
Hokkien word *chhōa*, which is used only for [+animate] entities. In SBrE,
when *fetch* is used with [+human] entities, the role relationship is very
important. The person fetched is generally in a lower role relationship and the
person who is to fetch, i.e. the addressee, is usually in a lower relationship too,
as seen in the examples given in 3 above. The usage exemplified in 5 is less
common.

In SgE, one can fetch anybody as the role relationship is not important.
Thus, for example, a teacher can say to a student:

Everything is ready now. Can you fetch the principal here?

This use of *fetch* would be considered rude in SBrE.

Fetch in SBrE is a bi-directional verb. Except for 3 tokens which show
bi-directionality, all the other 19 tokens used by 10 informants show uni-
directional movements with the verb *fetch*. Some non-standard examples
include the following:

T4.4. Like my taichi I stop temporary, because school holidays—right?
School holidays so—I don't have to *fetch* my son, my children to school,—
so I don't go taichi y'see.
A17.17. And he wanted to—me—to *fetch* (take) me to his house.

Sometimes *fetch* involves movement from one point to various other points:

A2.18. Why you want dem de family, de male family (the bridegroom's family)
to go and *fetch* you (the relatives) here and dere. (A → B → C → D)
A2.18. always during marriages ah, she will ask us to go *fetch* dem (the
relatives) dere (the restaurant) and *fetch* dem home. (A → B ⇔ C)
S20.10.—come home—de—de husband will *fetch* (my daughter) home for
me lah. (After work her neighbour's husband will go from his office to her
daughter's school to pick her up and take her home.) (A → B → C)

The following token is an unusual one:

O6.16. Of course the ferry will have to *fetch* you over.

It is classified as a non-standard token showing uni-directional movement as the ferry service starts from Jardine's Steps, waiting to take passengers across to Sentosa. If the token were considered as expressing bi-directional movement, then in SBrE (i.e. if we think of a case where a very rich man owns a boat and is living on an island) it would have to be rephrased as:

'I'll send my boat over to *fetch* you to-night.'

10

The Repetition of Verbs in Singaporean English

10.1 Introduction

The use of verbal repetition is a particularly interesting feature of Singaporean English. Ho has divided this repetition into six categories:

I Verbal repetition where a verb may be uttered twice or a few times, e.g. *blink blink, wait wait wait,* etc.

II Verbal repetition with *and,* e.g. *calculate and calculate.*

III Repetition of phrases, e.g. *quickly learn quickly learn, sell finish take again sell finish take again,* etc.

IV Repetition of phrases with *this/that, here/there, up/down,* e.g. *buy this buy that, look here look there, run here run there.*

V Onomatopoeic reduplication.

VI Repetition to show emphasis in SgE, where very often in SBrE stress and intonation would be used.

Table 10.1 shows the number of informants who used repetition of verbs (Types I to IV) and the frequency of such repetitions according to the educational attainment of the informants.

As shown in Table 10.1, most verbal repetitions fall under Type I. Altogether there were 63 tokens used by 33 of the informants. As expected, more informants with primary, sec. 1–3, and O level education used this type of verbal repetition than those with A level and tertiary education. Interestingly, there were 11 tokens in the tertiary group compared with 4 tokens in the A level group. It could be that those at the top were less careful and prescriptive than those at the level below. A parallel is seen in the hypercorrect behaviour of Labov's Lower Middle Class in New York.

There were only 12 tokens of verbal repetitions with *and* used by 11 informants. Notice that acrolectal speakers used this structure more than basilectal speakers. It is claimed that in many native varieties of English, verbal repetition with *and,* e.g. *he worked and worked,* is probably more frequently used than just repetition of the verb. More informants with primary and sec. 1–3 education used repetition of phrases (including phrases with *this/that, here/there, up/down*) than those with A level and tertiary education.

TABLE 10.1. *Number of informants who used repetition of verbs Types I to IV and frequency of such repetitions according to the educational attainment of the informants*

	I		II		III		IV	
	Informants	Tokens	Informants	Tokens	Informants	Tokens	Informants	Tokens
Tertiary	5	11	4	5	2	3	2	2
A level	4	4	1	1	1	1	—	—
O level	8	9	2	2	3	5	—	—
Sec. 1–3	8	22	1	1	1	1	5	5
Primary	8	17	3	3	4	4	1	3
TOTAL	33	63	11	12	11	14	8	10

10.2 Verbal repetition according to the number of times a verb is repeated

Table 10.2 shows the frequency of Type I verbal repetitions according to the educational attainment of the informants.

As can be seen from the table, twofold and threefold verbal repetitions have the highest number of tokens. Exemplifications of twofold verbal repetitions are as follows:

S20.10. ... change her—*wipe wipe* her up firs(t) lah. 'When my little daughter returns from school, I wipe her body quickly with a damp towel, and give her a change of clothes.'

A14.3. If you look clearly y'know sometime(s) dey *blin(k) blin(k)* deir eyes— 'know de kind of fearing atmosphere.
   'The eyes of the statues seemed to blink at you.'

S7.28. ... or make de lion nose itch, he can'(t) *scratch scratch* like dat lah.
   'The lion is unable to scratch its nose.'

Each of these utterances manages to give a visual impact of the situation; *blink blink*, for example, captures the physical sensation of the eyes blinking. The reduplicated verbs are said quickly with little or no pause, and show the rapidity and brevity of the actions.

The use of repetition without the conjunction *and* shows the influence of Chinese where verbs are reduplicated to give a vivid effect:

   Tiānkōng zhōng   diànguāng shánshan
   sky   middle lightning   flash flash
   'Lightning flashed in the sky.'

Repetition can also have an iterative function:

P19.4. Everytime see you *quarrel quarrel* each other—not nice lah.
   'You are always quarrelling. This is most unpleasant.'

TABLE 10.2. *Frequency of Type I verbal repetitions accord-ing to the educational attainment of the informants*

	Number of repetitions of verb			
	2	3	4	5
Tertiary	4	7	—	—
A level	3	—	1	—
O level	6	3	—	—
Sec. 1–3	11	8	2	1
Primary	10	7	—	—
TOTAL	34	25	3	1

P12.7. Yah everytime pushing ah, everytime dey *push push*—to work.
'They kept on pushing us to work harder.'

P7.21. Some people *delay delay* no house no house. Where I expec(t) to stay at the roadside. (The squatters kept on putting off shifting to new premises, giving the excuse that they had not been able to find a house.)

Repetition is often used in Chinese to convey an air of informality and casualness. Verbs which are uttered twice in SgE seem to share a similar function:

S10.16. (What she does when she is free.) Shopping [ɔ:] (particle). Den bring along my all dose nephew dey all go *walk walk*.
'When I'm free I go shopping and I often take my nephews out just to have a look around.'

S14.4. I like to sing, I like to draw, I like to *walk walk* around, like to see shows, like to see TV, like to see books.

P11.24. (In response to a question about what he does at the Katong Shopping Centre.) Nothing ah, *walk walk*, *see see*, see—aah what type of shirt lah, trousers.

In Mandarin as well as the Chinese dialects, when you are looking at a specific thing, the verb is not repeated. The following Hokkien examples are from Bodman (1955:118):

> guà bèq chhût khì khuǎ
> I   want out   go see   (our gloss)
> 'I'll go out to look' (implying looking at a specific thing).

However, when one is referring to things in general, the verb is reduplicated:

> guà bèq chût khì khuà khuǎ
> I   want to   go see see   (our gloss)
> 'I'll go out to take a look' (indeterminate and casual).

> guà bèq chût khì kiā kiá khuà khuǎ
> I   want out go walk walk see see   (our gloss)
> 'I'm going out to do some walking around and sightseeing.'

One of the verbal aspects in Chinese discussed by Chao (1968:204) is the tentative aspect:

An action repeated in the neutral tone can be regarded as one of its aspects, along with its progressive aspect, perfective aspect, and so on. Thus, *kannj* 'looking', *kannle* 'looked', *kann. kann* 'just look'. This last form, however, is connected with the syntactic construction of verb plus cognate object: *kann i-tsyh* 'look once', *kann₀yi₀kann* 'take a look', whence *kann.kann* 'just look'.

A number of sentences in the corpus reflect the idea of *just plus verb*, e.g.

P9.15. ... dey all *play play* only lah. Disturb a bit ah.
'I just joked with the girls a bit.'
P9.24. ... a(s) long you cleang for him—*cleang cleang* (clean) only.
'As long as you clean the milk can for him—just give it a rinse.' (Note that in colloquial SgE, *only* has the same function as *just*.)
P11.33. This one for *play play* (pray) de [ɪɒʔ] (god) one lah.
'The sugar cane is really just used as an offering to the gods.'

Exemplifications of verbal repetitions where the verb is repeated three times are given below. A dramatic effect is achieved by repetition:

P14.19. ... So you *do do do*, then wait—tsch—very hard lah. (This repetition manages to capture the working of the sewing machine as its needle moves furiously along.)
P18.15. Dey do—do gun. *Do do do*. (This repetition shows the informant's son at play, joining up the pieces of Lego and pretending it was a gun.)
T5.3. You *type type type* den you stop. (The iterative use of *type* gives the effect of the typist hitting away at the keyboard.)
T4.9. She was always pestering my y'know to *look look look* for (a house). (The iterative use of *look* shows the informant and his wife making various visits to different places to look for a suitable house.)
T17.6. In the studio all we did was—*design design design*. (Showing the architects hard at work, i.e. they kept on designing.)

In SBrE, instead of repeating the verb, adverbial phrases or additional verbs are more likely to be used:

> looked all over the place for a house
> typing away full blast
> all we did was—keep on designing.

In SBrE, repetition is usually only with monosyllabic words, as in *We worked, worked, worked—until dawn*. When a verb is repeated, there is often the suggestion of something boring, monotonous, and excessive. However, in SgE it is possible to have repetitions of disyllabic words or even trisyllabic words such as *calculate* and *underline*. The action need not necessarily be a boring one, as shown by the use of *design* above.

Perhaps the main difference between the use of repetition in SgE and SBrE is that in the latter it is more frequently used to show a sense of weariness, annoyance, or irritation. In the former, while repetiton can capture the emotions of a speaker, one of its main functions is to achieve vivid dramatic effects. The following SgE repetitions, which show the speaker or the person concerned engaged in active thinking, are not possible in SBrE:

T4.10. So she's—*ting ting*—'Yah!' she says, 'I got a client y'see I'm looking after the house for dem, looking for tenan(t) ...'

O12.8. Then later, I *ting ting*. Eh, maybe is you call up you know.
P19.16. And I was tingkings, sit down *ting ting ting*, over over again.

Verbs which are repeated four or five times are infrequent. They are used to highlight the action. For example:

S10.6. Some they *choose choose choose choose*. From here *choose choose choose choose choose* from—choose the whole (al)ready ah—whole shop already choose one. After a while he said, "Don(t) wan(t) already!" Wah! damn bang boy!

Here the speaker shows the customer picking up a spectacle frame and putting it down and then picking up another one and so on—this went on for a long time. The next example is similar:

S10.23. And den wear dose er ribbon ah, cororing (coloured) one 'know. Our school not allowed what. Only blue colour allowed. Dey don't care. Dey just *tie tie tie tie* like dat.

There is the suggestion that the girls flouted the school regulations and went on and on using coloured ribbons to tie up their hair. It also gives the idea that a number of girls did that—this girl did it, that girl did it, yet another did it too.

In SBrE, a verb is marked for tense even if it is repeated. In SgE, marking a repeated verb for tense is infrequent. Only one informant marked the last verb in a threefold verbal repetition for third person singular:

S14.9. ten rulers 'know—*bit bit bits* (beat) on your han(d) know.

It is noticed that in SgE *and* can be added after a verb has been repeated, e.g.

A13.4. the spirit is there y'know, you just *work work and work* harder and harder.
O18.2. She keeps *bargaining bargaining and bargain* lah.
S10.24. Stay back *sing sing and sing*, and sing sing sing until seven o'clock.

Sometimes a verb can be repeated after a repetition with and:

P19.16. the child *cry and cry cry cry*—I cannot sleep at night.

It is interesting that SgE does not take on all the features of Chinese. For example it is not possible to say in SgE:

*He wants to *see one see* that house.

In Chinese when a monosyllabic verb is used reduplicatively, the word *yī* 'one' can be inserted between the repeated verbs:

wǒ xiǎng kàn yī   kàn nèi-jiān wūzi[1]
I   want see one see that-CL house
'I'd like to have a look at that house.'

In SgE one can say:

I want to see see that house again before making a decision.

SgE does not follow Chinese rules strictly but at times creates its own. For example, in Chinese only the verb and not the object can be reduplicated in constructions like:

kàn kan shū
see see book
'Read books'

In SgE it is sometimes possible to repeat the object:

S1.11. So he get jealously 'know, always poke *fire fire fire fire.* (She got jealous and always caused trouble.)

10.3 Verbal repetition with *and*

In British English, reduplication with *and* is quite common e.g.

He *worked and worked and worked.*
He stood at the counter and *stamped and stamped* away (stamping books).

In SBrE, the repetition is slower and the verb is marked for tense, or number. In the corpus, only two informants made an attempt to mark the verb:

T5.5. and the rest of the time he just *reads and read and read and read* . . .
T19.8. Den we *walk and walk and walked*—walked until—we could find one.

Note that in each utterance only one of the repeated verbs has been marked for tense.

There are two non-standard repetitions with *and*:

P18.20. Don't *keep and keep and keep* . . .
S7.28. Make *join and join* . . .

Keep cannot be repeated in SBrE as *keep* refers to a continuous state. However, one can say *to keep something for a long time. Make join* means 'to cause to be joined up'.

---

[1] In Standard Mandarin,   yì-jiān   wūzi
                              one-CL room

refers to a room, while   yì-suǒ   fángzi
                          one-CL house

refers to a house. In Singapore Mandarin there is often no distinction between the two. It is more common, however, to refer to a house as *wūzi*.

10.4 Repetition of phrases

Reduplicated phrases show the repetition of actions, e.g.

O12.9. Every now and then you have to *read books read books* (keep on reading books).

O15.3. Dey always *come back come back*, and they recommend ah friends to come and buy lah.

They also give a sense of urgency:

T18.8. you just want to *fast and pray fast and pray* until your prayer is answered . . .

and a sense of immediacy:

T18.9. Let us *lay hands on you, lay hands on you, lay hands* until you speak in tongues and how do you know whether dis is gibberish or not y'know.

In SBrE an adverbial phrase and the phrase *kept on* are more likely to be used instead of repetition:

We *kept on* praying and fasting *all the time.*
They *kept on* laying their hands on you.

Sometimes in SgE new verbs are coined and repeated:

O16.22. Dat's why we just keep quiet lah. *We friend we friend.* 'We continued to be her friend.'

Sometimes word order is changed in the verb phrase and this clearly shows the influence of Chinese:

A2.19. She very impatient in teaching us y'know—said 'Quickly learn quickly learn!'

10.5 Repetition of phrases with *this/that, here/there, up/down*

In SBrE it is common to hear expressions like:

I looked here, there, and everywhere.
I looked here and there.

Very often in SgE, the whole phrase is repeated:

T13.6. I want this I want that

Sometimes the subject is deleted:

T18.4. And I open up de—ah—de bonnet and *I look( ) here, (I) look( ) dere,* check my (c)ompression.

P9.7. (Referring to his safety boots which were badly corroded but the foreman said that he could not have them changed until he had worn them

for 9 months.) You walk also like old man like dat waah—*(you) walk here,
(you) walk dere* can't walk quick—like—you scared fall down or what. (As
you move from place to place you are afraid to walk quickly, in case you fall
down because of the badly damaged boots.)

This sort of structure reflects Chinese syntax:

tā   pǎo lai   pǎo qu
3sg run come run go
'S/He ran here and there.'

tā   zǒu shang zǒu xia
3sg walk up   walk down
'S/He walked up and down.'

In SBrE it is probably less likely that repetition would be used. Instead, the
verb phrase is more likely to be a structure such as. *V* + [*demonstrative/
adverbial*] + *and* + [*demonstrative/adverbial*]

The following are exemplifications from SgE with the SBrE equivalent of
the repetition in brackets:

T13.6. I can't keep pestering, say y'know 'I want—I *want dis I want dat* ('I
want this and that') you see.'

S6.22. Because my house dere, dere a lot of spaces to hide 'know. Because he
can *enter from here, enter from dere* (enter from here and there). So de police
enter front, de front, de—all de boys run from de back, see.

S15.7. . . . everytime *walk up walk down* ('walk up and down') also de same.

S16.21. Dis (referring to the chef's hat) is for operational staff who *run here
run dere* ('run here and there') to get tings ready for de offloading.

S20.15. My kids you, dey went to emporium or Yaohan or what ah, touch dis
touch dat ('touch this and that'). But dey din ask to buy. Dey din—dey just
see y'know.

10.6 Onomatopoeic reduplication

In Chinese, onomatopoeic reduplication such as the following is common:

pùtōng pùtōng
splash splash.

Two tokens of such reduplication are found in the corpus:

T15.10. He was a very good lecturer and he was—he has dis very powerful
voice Oxford accent y'know so de girls just *woo woo* (swooned) over him.

P18.25. If not mah-jong then lau gau, then [lɒʔlɒʔlɒʔ] (rattling sounds)—
also can play money lah. Also gamble lah. ([lɒʔlɒʔlɒʔ] captures the
rattling of the dice before they are thrown.)

10.7 Repetition to show emphasis in SgE, where very often in SBrE stress and intonation would be used

Some of the repetition showing emphasis is similar to that used by SBrE except that in SgE the repetition is much faster, e.g.

A16.18. I: They don't bargain at all?
　　　　 J: They bargain, they do bargain.
A11.6.　I: What about the Pre-U students. They don't join the X group?
　　　　 J: No, they do they do.

In British English *do* in *they do they do* will be said with a proclaiming tone (i.e. rise and fall) but in SgE it is said with a level tone. Similarly, *do* will have a rise fall tone to show emphasis. It is said with a level tone in SgE.

Sometimes phrases are repeated quickly to show emphasis:

A6.11. I: Did you study Malay at all?
　　　　 J: Yah I *studied I studied*—up to Sec two.

In SBrE *studied* would either be said once with stress, or when the verb is repeated, *did* would be added, e.g.

Yes, I *studied* Malay, I *did* study Malay up to secondary two.

In the example below the same level tone is used by the informant to emphasize the fact that he has hobbies.

A16.9. Ah *I have I have*. I use to collect stamps.

In SBrE A16.9 would be rephrased as:

Yes I *have* hobbies.

or

Yes I *have* hobbies, I *do* have hobbies (said with a proclaiming tone for *have* and *do*).

Similarly A6.10 in SBrE will have a rise fall on *see* and *know*. It is most probable that only one *see* and one *know* would be used.

A6.10. I: How about markets? What would you use there?
　　　　 J: Are you referring to dose ah?
　　　　 I: Not the supermarkets you know . . .
　　　　 J: I *see I see I know I know*.

Other examples showing an emphatic use of repetition include the following:

P4.4. I: Do you have to pay anything to get into the CBD (Central Business District)?
　　　　 J: No need no need
　　　　 I: Four dollars?

J: Pay aah—the four dollar ah yah yah *must pay must pay. Enter no need already* lah, *enter no need already*. Enter the restricted zone *no need already*.

In SBrE if it is a single utterance either the stress will be on *must*:

Yes, you *must* pay;

or, if the verb is repeated, the second utterance has to be worded differently:

Yes you *must* pay, you *do have* to pay.

'Enter no need already . . .' would have to be rephrased in British English as:

If you have already entered the CBD, you *don't need* to pay again. No, you *don't have* to pay.

Other constructions which are similar to British usage include the following:

T13.4. I just *cry, cry* the whole day (note that there is a pause after the first cry).

Syntactically, the above utterance, as well as T19.2 and A10.5 given below are fairly close to SBrE except that the verbs are unmarked for past, although there is reference to the past:

T19.2. And—and *rus* ah, *rush* all the way we—by train and we reach dere.

A10.5. We went on tour—mainly on South Island just to—y'know—walk, *walk* around to see de country.

There is also repetition as an afterthought which is similar to British usage:

O19.13. dey pick you know—my unopen brandy, my unopen whisky. All the other things that were half open *dey din take* you know. Dat, *dey din take*. (Referring to what the burglars took away with them when the informant and her family were away on holiday.)

T14.10. So normally we *take turn*. De library officer will *take turn* in the first place. Every month we change the display.

Sometimes an afterthought can be expressed quite differently from British English, e.g.

S14.19. Then my brother help my sister cook, cook also.

In SBrE it would be expressed differently:

Then my brother helps my sister to cook—mmm, yes he does.

with a rise fall on *does*.

11

Quantitative Investigations and Second Language Acquisition

11.1 Noun plural marking

Data on noun plural and third person singular marking (Platt 1977a, Ho 1981, Wolfram 1969) seem to point to the importance of semantic-syntactic relationships. The research carried out for all three works found third person singular marking to be lower than noun plural marking. As there is no obvious special relationship between third person singular subjects and the verb as compared with the relationship between other possible subjects and the verb, marking is naturally less quickly internalized. Furthermore, there is no distinct marking of third person singular for modal verbs or for past tense (*be*, of course, has separate forms for singular and plural: *was* and *were*). The importance of semantic-syntactic environments for the SgE noun plural data has been discussed in Chapter 4. In general, with the New Englishes, investigations have shown that noun plural marking is higher when nouns are preceded by quantifiers than when not. One cannot overemphasize the value of quantitative data: the ordering of environments in terms of difficulty of acquisition of a variable and the ordering of data by means of implicational scaling for any linguistic variable(s) can certainly provide much-needed insights and short cuts in the teaching/learning processes (Platt 1976).

11.2 *Be* insertion and omission

It is apparent from Ho's investigation that whereas the preceding environment influencing the omission or insertion of *be* is largely a phonetic one, that influencing the following environment is a semantic-syntactic one, showing an undeniable influence from Chinese.

The omission of *be* in the various syntactic environments is also found in Ho W. K.'s (1972) investigation of the written work of Chinese-stream students. The omission of *be* is a feature found in the written compositions of English-stream Chinese students as well.

To recapitulate, two of the most difficult environments are *be* + *Adj* and *be* + *V-ing*. The percentage omission of *be* for both environments is about the same. For the *be* + *Adj* environment, it is to be noticed that in Chinese, adjectives are stative verbs and hence *be* is omitted. Secondly, in Chinese,

FIG. 11.1 The production of non-standard structures as a result of interactions among verb forms (*Source*: George 1971:277)

modifiers such as *very, not, also,* etc. are obligatory if no contrast is intended. SgE has a large number of such modifiers. These modifiers act as elements of emphasis. If they are omitted, then a particle is often found in phrase or sentence final position. This particle acts as a completive marker. It is found that contraction does occur with pronouns, e.g. *he, she, I,* preceding *be.* If more emphasis were given to the teaching of contraction and secondary stress put on such pronouns, then *he's, she's,* and *I'm* could gradually be internalized as single lexical units. This is a suggestion that may help weaker learners to remember the use of *be* with adjectives.

George (1971:276) comments that when language items are introduced in the classroom 'regardless of their frequency of occurrence in ordinary English, interactions among the forms are predictable', resulting in the production of non-standard structures. This is shown in Fig. 11.1.

Ho W. K. (1972:88, 104) gives instances of such structures in the written English of Singaporean students:

the students *are study* at night.
One *is work* in Jurong.
she just *staring* at me for a long time.
Every morning and evening I *watering* all the plants.

Naturally such forms are also reinforced by L1 syntax. As George (1971) suggests, presentation of *be + V-ing* forms as 'predicative adjuncts to the sentence subject' may help the mastery of standard *be + V-ing* structures. Likewise, presentation of passives can be shown in the same way:

```
              sad
       is
She          crying
       was
              trained
```

(adapted from George 1971:277)

However, as *be* tends to be omitted in the environment preceding adjectives, it is best to present the contracted or reduced forms first. The contracted form is certainly less jerky in rhythm and less formal and is what is normally used in speech in native varieties. The full forms of *be* can be taught later. Attention should be given to the teaching of contracted forms such as *they're* and *we're* as well. Emphasis should also be given to the teaching of liaison with nouns ending in an alveolar fricative, in preceding environments, where omission of *be* is high.

Implicational scaling is beneficial for pedagogical purposes since it shows the order of acquisition of *be* in preceding and following environments. Since *be + Nom* is acquired before *be + Adj* and *be + V-ing*, it should be taught first before teaching the latter two structures.

11.3 Past tense marking

11.3.1 The bioprogram versus mother tongue interference and L2 influence

Bickerton's hypothesis of a bioprogram grammar in the human species certainly has far-reaching implications for second language or non-primary acquisition of language. Among the important distinctions made are those between state and process, punctual and non-punctual, specific and non-specific referents, and causative and non-causative.

To what extent is the interlanguage of the L2 learner influenced by the bioprogram and by L1? Are the interactions of both factors equally important in the acquisition process? These are questions which Bickerton poses when he gives possible examples of sentences which might be produced by Spanish-speaking learners of English:

an English sentence such as *For many years he lived in Pennsylvania but he studied French in Montreal* would be rendered as *Vivía en Pennsylvania durante muchos años pero estudiaba el francés en Montreal* rather than **Vivió en Pennsylvania durante muchos años pero estudió el francés en Montreal.* If a Spanish-speaking learner of English then produces **For many years he was living in Pennsylvania but he was studying French in Montreal*, are we to assume that this is due to first-language interference or to continuing influence from the bioprogram, or to a mixture of the two? (Bickerton 1984*b*:155)

Bickerton then cites an example which runs counter to the bioprogram and shows the strong influence of the mother tongue:

In the course of nonprimary acquisition of English, native speakers of Hindi frequently make mistakes such as **I am liking it* or **He is wanting to see you* (Gordon Fairbanks, p.c.). Use of nonpunctuals with statives is a bioprogram as well as an English violation; Hindi speakers apparently commit it because in Hindi imperfective marking can be used with statives. (Bickerton 1984*b*:155–6)

It is true that the background language could have an influence on the use of such structures. However, as shown in Platt, Weber and Ho (1984:73) there are other influences at work too, such as overteaching of the *-ing* form in school, and there is also the extended use of *-ing* constructions in the established varieties of English:

I'm having a good time.
She's having her breakfast now. Please call back later.

Such usage has led to overgeneralization by Singaporean learners of English. The following are common expressions in SgE:

I'm having a running nose.
At present I'm having a house with four rooms.

However, in general, the state–process distinction holds for Singaporean Chinese learners of English. This is, of course, also explained by the fact that the progressive marker is incompatible with statives in Chinese.

With regard to the punctual–non-punctual distinction, empirical evidence as tabulated in Table 11.1 shows that both influences—the bioprogram and L1 background language of the learners of English—are important.

Andersen (1984:84–90) refers to findings by Kumpf and Flashner. The former's investigation of the English IL (Interlanguage) of a Spanish and a Japanese speaker reveals that a zero-ING opposition is used to encode perfective–imperfective distinctions while the latter's research on the English of three Russian speakers shows a PAST–zero opposition.

In the following written text (an account of the past, as the writer's parents had since then been separated) by a Navajo Indian, Bartelt shows the use of the non-past forms to express the Navajo usitative mode, a mode denoting [+habitual] actions. The past tense is used to denote the perfective mode:

She never wanted to get married, because it was a lot of problems, for them to stay together. Beside the problem they had was my dad drink a lot. when he comes home drunk. He always starts fighting with my mother. which we didn't like at all. He never comes back, when he goes to town. My dad stays out in town for a week or two weeks. We all get worried about him. Instead, he comes back all drunk which we don't like. And finally she couldn't put up with him. The reason why she gave up was because he

TABLE 11.1. *How punctual and non-punctual events with past reference are encoded by learners of English with different background languages*

L1 of informants	Researcher	Punctual events	Non-punctual events
Group I			
Spanish	Kumpf	0	-ING
Japanese	Kumpf	0	-ING
Group II			
Russian	Flashner	PAST	0
Navajo and Western Apache	Bartelt	PAST	0
Chinese	Ho	PAST	0

was too mean to her. He didn't want my mother to spend time with us kids when we want something he doesn't buy it for us. The part that got mom really mad was when he didn't let her go to the store and get something to eat. he always hit us kids around for no reason. Probably we get on his nerves. (Bartelt 1982:201–2)

The marking of non-punctual habitual actions for third person singular, instead of past, a feature found in SgE, is also present in the same text.

Table 11.1 shows the way past events are marked according to two semantic categories by informants with different background languages. The evidence given in the table shows aspect rather than tense morphology. Clearly the informants are marking verbs according to semantic categories— perfective–imperfective, or in Bickerton's terminology, punctual–non-punctual.

In the Singapore context, the semantic factor has tremendous weight, so much so that non-marking for past is extended to pre-verbal markers. Thus *be* in *be + stem* is often not marked for past, mainly in the environment of statives and habituals.

11.3.2 Pedagogical implications

From Table 11.1 it may be seen that learners of English whose L1 is Russian, Navajo, Western Apache, and Chinese (i.e. those in Group II) tend to mark punctual events with past forms. Those whose L1 is Spanish or Japanese (Group I) tend to use the non-past forms. It would be interesting to see what a longitudinal study of English language acquisition by speakers of Spanish and Japanese revealed—whether punctual verbs are better marked than non-punctual ones for past.

For the learners in Group II, where it is overwhelmingly clear that punctual verbs are better marked for past than non-punctual verbs, it is important that this distinction should be borne in mind in the planning and designing of instructional programmes. Special emphasis should be given to the teaching of past tense marking in non-punctual contexts.

One should also remember positive and negative transfer from L1 and interference from L2. For the Chinese learner of English, the perfective aspect marker -*le* (much as it aids in the marking of punctual verbs for past as it occurs in the environment immediately following the verb) is often transferred to the interlanguage as *already*, resulting in a proliferation of expressions like *eat/ate already*. Note that in English the adverb *already* often occurs with the pluperfect and the present perfect. It is crucial not to introduce the teaching of such perfective forms too near to the teaching of past forms. It must be remembered that *le* in Chinese in sentence final position has the meaning 'current relevant state'. One realizes how a potential positive transfer from L1 can be tapped here. One can see a parallel with the English use of *already* in the teaching of the perfect tenses which have the semantics of 'current relevance'. Naturally, special attention should be given to the teaching of the auxiliaries *have* and *had* and particularly the contracted forms *'ve* and *'d* (bearing in mind that fricatives and stops in final position are particularly difficult for Singaporean learners of English). It can be seen in Ho's corpus that such forms in expressions like 'I already *seen/given* him' (which are also present in non-standard native varieties) are already becoming fossilized in basilectal SgE.

11.3.3 Past tense marking with particular reference to CC verbs

Although Ho's analysis shows that the overriding factor which influences past tense marking is a semantic one, the phonological factor should not be ignored. Special attention should be directed towards the teaching of verbs ending in consonant clusters. Marking for past, irrespective of semantic categories, is very low indeed. Failure to mark verbs in such environments is also reflected in the written English of ethnically Chinese Singaporean students:

> So I spent my holiday on doing nothing only read book *watch* television and went out sometime. (From a Secondary 1 student.)

When we *return* home, it was about 1.00 am. (From a Secondary 2 student.)

I show to him he *call* (asked) me to take a look at it. (From a Secondary 2 student.)

I changed into my school uniform, *pick* up my school bag and run out of the house. (From a Secondary 4 student.)

Although they *look* funny, they were ferocious and behaved very unfriendlily. (From a Secondary 4 student.)

An investigation by Bickerton (1971*b*), who examined the essays written by 12-year-old Guyanese school children, revealed the percentage scores shown in Table 11.2 for the three phonetic environments for the marking of verbs

TABLE 11.2. *Past tense marking of verbs in the written English of Guyanese schoolchildren*

	N	CPW	IPW	Error (%)
Weak-syllabic verbs	128	111	17	13.3
Strong verbs	551	471	80	14.5
Weak-non-syllabic verbs	321	169	152	47.4

N = number of verbs.
CPW = correctly produced in writing.
IPW = incorrectly produced in writing.
Source: Bickerton 1971*b*:137.

for past. Note that the percentage error for the weak-non-syllabic verbs is very high compared to the other two environments.

Another survey, by Ho W. K. (1972:78) on the written compositions of pre-university Chinese-stream students, shows that the same phonetic problem has given rise to an omission of *t* and *d* endings in past tense verbs and past participle forms.

It appears that the omission of consonant clusters in final position in speech is also transferred to the written form and, as suggested by Bickerton for the Guyanese situation, which is equally applicable to the Singapore situation, 'an improvement in specific oral skills might lead to a corresponding improvement in writing' (Bickerton 1971*b*:139).

11.4 Verbs of movement and repetition of verbs

The strong influence of Chinese in the use of verbs of movement and the repetition of verbs has already been discussed. Attention should be focused on verbs of movement, as the non-standard use of *bring* and *take* can lead to misunderstanding and a breakdown in communication and certainly the use of 'to send someone home' can be misconstrued as an impolite gesture. It should be noted that the deictic system in Chinese is very different from that of English. In Chinese, direction is indicated by directional postverbs. Thus in *ná lai* 'take come' and *ná qu* 'take go', *lái* and *qù* indicate direction towards and away from the speaker respectively. The preceding verb *ná* has no deictic function. However, in English, the choice of *bring/take* and *come/go* shows direction towards or away from the speaker or some other point of reference. The use of postverbs is not confined to spoken SgE. It is also found in the written assignments of students (cf. Ho 1987), e.g. 'I took plane go back to Singapore from Perth' (from a Secondary 1 student). Expressions with postverbs are stigmatized structures and are often avoided by speakers with higher levels of education. However, as shown in the discussion in Chapter 9, the non-standard use of *bring* and *take* is very high because of the semantic differences between the Chinese verbs *ná* and *dài* and the English verbs *take* and *bring*. The repetition of verbs is another area which merits attention since verbs which are repeated are almost categorically unmarked for past.

11.5 Concluding remarks

It seems appropriate to conclude with a relevant quotation from Bickerton (1971*b*:139–40):

Finally, we should beware of over-rigid methods of error analysis, and remember that the purpose of such analysis should not be merely the classification of different types of error, nor even the establishment of their relative frequencies; these are sterile exercises unless at the same time we are trying to find out why errors are made. Unless we fully understand the causes behind specific errors, we are dealing with the symptom rather than the disease.

Dynamics of a Creole System (1975) illustrates the fluid but systematic nature of the acquisition of more standard structures in a post-creole situation. The present work illustrates the high degree of systematicity in the continuum of an indigenized variety of English.

Appendix A

Sex, Age, Occupation, and Educational Qualifications of Informants

1. Informants with tertiary-level education

Informant	Sex	Age	Occupation	Educational qualifications
T1	M	32	investment officer	BScHons (Sing), MBA (Aus)
T2	M	35	financial controller	BSc (Sing), CA (UK)
T3	M	37	medical officer	MBBS (Sing)
T4	M	36	civil engineer	BEng (Malaya)
T5	M	27	administrative officer	BEng (UK)
T6	M	26	medical officer	MBBS (Sing)
T7	M	36	medical officer	MD (Canada)
T8	M	34	administrative officer	BSc, Dip Bus Adm (Sing)
T9	M	27	administrative officer	BCom Hons (UK)
T10	M	24	bank officer	BBA (Sing)
T11	F	29	lawyer	LL B (UK)
T12	F	29	statistician	BSc (Sing), MBA (Aus)
T13	F	22	financial analyst	BCom Hons (UK)
T14	F	25	librarian	BA (Sing)
T15	F	32	investment manager	BA, Dip Bus Adm (Sing)
T16	F	26	internal auditor	BAcc (Sing)
T17	F	28	architect	B. Arch. (Sing)
T18	F	30	financial controller	BBA (Sing)
T19	F	32	financial controller	BA Hons., M. Admin. (Aus)
T20	F	28	teacher	BAcc (Sing)

Notes: Sing.—Singapore; Aus.—Australia; UK—United Kingdom.

2. Informants with A level education

Informant	Sex	Age	Occupation
A1	M	31	systems analyst
A2	M	24	tax assistant trainee
A3	M	24	sales representative
A4	M	29	organization and methods officer

2. Informants with A level education (*cont.*)

Informant	Sex	Age	Occupation
A5	M	20	clerk (National Service)
A6	M	20	clerk (National Service)
A7	M	23	executive officer
A8	M	26	reservations officer
A9	M	30	sales manager
A10	M	20	corporal (National Service)
A11	M	21	bank clerk
A12	F	24	key punch operator
A13	F	19	relief teacher
A14	F	22	clerk
A15	F	21	clerk
A16	F	21	nurse
A17	F	36	teacher
A18	F	19	teller
A19	F	21	manageress
A20	F	25	flight stewardess

3. Informants with O level education

Informant	Sex	Age	Occupation
O1	M	28	bandsman
O2	M	22	technician
O3	M	33	renovation contractor
O4	M	46	laboratory technician
O5	M	26	sales engineer
O6	M	28	production manager
O7	M	26	draughtsman
O8	M	31	oil exploration assistant
O9	M	25	navigator
O10	M	25	port operation assistant
O11	F	23	nurse
O12	F	21	secretary
O13	F	28	security officer
O14	F	26	personnel assistant
O15	F	21	sales assistant
O16	F	20	sales assistant
O17	F	29	nurse
O18	F	19	accounts clerk
O19	F	40	personnel manageress
O20	F	20	X-ray assistant

4. Informants with sec. 1–3 education

Informant	Sex	Age	Occupation
S1	F	28	sales assistant
S2	M	24	workshop assistant
S3	F	25	music teacher
S4	F	27	production operator
S5	F	30	pre-set hand (catering)
S6	F	24	material handling operator
S7	F	29	parking warden
S8	M	43	mini bus operator
S9	F	38	typist
S10	F	22	sales assistant
S11	F	24	waitress
S12	F	20	cashier
S13	F	20	sales assistant
S14	F	18	cashier
S15	M	17	waiter
S16	M	40	production operator
S17	M	19	construction worker
S18	F	25	captain (head waitress)
S19	M	27	driver
S20	F	31	waitress

5. Informants with primary-level education

Informant	Sex	Age	Occupation
P1	M	32	vehicle receptionist
P2	M	40	odd-job man
P3	M	30	odd-job man
P4	M	31	taxi driver
P5	M	34	shop proprietor
P6	M	18	army recruit
P7	M	18	army recruit
P8	M	21	cook
P9	M	20	mechanic
P10	M	39	hawker
P11	M	26	shop assistant
P12	F	26	line leader (at a factory)
P13	F	30	catering hand
P14	F	36	shop assistant
P15	F	33	pantry maid
P16	F	16	factory operator
P17	F	34	washerwoman
P18	F	27	amah (nursing assistant)
P19	F	36	pantry maid
P20	F	32	pantry maid

Appendix B
A List of 'Static Idea' Verbs Occurring in Ten Well-known Handbooks of Grammar

VERBS	Z	S	O	J	Je	P	C	H	Sc	Q
abhor			●							●
accept										
adjoin				●						
adore										●
agree			●					●		
appear								●		
apply			●							●
astonish										●
be			●	●						●
be conscious				●						
be ignorant				●						
believe	●	●	●	●		●	●	●	●	●
belong (to)	●	●	●			●	●	●	●	●
be supposed to				●						
border on				●						
care			●							
come to				●						
complete				●						
complicate				●						
comprehend				●						
comprise				●						
concern										●
consist (of)						●	●	●	●	●
contain				●		●	●	●	●	●
correspond				●						
cost										●
demonstrate				●						
depend (on)			●	●		●		●		●
deserve	●					●	●	●		●
desire		●		●				●		●
detest		●						●		●
differ				●						
disapprove									●	
doubt								●		●
equal								●	●	●

VERBS	Z	S	O	J	Je	P	C	H	Sc	Q
exclude				•						
extend				•						
fail				•						
feel		•	•		•	•	•	•		•
fill				•						
find			•					•		
fit										•
follow				•						
foresee								•		
forget		•	•			•	•	•		
forgive								•		•
guess			•							•
hang					•					
hate	•			•	•			•		•
have				•						•
have to			•							
hear	•	•	•	•	•	•	•			•
hold				•						
hope		•	•		•	•		•		
imagine						•	•	•		•
impress										•
include			•	•						•
intend				•						•
intersect				•						•
involve										•
know	•		•	•			•	•		•
lack										•
lie			•		•					
like (and dislike)		•	•	•	•			•		•
look				•						
love	•	•	•		•			•		•
make a difference				•						
make				•						
match				•						
matter						•	•	•	•	•
mean	•	•	•				•	•		•
mind			•				•	•		•
need			•					•		•
notice								•		
owe										•
own	•					•	•			•
perceive				•						•
pity					•					
please	•					•	•	•		•
plan							•			•
possess	•						•	•	•	•
preclude				•						
prefer	•							•		•

VERBS	Z	S	O	J	Je	P	C	H	Sc	Q
presuppose										●
reach				●						
realize			●							●
recall			●							●
recognize	●							●		●
recollect		●						●		
refuse		●								
regard			●	●						●
remain (copula)			●							●
remember	●	●	●				●	●		●
represent			●							
require			●							●
resemble	●			●			●	●	●	●
result								●		
satisfy	●									●
see		●	●	●	●	●	●			●
seem	●		●					●		●
show				●						
signify									●	
sit					●					
smell		●			●	●	●			●
sound	●		●	●						●
stand					●					
suffice	●							●	●	●
suit	●		●				●			
suppose			●	●				●		●
surprise	●									
suspect			●							
taste						●	●			●
tend			●							●
think		●	●	●	●	●	●	●		●
trust			●							
understand	●		●	●			●	●		●
vitiate				●						
want		●	●	●				●		●
wish		●	●					●		●
wonder			●							

Z   Zandvoort (1975)
S   Scheurweghs (1959)
O   Ota (1963)
J   Joos (1964)
Je   Jespersen (1961)
P   Palmer (1965)
C   Christophersen and Sandved (1969)
H   Hornby (1954)
Sc   Schibsbye (1965)
Q   Quirk, Greenbaum, Leech, and Svartvik (1972)

Source: Scheffer 1975: 61–4.

References

AITCHISON, J. (1983), 'Review of Derek Bickerton, *Roots of Language*', *Language and Communication*, 3.1:83–97.

ALLEYNE, M. C. (1980), *Comparative Afro-American* (Ann Arbor, Mich.: Karoma).

ANDERSEN, R. W. (1978), 'An Implicational Model for Second Language Research', *Language Learning*, 28.2:221–82.

—— (1979), 'Creolization as the Acquisition of a Second Language as a First Language' (from the Conference on Theoretical Orientations in Creole Studies, 28 March–1 April 1979, St Thomas, Virgin Islands).

—— (1984), 'The One to One Principle of Interlanguage Construction', *Language Learning*, 34.4:77–95.

ANTINUCCI, F., and MILLER, R. (1976), 'How Children Talk About What Happened', *Journal of Child Language*, 3:167–89.

BARTELT, H. G. (1982), 'Tense Switching in Narrative English Discourse of Navaho and Western Apache Speakers', *Studies in Second Language Acquisition*, 4.2:201–4.

BAILEY, B. L. (1966), *Jamaican Creole Syntax* (London: Cambridge University Press).

BAILEY, C.-J. (1973), *Variation and Linguistic Theory* (Arlington, Va.: Center for Applied Linguistics).

—— and SHUY, R., eds. (1973), *New Ways of Analyzing Variation in English* (Washington, DC: Georgetown University Press).

BAUGH, J. (1980), 'A Reexamination of the Black English Copula', in Labov 1980: 83–107 (q.v.).

BICKERTON, D. (1971a), 'Inherent Variability and Variable Rules', *Foundations of Language*, 7:457–92.

—— (1971b), 'Cross-Level Interference: The Influence of L1 Syllable Structure on L2 Morphological Error', in Perren and Trim 1971:133–40 (q.v.).

—— (1973a), 'The Structure of Polylectal Grammars', in Shuy 1973:17–41 (q.v.).

—— (1973b), 'The Nature of a Creole Continuum', *Language*, 49.3:640–69.

—— (1975), *Dynamics of a Creole System* (Cambridge: Cambridge University Press).

—— (1977), *Creole Syntax*, vol. ii of Final Report on NSF Grant No. GS-39748 (University of Hawaii, mimeo.).

—— (1981), *Roots of Language* (Ann Arbor, Mich.: Karoma).

—— (1984a), 'The Language Bioprogram Hypothesis', *The Behavioral and Brain Sciences*, 7:173–221.

—— (1984b), 'The Language Bioprogram Hypothesis and Second Language Acquisition', in Rutherford 1984:141–61 (q.v.).

BINNICK, R., DAVISON, A., GREEN, G., and MORGAN, J., eds. (1969), *Papers from the Fifth Regional Meeting of the Chicago Linguistic Society* (Chicago: Department of Linguistics, University of Chicago).

BLISS, A. (1984), 'English in the South of Ireland', in Trudgill 1984:135–51 (q.v.).

BLOOM, L., LIFTER, K., and HAFITZ, J. (1980), 'Semantics of Verbs and the Development of Verb Inflection in Child Language', *Language*, 56.2:386–412.

BODMAN, N. C. (1955), *Spoken Amoy Hokkien*, vol. i (Kuala Lumpur: Charles Grenier and Son Ltd.).

BRADSHAW, J., and HEW, Y. L. (1988), 'Talking to Children in a Multilingual Household', in Foley 1988:100–14 (q.v.).

BRONCKART, J., and SINCLAIR, H. (1973), 'Time, Tense and Aspect', *Cognition*, 2:107–30.

BUDGE, C. (1986), 'Variation in Hong Kong English' (Ph.D. thesis, Monash University, Melbourne).

CAPELL, A. (1979), 'Ups and Downs', *Talanya*, 6:14–27.

CEDERGREN, H., and SANKOFF, D. (1974), 'Variable Rules: Performance as Statistical Reflection of Competence', *Language*, 50:333–55.

CHAO, Y. R. (1968), *A Grammar of Spoken Chinese* (Berkeley, Calif.: University of California Press).

CHIANG, K. C. (n.d.), *A Practical English–Hokkien Dictionary* (Singapore: The Chin Fen Book Store).

CHRISTOPHERSEN, P., and SANDVED, A. O. (1969), *An Advanced English Grammar* (London: Macmillan).

COMRIE, B. (1976), *Aspect* (Cambridge: Cambridge University Press).

CREWE, W. J., ed. (1977a), *The English Language In Singapore* (Singapore: Eastern Universities Press).

—— (1977b), *Singapore English and Standard English* (Singapore: Eastern Universities Press).

CROWLEY, T., and RIGSBY, B. (1979), 'Cape York Creole', in Shopen 1979:153–207 (q.v.).

DeCAMP, D. (1971), 'Toward a Generative Analysis of a Post-Creole Speech Continuum', in Hymes 1971:349–70 (q.v.).

DAY, R. (1972), 'Patterns of Variation in Copula and Tense in the Hawaiian Post-Creole Continuum' (Ph.D. dissertation, University of Hawaii).

DeFRANCIS, J. (1976), *Beginning Chinese* (New Haven, Conn.: Yale University Press), 2nd edn.

DE SOUZA, D. P. (1977), 'Language Status and Corpus Planning in Post-Independence Singapore' (unpublished project, SEAMEO Regional Language Centre, Singapore).

DOWTY, D. (1977), 'Toward a Semantic Analysis of Verb Aspect and the English "Imperfective" Progressive', *Linguistics and Philosophy*, 1:45–77.

ELLIOT, D., LEGUM, S., and THOMPSON, S. (1969), 'Syntactic Variation as Linguistic Data', in Binnick, Davison, Green, and Morgan 1969:52–9 (q.v.).

FASOLD, R. W. (1970), 'Two Models of Socially Significant Linguistic Variation', *Language*, 46:551–63.

—— (1972), *Tense Marking in Black English* (Arlington, Va.: Center for Applied Linguistics).

—— (1973), 'The Concept of "Earlier–Later": More or Less Correct', in Bailey and Shuy 1973:183–97 (q.v.).

—— (1975), 'The Bailey Wave Model: A Dynamic Quantitative Paradigm', in Fasold and Shuy 1975:27–58 (q.v.).

—— (1990), *The Sociolinguistics of Language* (Oxford: Basil Blackwell).

FASOLD, R. W. and SHUY, R. W., eds. (1975), *Analyzing Variation in Language* (Washington, DC: Georgetown University Press).

FOLEY, J., ed. (1988), *New Englishes: The Case of Singapore* (Singapore: Singapore University Press).

GEORGE, H. V. (1971), 'English for Asian Learners: Are We on the Right Road?', *English Language Teaching*, 25.3:270–7.

—— (1972), *Common Errors in Learning English* (Rowley, Mass.: Newbury House).

GRANGER, S. (1983), *The Be + Past Participle Construction in Spoken English with Special Emphasis on the Passive* (Amsterdam: Elsevier Science Publishers BV).

GUPTA, A. F. (1986), 'A Standard for Singapore English?', *English World-Wide*, 7.1: 75–99.

GUTTMAN, L. (1944), 'A Basis for Scaling Qualitative Data', *American Sociological Review*, 9:139–50.

HEATON, B. (1979), 'Communication in the Classroom', *Singapore Journal of Education*, 1.2:57–60.

HILL, K. C., ed. (1979), *The Genesis of Language: The First Michigan Colloquim, 1979* (Ann Arbor, Mich.: Karoma).

HO, M. L. (1981), 'The Noun Phrase in Singapore English' (MA thesis, Monash University, Melbourne).

—— (1986), 'The Verb Phrase in Singapore English' (Ph.D. thesis, Monash University, Melbourne).

—— (1987), 'Non-Standard Use of Verbs of Movement in Singaporean English' (paper presented at the Conference on Variation and Second Language Acquisition, Ann Arbor, Mich.).

—— (1989a), 'Singaporean English: The Indian Connection?' (paper presented at the International Conference on English in South Asia, Islamabad).

—— (1989b), 'The Acquisition of Past Tense Marking by Chinese Singaporeans' (paper presented at the Conference on Syntactic Acquisition in the Chinese context, Hong Kong).

—— (1990), 'Variation in Singaporean English' (paper presented at the 9th World Congress of Applied Linguistics, Thessaloniki).

HO, W. K. (1972), 'An Investigation of Errors in English Composition of Some Pre-University Students in Singapore, with Suggestions for the Teaching of Written English' (unpublished project, SEAMEO Regional English Language Centre, Singapore).

HOLM, J. (1975), 'Variability of the Copula in Black English and Its Creole Kin' (unpublished MS, subsequently revised and published in Holm 1984).

—— (1982), 'Review of Derek Bickerton, *Roots of Language*', *English World-Wide*, 3:112–15.

—— (1984), 'Variability of the Copula in Black English and Its Creole Kin', *American Speech*, 5.4:291–309.

—— (1988), *Pidgins and Creoles*, vol. i: *Theory and Structure* (Cambridge: Cambridge University Press).

The Holy Bible (Revised Standard Version) (1957) (Edinburgh: Thomas Nelson and Sons Ltd.).

HORNBY, A. S. (1954), *A Guide to Patterns and Usage in English* (London: Longmans).

HUEBNER, T. (1982), 'From Topic to Subject Dominance in the Interlanguage of a Hmong Speaker' (Ph.D. dissertation, University of Hawaii).

HYMES, D., ed. (1971), *Pidginization and Creolization of Languages* (Cambridge: Cambridge University Press).

JESPERSEN, O. (1961), *A Modern English Grammar on Historical Principles*, part iv (London: G. Allen and Unwin).

JOOS, M. (1964), *The English Verb* (Madison, Wis.: University of Wisconsin Press).

KACHRU, B. B., ed. (1982), *The Other Tongue: English across Culture* (Urbana, Ill.: University of Illinois Press).

KENNY, A. (1963), *Action, Emotion and Will* (London: Routledge and Kegan Paul).

KHOO, C. K. (1980), *Census of Population 1980, Singapore*, Releases 1 and 2 (Singapore: Department of Statistics).

KING, H. V. (1969), 'Punctual Versus Durative as Covert Categories', *Language Learning*, 19:183–90.

LABOV, W. (1969), 'Contraction, Deletion and Inherent Variability in the English Copula', *Language*, 45:715–62.

—— (1972), *Language in the Inner City* (Philadelphia: University of Pennsylvania Press).

—— ed. (1980), *Locating Language in Time and Space* (New York: Academic Press).

—— (1982), 'Objectivity and Commitment in Linguistic Science: The Case of the Black English Trial in Ann Arbor', *Language in Society*, 11.2:165–202.

LAKOFF, G. (1970), *Irregularity in Syntax* (New York: Holt, Rinehart and Winston).

LE PAGE, R. B. (1983), 'Review of D. Bickerton, *Roots of Language*', *Journal of Linguistics*, 19.1:258–65.

LESLIE, A. (1981), *Oddities in language* (Singapore: Federal Publications).

LEVIN, S. (1985), 'Review of D. Bickerton, *Roots of Language*', *General Linguistics*, 25.1:41–50.

LI, C. N., and THOMPSON, S. A. (1981), *Mandarin Chinese: A Functional Reference Grammar* (Berkeley, Calif.: University of California Press).

LIM, S. (1981), 'Baba Malay: The Language of the "Straits-Born" Chinese' (MA thesis, Monash University, Melbourne).

LOMAN, B. (1967), *Conversations in a Negro American Dialect* (Washington, DC: Center for Applied Linguistics).

Longman Dictionary of Contemporary English (1978) (Harlow and London: Longman).

LYONS, J. (1977), *Semantics*, vol. ii (Cambridge: Cambridge University Press).

MINDERHOUT, D. I. (1977), 'Language Variation in Tobagonian English', *Anthropological Linguistics*, 19.4:167–80.

NEWBROOK, M., ed. (1987), *Aspects of the Syntax of Educated Singaporean English: Attitudes, Beliefs and Usage* (Frankfurt: Peter Lang).

OTA, A. (1963), *Tense and Aspect of Present-Day American English* (Tokyo: Kenkyusha).

PALMER, F. R. (1965), *A Linguistic Study of the English Verb* (London: Longmans).

PERREN, G. E., and TRIM, J. L. M., eds. (1971), *Applications of Linguistics* (Cambridge: Cambridge University Press).

PLATT, J. T. (1975), 'The Singapore English Speech Continuum and Its Basilect "Singlish" as a "Creoloid" ', *Anthropological Linguistics*, 17.7:363–74.

—— (1976), 'Implicational Scaling and Its Pedagogical Implications', *Working Papers in Language and Linguistics*, 4:47–60.

—— (1977*a*), 'The "Creoloid" as a Special Type of Interlanguage', *Interlanguage Studies Bulletin*, 2.3:22–38.

—— (1977*b*), 'English Past Tense Acquisition by Singaporeans: Implicational Scaling

Versus Group Averages of Marked Forms', *ITL: Review of Applied Linguistics*, 38: 63–83.

PLATT, J. T. (1978), 'The Concept of a "Creoloid". Exemplification: Basilectal Singaporean English', in *Papers in Pidgin and Creole Studies*, Series A, No. 54:53–65 (Canberra: The Australian National University).

—— (1979), 'Variation and Implicational Relationships: Copula Realization in Singapore English', *General Linguistics*, 19.1:1-14.

—— (1989), 'The Nature of Indigenized Englishes: Interference—Creativity—Universals', *Language Sciences*, 11.4:395–407.

—— and Ho, M. L. (1982), 'A Case of Language Indigenization: Some Features of Colloquial Singapore English', *Journal of Multilingual and Multicultural Development*, 3.4:267–76.

—— and —— (1988), 'Language Universals or Substratum Influences? Past Tense Marking in Singapore English', *English World-Wide*, 9.1:65–75.

—— and —— (1989), 'Discourse Particles in Singaporean English: Substratum Influences and Universals', *World Englishes*, 8.2:215–21.

—— and WEBER, H. (1980), *English in Singapore and Malaysia Status: Features: Functions* (Kuala Lumpur: Oxford University Press).

—— —— and Ho, M. L. (1983a), *Text Volume of Singapore and Malaysian English* (Amsterdam: Benjamins).

—— —— and —— (1983b), 'Some Verbs of Movement in Standard British English and Singapore English', *World Language English*, 2.3:156–60.

—— —— and —— (1984), *The New Englishes* (London: Routledge and Kegan Paul).

PRIDE, J. B., ed. (1982), *New Englishes* (Rowley, Mass.: Newbury House).

QUIRK, R., GREENBAUM, S., LEECH, G., and SVARTVIK, J. (1972), *A Grammar of Contemporary English* (London: Longman).

RAMISH, L. M. (1969), 'An Investigation of the Phonological Features of the English of Singapore and Their Relation to the Linguistic Substrata of Malay, Tamil, and Chinese Languages' (Ph.D. thesis, Brown University, 1973; microfilm-xerox).

RICHARDS, J. C. (1982a), 'Rhetorical and Communicative Styles in the New Varieties of English', in Pride 1982:227–48 (q.v.).

—— (1982b), 'Singapore English: Rhetorical and Communicative Styles', in Kachru 1982:154–67 (q.v.).

—— and TAY, M. W. J. (1977), 'The *LA* particle in Singapore English', in Crewe 1977a:141–56 (q.v.).

RITCHIE, W. C. (1986), 'Second Language Acquisition and the Study of Non-Native Varieties of English: Some Issues in Common', *World Englishes*, 5:15–30.

ROMAINE, S. (1979), 'On the Decisiveness of Quantitative Solutions: Why Labov was Wrong about Contraction and Deletion of the Copula', *Work in Progress*, 12:10–17 (Department of Linguistics, University of Edinburgh).

—— (1980), 'The Relative Clause Marker in Scots English: Diffusion, Complexity and Style as Dimensions of Syntactic Change', *Language in Society*, 9:221–49.

—— (1982), *Socio-Historical Linguistics: Its Status and Methodology* (Cambridge: Cambridge University Press).

—— (1988), *Pidgin and Creole Languages* (New York: Longman).

ROSS, J. (1973), 'A Fake NP Squish', in Bailey and Shuy 1973:96–140 (q.v.).

RUTHERFORD, W. E., ed. (1984), *Language Universals and Second Language Acquisition* (Amsterdam: Benjamins).

SCHEFFER, J. (1975), *The Progressive in English* (Amsterdam: North Holland).

SCHEURWEGHS, G. (1959), *Present-Day English Syntax* (London: Longmans).

SCHIBSBYE, K. (1965), *A Modern English Grammar* (London: Oxford University Press).

SCHUMANN, J. H. (1974), 'Implications of Pidginization and Creolization for the Study of Adult Second Language Acquisition', in Schumann and Stenson 1974:137–52 (q.v.).

—— (1979), 'The Genesis of a Second Language', in Hill 1979:48–61 (q.v.).

—— and STENSON, N., eds. (1974), *New Frontiers in Second Language Learning* (Rowley, Mass.: Newbury House).

SEUREN, P. (1984), 'The Bioprogram Hypothesis: Facts and Fancy', in 'Open Peer Commentary' following Bickerton 1984a:208–9 (q.v.).

SHOPEN, T., ed. (1979), *Languages and Their Status* (Cambridge, Mass.: Winthrop Publishers).

SHUY, R., ed. (1973), *Sociolinguistics: Current Trends and Prospects* (Georgetown University Round Table on Languages and Linguistics 1972. Washington, DC: Georgetown University Press).

SMITH, I. (1985), 'Multilingualism and Diffusion: A Case Study from Singapore English', *Indian Journal of Applied Linguistics*, 11:105–28.

STOLZ, W., and BILLS, G. (1968), 'An Investigation of the Standard–Nonstandard Dimension of Central Texan English' (unpublished MS).

SONG, O. S. (1923), *One Hundred Years' History of the Chinese in Singapore* (London: Murray; repr. Singapore: University of Malaya Press, 1967).

The Straits Times, 10 July 1984.

The Sunday Monitor, 22 July 1984.

TAY, M. W. J. (1982), 'The Phonology of Educated Singapore English', *English World-Wide*, 3.2:135–45.

TONGUE, R. K. (1974), *The English of Singapore and Malaysia* (Singapore: Eastern Universities Press; 2nd edn., 1977).

TRUDGILL, P., ed. (1984), *Language in the British Isles* (Cambridge: Cambridge University Press).

—— and HANNAH, J. (1982), *International English: A Guide to Varieties of Standard English* (London: Edward Arnold).

T'UNG, P. C., and POLLARD, D. E. (1982), *Colloquial Chinese* (London: Routledge and Kegan Paul).

VENDLER, Z. (1967), *Linguistics in Philosophy* (Ithaca, NY: Cornell University Press).

VERKUYL, H. J. (1971), *On the Compositional Nature of the Aspects* (Amsterdam: University of Amsterdam).

WOLFRAM, W. A. (1969), *A Sociolinguistic Description of Detroit Negro Speech* (Washington, DC: Center for Applied Linguistics).

—— (1974), 'The Relationship of White Southern Speech of Vernacular Black English', *Language*, 50:498–527.

Webster's Third New International Dictionary (1976), 2 vols. (Springfield, Mass.: G. and C. Marriam Company).

WOLFSON, N. (1982), *CHP: The Conversational Historical Present in American English Narrative* (Dordrecht: Foris Publications).

ZANDVOORT, R. W. (1975), *A Handbook of English Grammar*, 7th edn. (London: Longmans).

Index